Ridiculous World (Trip)

Matt Bishop

with Reece Gilkes

Sidecar Press

An imprint of As Seen from the Sidecar,
a United Kingdom Community Interest Company (CIC)

Copyright © 2020 Matt Bishop and Reece Gilkes

First Printing

ISBN: 978-1-8381329-0-3

This book is dedicated to the millions of people still trapped in slavery. Although reading this book will not free those trapped, we hope it will help more people to understand how the issue still persists in 2020—and what to do to stop it.

CONTENTS

PROLOGUE

"Welcome to Russia guys—don't do it, you will die!"

The words from a Facebook message I received from a Russian biker in Moscow play over and over in my head as we drive out of Mogocha, headed for the wilderness of Russia's Far East. It's −30°C and we're driving our beat-up scooter and sidecar along the most remote part of the Trans-Siberian Highway. Villages come every 100 km or so and, when they do, they are usually just four or five houses by the roadside. We're completely alone and if we're to survive this section of the trip, everything has to go exceptionally well.

I sit in the sidecar, with no heated kit, waiting for the cold to start its work. I begin the ride with my visor up but after two minutes the frozen wind whipping against my eyes is too much to bear. I flick my visor down. I breathe. I can still see. I breathe again. The visor's misty. I breathe again and ice starts to form. A few minutes pass and all I can see is a layer of ice on the inside of my visor.

"Arghh, shit!" I shout, as the scooter slips out beneath us and we momentarily slide sideways. I brace for impact. It doesn't come. I flick up my visor and see that we're still bouncing along the snowy road. As I do, a truck steamrolls past us going at least 50 mph. I look to my left and get snow and grit chucked in my face. The lorry presses on, headed for Moscow. I wipe myself down. Shut my visor and breathe. I can still see. I breathe again. Mist forms. I breathe again and it's ice. The cycle repeats. I sit there worried that the next lorry will come at the same time as the next slip. I feel worn down and scared. I've been doing this eight hours a day for a week. I've got to do it for at least another month until Moscow. The guy from Moscow is right. We're going to die. Why are we doing this?

* * *

"Welcome to Flight Centre, this is Matt."

It's February 2015 and I've been a travel agent for around four months. I sell the dream. I'm the person you come to for that big summer holiday or that gap year you've been planning. I make trips happen. I am the voice of adventure, but my personal dreams of adventure seem like a distant memory.

Seven a.m. My alarm rings. Groan. Snooze. Repeat. Eight a.m. I peel myself off the bed. I take a minute to stare at the mold creeping down the wall, rush to get ready and then run through the dark to catch the Tube. Crammed in the lift with twenty or thirty other commuters, it feels like we're descending into a modern, inner-city mine. Spluttering from the cold that I seemingly always have, I'm careful not to sneeze on the other city miners as we descend into the tunnels that transport us to the various streets, where we undertake our daily grind.

Dreams sold. I walk back down along a dark Oxford Street. Get back in the tunnel. Go back up the mine shaft and return home. I pass my flat mate, Reece. He's just on his way out to the mine.

"Welcome to Meat Liquor guys, my name's Reece, I'll be your waiter this evening."

Reece is pushing tables at one of London's hippest burger joints. Here, top-quality, overpriced burgers are wolfed down by the better paid miners. It's verging on pitch-black and most days the gent's toilet floods, so it stinks. Fortunately, the majority of the restaurant's patrons have repurposed their noses from smelling devices to cocaine inhalers, so the stench doesn't affect business much.

Reece returns to the flat about midnight. I've been sitting drinking beers and applying for jobs that I'll never get. The evening routine begins. Four games of Arsenal vs. Man United on FIFA, with more tins. One of us triumphant and the other in need of drowning his sorrows, we jump on the bus and head down into Camden for a night on the tiles.

Seven a.m. and the cycle repeats.

We're sleepwalking through life. Changing nothing. Moaning a lot, but generally enjoying the view from the inside of our comfort zones and doing nothing to achieve our dreams.

I pick up the *Evening Standard* and an article momentarily wakes me from my slumber. It's a picture of a long line of people walking through a non-descript European field with the caption: "BREAKING POINT—the EU has failed us."

The UK Independence Party's poster boy, Nigel Farage, is pointing at the line and, in turn, pointing the blame at vulnerable, normal people just looking for a better life. Along with many others in the media, he's blaming everything that's wrong in Britain on immigration.

"For heaven's sake, Nigel," I think to myself.

I get home and bang on the news.

"'There is a swarm of migrants and refugees trying to get into Britain' is the message from the Prime Minister David Cameron. "

"Oh, for Christ's sake, Dave," I mutter under my breath. "Not you, too!"

Reece gets in and I instantly vent about what I've been seeing in the news. We talk about how absurd it is that the media are painting these people as trouble, when in fact they are just in trouble and need help. We do some research into it and find that the same thing is happening all over the world. It is not just the UK that seems to be governed by fear-driven politics. There is seemingly a rise in it worldwide, with the Far Right making ground in Europe and a TV character at the helm in the States.

We decide we should break from our norm of moaning and doing nothing. Instead, this time we will do something about it. We will push back against that negative stuff in the press and tell some good stories. We know we won't really make an impact, but we think there's no harm in trying.

Conveniently, we are both off work the following day, so we start brainstorming. Just bouncing ideas around. We begin by putting everything down on paper, but that isn't enough, ideas are flowing at the rate of knots and we need more room to write. It feels like we can fill the whole room with ideas, so we decide we will do exactly that and buy four whiteboards, which turn our dingy living room into a living, breathing mind map. Our other flat mate, John, isn't too keen on the transformation but, at the end of the day, John is a bit of a prick and he always leaves the heating on.

Over the next few days we start to form our ideas and begin to work out what we should do. We come to the conclusion that the best thing we can do is try to remind everyone that *no matter where we're from or where we're going, we're all human,* and despite what's in the news, *people are generally good.* We decide that the easiest way to do that is to let strangers help us.

We agree to bite off a challenge which could only be achieved through the help of complete strangers all around the globe. We would travel on the most ridiculous vehicle imaginable through the world's toughest environments and see whether strangers in far-flung places will help us.

After much deliberation and many ridiculous ideas, including going around the world in a Flintstones-style car, we decide to undertake our journey on a scooter with a sidecar.

Neither of us can ride a motorbike, we know nothing about mechanics, and we've never sat in a sidecar. It seems suitably stupid, then, to attempt to be the first people to ever circumnavigate the globe on a scooter with a sidecar. That should grab some attention!

And so begins the completely ridiculous story of how Reece and I circumnavigate the globe on a scooter with a sidecar, and more importantly the story of the world as seen from the sidecar. The stories of everyone we meet. Stories of what it means to be human. A few stories of greed and cruelty and some of despair and destitution but, overwhelmingly, the majority of the stories are of adventure, laughter, and kindness.

I hope you enjoy the ride.

– 1 –

"YEAH RIGHT, THAT'LL NEVER HAPPEN."

"Sorry sir, you're here for a blister?" said the nurse in a thick, disapproving, Scottish accent.

"Yeah, it's really nasty," replied Reece. "I think someone should take a look at it."

We were at Inverness Accident & Emergency and I was standing a couple of steps back trying to contain my laughter. I was laughing because Reece really had come to hospital for a blister. It was a true mark of the man. If you ever needed an example of a situation that would describe Reece, this was it. Absolutely ridiculous, but yet, somehow, justified.

It was around 7 p.m. on December 8, 2016. The weather was horrific; it was absolutely crapping it down with icy, cold rain. It was a particular band of rain that we'd grown to know quite well because it had been riding with us for the last week. We first met it at Land's End and for the last 800 miles or so it had decided to join us on our first-ever motorcycle adventure.

We were not on this adventure for fun. Riding a Yamaha YBR through freezing rain, equipped only with my grandad's hand-me-down leather jacket, was not my idea of a holiday. I found myself here in Inverness in a desperate attempt to prove a point. A woefully thought-through effort at drumming up support for our grand idea: the first-ever circumnavigation of the globe on a scooter with a sidecar.

Around a year prior to winding up in A&E with Reece's blister, we had decided that we would be the first people to ever circumnavigate the globe on a scooter with a sidecar. Neither Reece nor I had ever really ridden a motorcycle, we had never been in a sidecar, and we had zero mechanical expertise. We were, and still are, really average kind of blokes. Mid-level achievers. We had never really tried that hard at anything unless we were playing football or FIFA. A bit flabby, over comfortable, enjoyed a pint too much, and our conversations typically ranged from the transfer window to who we had found on Tinder. We had never taken ourselves too seriously. I did a degree at Plymouth University in Human Geography because I could get in and they had Cornish pasties on the open day. Reece studied film at University of East London because at the time it was the worst uni in the country on paper and it would accept his straight Ds so he didn't have to re-sit sixth form.

Reece's readiness to opt for the worst course in the country rather than re-sitting did, however, set us down the path for circumnavigating the globe on a scooter with a sidecar. It meant that we both went "travelling." We did a standard "gap yah" in 2010-2011 with our school pal, Tama, travelling around New Zealand and Southeast Asia. We were from run-of-the-mill backgrounds and we had to work to go away which, in the end, made it all the sweeter.

We earnt our travels in our hometown of Banbury, which has a lot of demand for cheap labour in its factories—I spent six months in them. It was an eye-opening experience. I had a summer of mixing spices for the tops of M&S pies and mopping up melted Cadbury's buttons in a chocolate factory. A word of warning: if you bought an M&S shepherd's or cottage pie in 2010, you probably ate my sneeze. Sorry about that—you try pouring a 25-kg sack of chili powder into a mixer and see what happens. Reece went down another route and did a lot of work in hospitality. He pot-washed in a Pizza Hut and bog-washed in our local night club. In fact, I think I remember him having to unblock a toilet with his hands in that job. Yeah, I think Reece actually had to punch a shit to go on that trip, so we'd really earnt our adventures.

Our "gap yah" gave us a taste of what the world was like. Full of incredible people doing really weird stuff. Normal stuff like eating, drinking, working, flirting, but doing it in really weird ways. From dating over a skewer of BBQ'd chicken feet, to partying with a glass of fermented saliva, we found that people really did do stuff wildly differently to us and we loved it. Couldn't get enough of it. Finding all of the quirks and peculiarities in different cultures became a passion of mine and I don't think I'll ever get bored of it. We had planned to go away for the best part of a year and we came back after four months having blown our budget on booze, but boy did we have a blast. I think those four months were pretty life-changing for us. We were from a small town. We had a small-town mentality, but that trip gave us a massive whack with the "there's-a-whole-world-out-there" stick and we wanted to explore it.

The trip had also given us confidence. Confidence in our own abilities to go to far-flung places and not die (although in reality we were probably never more than ten miles from the refuge of a McDonald's) but, more importantly, confidence in the world. Confidence that the world is a good place. In our minds, we had met people from all walks of life, and everyone was great. There's always the odd bad apple but, generally speaking, everyone we had met had just been happy to welcome us to their part of the world. That stuck with us.

Cut to five years later and we had grown up a touch, but hadn't forgotten our trip. How could we? We had matching tattoos, after all (no regrets . . . honest). We ended up living together in a dingy flat in North London. We were doing alright. Reece was still smashing it in hospitality; he had moved up in the world from Pizza Hut and was pushing tables in a hip joint called Meat Liquor. I was working in the travel industry as an International Travel Consultant at Flight Centre. To be honest, despite the over-dramatic prologue to this book, they were both actually pretty good jobs. Not our dream jobs, but it could have been a lot worse. Nobody's punching shit or mixing chili spices. Working as a travel agent has serious perks, and I was earning decent money and getting free holidays. Reece was doing okay, too, and earning as much as I was, plus he had all the burgers and chicken wings he could scoff.

We were both doing fine but were fairly unfulfilled. We hadn't lost that spirit of adventure, but as of yet we hadn't had the *umph* to do anything about it. Then came Nigel Farage, the European Migrant Crisis, and the Brexit debate. Now that really pissed us off. We were watching the news and seeing thousands of really vulnerable, desperate people embarking on the most horrendous journey in the hope of a better life. Just looking for a safe place and a future for themselves and their loved ones. Nigel Farage and his mates in the press saw them as a stream of terrorists, rapists, and murderers coming to threaten Britain. Well that's the story they sold. In reality, they probably just saw them as an opportunity for political gain. Now, we're not particularly political guys and this project was not politically charged at all, but when someone goes out and uses somebody else's vulnerability for their own gain, on such a massive scale, it really gets our backs up. And more importantly the hate they were preaching was well-received by a disenfranchised, angry British public who had been beaten down by austerity for the past ten years and was looking for somebody to blame.

If you asked a fair chunk of the British public at the time, they'd tell you that the devil was at the doorstep and the people in the Calais Jungle refugee camp were a real danger. There was only one answer. Take control of the borders again and leave the EU! In my opinion it was a horrendous misrepresentation of the facts that ultimately had nothing to do with the EU and, in the end, needlessly led to the divide of the country into "in" or "out" at the same time it distracted from real issues, like the fact there were thousands of normal people in a desperate situation at our border.

Well, that night in 2015 we'd had enough, and we decided we had to do something about it. The bit that pissed us off the most was the way people stuck in the migrant crisis were being portrayed in the media, so initially we decided we would go and meet them and show what they're really like. But we did more research and realised this wasn't just a British problem. It was going on the world over. There was, and still seems to be, a global rise in hate-preach, scaremongering, and the like.

We thought if we could show people at home that everyday people from different places are generally good, then maybe we could remind everyone that the world isn't that scary after all and we would just pour a tiny bit of cold water over this burning pandemic of fear-driven politics. We figured that the simplest way to do that would be to let people help us. We reasoned that, if we went to places all around the world in a really silly way, and got ourselves in sticky situations, then one of two things would happen: Farage et al would be right and we'd be "raped and terrorised," or people would take us in, help us out, and send us on our way, thus proving they are good and in turn that your average person, no matter where they are from, is generally good. Plus, this idea would finally give us the chance to scratch that travel itch and go on the adventure of a lifetime.

After much discussion, we decided the optimum vehicle for embarking on such a trip would be a scooter with a sidecar. Firstly, it would look silly and not at all threatening or flashy, but most importantly it would be unsuited, impractical, and would break a lot, which would render us in need of help. Plus, doing a first-ever Guinness World Record attempt would capture people's attention and get our stories heard. At the same time, we reasoned that a trip this foolhardy would be a good way to raise money for a good cause. We decided to support charities that were fighting human trafficking and modern slavery, as human trafficking was and still is a major issue for people caught up in the European Migrant Crisis.

So, we had a plan. But saying you're going to circumnavigate the globe on a scooter with a sidecar is one thing, actually doing it is another matter altogether. By the time Reece's blister had taken us to Inverness A&E, we'd been in planning for about a year and we were getting nowhere with it. Everyone was fairly confident it would never happen. To be fair, planning a trip like this is quite the task. There are so many elements to it. There is a seemingly endless list of questions you have to answer. Even seasoned pros have to ask stuff like: Which way will I go? How will I pay for it? Is it safe? Can I get the necessary visas? What insurance do I need? Can I ship that route? Etc., etc. For us though, the list was somewhat longer. Ours started with: What exactly is circumnavigating the globe on a scooter with a sidecar? I mean, what is a circumnavigation of the globe? Sure, you have to go around it, but how? Can you fly? How many miles do you have to do? Do you have to go to a certain amount of countries? What are the rules here? Then the other side to that question is: What exactly is a scooter and sidecar? Can you just buy one of these puppies? How does a sidecar even work? Christ, is it a motorbike? Do I have to get a motorbike license?

The answer to that question was, of course, yes, it is a motorbike. And yes, you do need a full motorcycle license. Well, we didn't sign up to that. Motorbikes have always scared me to death. All I knew about motorbikes was what my mum had told me as a kid. They're loud, people ride them for a short time, and then they die on them. Thankfully, I don't think my mum had given me the full picture. They are kind of loud, but you don't necessarily have to die on them, plus ours would have a giant stabiliser in the form of a sidecar, so should be a bit safer too, right?

The other fairly major problem we had to solve before we could think too much about all of the smaller questions was working out how to pay for it. After a fair bit of research, we figured that an around-the-world trip by scooter and sidecar would probably cost around fifty big ones. Now our personal financial situation was what you'd kind of expect from a couple of average Joes living in London. We picked up a decent wage of around £1,700 a month but we blew the first £700 of that on rent and the next £900 on bills, the Tube, food, and pints after work. Which left around £100 a month to chip away at our massive student overdraft. So, doing the math, if we carried on like that, we'd have the money saved and be ready to go in just over twenty years' time (genuinely). I'm all about "patience is a virtue" and "good things come to those who wait," but that's just too long. The only way we were going to get this thing off the ground was with a lot of sponsorship.

Getting sponsorship is hard. It's a relentless, demoralising task but if you stick it out and you're adaptable enough, then it's out there. Everyone says to start with the Colonel Sanders philosophy. Have you heard that one? Apparently, the story goes that a bloke called Colonel Sanders had developed the best fried chicken recipe in all of the world. He just knew that it was going to take the world by storm, but he didn't have the capacity to get it out there himself, so he started trying to get restaurants to sell his chicken. He went into his first restaurant thinking it would be easy and everyone would buy his chicken. He was wrong. The first restaurant said no. "Shoot, onto the next." Another no. Ten noes passed, then a hundred noes, then 500 noes. Now, after 500 rejections, any sane person would have to sit and think, "Actually, maybe fried chicken isn't for me." But after 1,000 noes, the Colonel got a yes and that yes grew into the biggest high-street chicken shop in the world, KFC. Thank Christ he stuck it out— imagine a world without the Wicked Zinger Box Meal.

So, with the Colonel's story in mind, sometime in early 2016 I sat down with my mobile and decided I would start trying to get sponsorship for our mission. The first thing on my list was our motorcycle tuition. It costs a grand to get through your test so we figured if we could get that sponsored it would be a great start. I searched "learn to ride a motorbike" in Google and just started ringing training centres. The first one I rang was a straight, "No chance mate, I can do you five percent off." No bother, the Colonel had warned me of this—onto the next 999 calls. The second one I called was Metropolis Motorcycles London.

"Hi, I was wondering if I could speak to the manager of the training centre, please."

"You'll want Chris, just a minute," said the receptionist.

"Hello, Chris Spinks speaking," said a soft, Cockney voice.

"Hi Chris, my name's Matt. I've got a bit of a funny request. Next year I'm going to be setting off around the world on a scooter and sidecar raising money for charities fighting modern slavery, but before I go I need to be able to learn to ride a bike. I'm looking for a company to sponsor the training and I was wondering if you'd be interested."

"Matt, Charley Boorman, Ewan McGregor, Long Way Round —do you know of it?"

"Yeah, of course."

"I trained them. Had the lot in here—that von Planta fella, too, and Ewan's missus, taught her to ride as well!"

"No way—that's incredible!" I replied and then proceeded to ask a hundred questions on what the Long Way Round team were like.

We had a five minute back-and-forth in which Chris told me that Charley was a good bloke, Claudio couldn't pass his test, and Ewan's wife was fit, before I said, "Well, what do you reckon Chris, want to add us onto your list of celebs?"

"You going to get me on the telly?"

"I'll try."

"Alright then, let's do it."

Take that, Colonel. Second bloody call, £2,000 worth of sponsorship in the bag. I rang back to book our Compulsory Basic Training tests a week later. Chris answered. "Matt . . . two words: Tom . . . Hardy." The bloke seemed to have a conveyor belt of celebs going through the door. I thought he was talking rubbish before he sent me the pictures. I don't know how he did it, I guess it was his Del Boy-esque charm combined with the fact he would chuck free tuition at anyone who might get him on the telly one day. What a legend.

We did our CBTs about a week later. Nailed it. John, our trainer, had us racing around that school car park like Valentino Rossi in no time, Doctors Dangle and all. I promised Chris a film crew on day one, so Chelsea, my girlfriend, came along and filmed off the back of John's bike, so don't say we don't deliver on our sponsorship deals. Plus, the footage eventually got used on BBC Oxford's Facebook page. I reckon that counts as the telly.

A couple of weeks later we had our intensive course, which was two weekends of bricking it on a 700cc Yamaha. The Monday after the second weekend was test day. We had passed mock tests in training, but we were both completely sick with nerves. The test in the UK is split into two modules. Module 1 is riding around cones and an emergency stop in what is essentially a school playground. Module 2 is just a drive around town and an examiner follows behind, giving you instructions.

I was up first. I plucked up the courage, got on the bike, and was ready to nail it. The low-speed control element had been keeping me up at night but, on the day, I nailed it and didn't touch the floor once. I was pretty much out of the woods and just had to perform an emergency stop to get on to Module 2. All I had to do was go past a speed gun at 30 mph and then slow down quickly in order to stop in a designated area. I drove up to the top of the pad, talking to myself, saying, "Come on Matt, you can do this, you can do this." I went around the corner. Hit full throttle and sped past the speed gun at 50 mph. I freaked out, slammed on the brakes but missed the back one and just hit the front. The next thing I knew, I was doing an endo and my back wheel was at shoulder height. Thankfully, I let go of the brake and came crashing back down. I landed on two wheels and the only injury was that my balls went into my stomach. The instructor kindly asked me to leave the testing area and I got an instant fail. He said I was around two inches from flipping the bike over and tumbling down the pad. I told him that it was a shame the DVLA didn't appreciate flamboyance and calmly went to sit down next to a completely stunned Louis, who had been training us that day.

Reece was up next. Somewhat relaxed by just how badly I had done, he nailed Module 1. But on Module 2, he pulled out in front of a car at a roundabout and nearly got killed. An hour or so later, we were sat in front of a disappointed Chris who advised we both get some more practice under our belts before trying again.

Chris' advice was what had led us to the waiting room at Inverness A&E. He was right. We did need some practice, but more than that we had to do something to convince people we were for real. It was unbelievable good fortune to get the sponsored training from Chris and we'd all but wasted that. At the same time, no other potential sponsors were biting, and we were no closer to getting on the road. It made sense; how could we possibly expect anyone to believe that we were actually going to do it? We were saying we were going to do something that nobody had ever, *ever,* done before. I mean imagine getting approached for sponsorship for a first-ever scooter-and-sidecar trip by two blokes who couldn't ride a motorcycle, who had never sat in a sidecar, who had zero mechanical expertise, and who had never done any form of overland travelling. You would think they were nuts and just delete the email. We knew we had to do something to get some credibility. We knew we had to get serious about it, and the most sensible way to get serious about something as silly as circumnavigating the globe on a scooter with a sidecar is to do something almost as silly.

We decided that a stupid motorcycle trip in the UK would kill two birds with one stone. We'd get some practice on the bikes and make people think we were the real deal at the same time. The toughest UK challenge we could think of was to take our learner bikes from our houses in London to Lands' End, to John O'Groats, and back to London . . . in mid-winter. By the time we got to Inverness we had been on the road for ten days and we were hating every minute of it. We were spending long days winding around the country's A and B roads, soaking wet, and freezing cold. Thankfully, we had plenty of friends dotted around so we only had to do a couple of nights in the tent, but it really was a miserable affair. The trip was genuinely a lot harder than we had ever imagined. It was ridiculously cold and frighteningly dangerous. We were pushing our riding capabilities way past their limits and had some really close shaves. The thing that got us in the end, though, was poor hygiene. Reece had been wearing stinking, sodden wet socks and boots for a week and it had caused him to get an infected blister. It was rank.

After the nurse at Inverness hospital had squeezed a solid litre of pus out of Reece's infected foot (genuinely, that much), we went on to make it to John O'Groats and back down to London just in time for Christmas. The trip took us two weeks and I don't think we could have done it a second quicker. We arrived back to our second-ever fundraising night. It was called "UK Tour No More" and we told people a bit about the ride and raised a solid £400 for the modern slavery charities we would find en route. We also arrived back to a £500 dent into both of our non-existent savings and seemingly further away from getting around the world than we were before we set off. That was until Reece checked his work emails.

By this time, Reece had got out of Meat Liquor. I had referred him for a job at Flight Centre and he had ended up working in the same team as me. Lucy Clifton, who was Head of Sales at Flight Centre UK at the time, had emailed Reece and said, "I think it's amazing what you and Matt are doing, let's get together when you're back in the office and we'll see how Flight Centre can support you." Boom! That was massive. Somebody believed. Aside from Chelsea, and Anuschka, Reece's girlfriend at the time, Lucy Clifton was probably the only person in the world who believed the trip might happen. We had told our friends and family what we had planned, and the response was essentially the same from everyone: "Yeah right, that'll never happen." There were varying reasons for why people came up with a version of that answer. Some people thought there's just no way it could be done, some people thought there's just no way that Reece and I could do it, and some people, mainly our parents, just really didn't want us to do it.

But they didn't matter. What mattered was Lucy was a believer! We didn't even know Lucy. She was a bigwig and you don't ordinarily exchange emails with Head of Sales as a part-time foot soldier like Reece. By the time this happened I was actually no longer a Flight Centre employee. We had spent a good year planning the trip in our spare time while working at Flight Centre. We would get into work at 5 a.m. and use the big map on the wall to plan routes before donning our uniforms and selling the dream on the 7 a.m. shift, and other days we would get a four-pack in and crack on researching after the late shift finished. It worked well, but we felt we needed to take the plunge to living back with our parents and getting jobs where we could save every penny. So, reluctantly, I handed in my notice, left my lovely house with my lovely girlfriend in London, and went back to my parents' house in sleepy Sibford Ferris to work full-time on the project. Reece said he would hand in his notice two weeks later because the timings worked out better. That was in August; by Christmas he was still a Flight Centre employee.

He had bottled it. Anuschka had said he could live at her gaff for a couple of hundred quid a month and then he could work part-time in London without having to move home. Thank heavens for Anuschka. At the time, I was a bit annoyed that I'd been left high and dry in the Cotswolds but had Reece not stayed on at Flight Centre, I probably wouldn't be writing this book. It meant he could stay on and it meant that when he went out of the office for two weeks, to nearly kill himself on icy Scottish mountain passes, people paid attention.

A couple of months later and we had passed our motorbike tests and found ourselves sat down with a couple of Lucy's colleagues, namely a guy called David Owen, who agreed to support the trip. The first commitment was that they would give us £5,000 to buy the bike if we put the £5,000 in to buy the sidecar. We thought that was great, I mean we didn't have £5,000 to buy a sidecar but we thought if we bought the bike, we'd have a much better chance of blagging a sidecar on the cheap. The next thing we knew we had the cash sat in our bank account, ready to be spent on a bike but absolutely no idea what to buy and no idea how we would put a sidecar on it.

At this point we were stumped. We had got in touch with all of the potential UK sidecar manufacturers and none of them would or could help us. The first we approached was Watsonian Squire. These guys are the real McCoy. The maker of the sidecar you're thinking of. That cool one. The one that Hagrid drives in Harry Potter. The guys at Watsonian aren't too keen on change though. They make one or two really good sidecars and are very reluctant to stray from them. They were even more reluctant to drag their good reputation through the mud and associate themselves with an impossible mission led by a complete couple of berks who had never even sat in a sidecar. Fair enough really but I'm sorry to say it guys, you are now KTM rather than BMW in this little Long Way Round project. After Watsonian, there was very little choice, we were down to trying to find individuals and tiny companies.

The closest we came to getting someone on board was a guy called Rod Young who owned a company called 3 Wheels Better. I went to see Rod in his little barn in rural Oxfordshire and he was exceptionally enthusiastic and full of advice but sadly he had decided to move to Croatia so couldn't join the team. We were really running out of options. We had £5,000 ready and waiting to buy an outfit with, and no idea what to spend it on.

However, one of the key lessons we learnt through this project is that if you stick it out and keep going, something will turn up. Eventually, the universe will help you out and you'll be presented with exactly what you need. Well, in this case, exactly what we needed was a 74-year-old man named Charlie Prescott.

One day in early 2017, Charlie walked into TSB bank in Banbury and undertook his banking as usual with one of the team he'd been banking with for years. That team member was Reece's step-mum, Cindie, and, in their conversation, she happened to mention that her stepson had come home one day and said, "I'm planning on going around the world on a scooter with a sidecar."

"Yeah right, that will never happen," was the unanimous response from Cindie and Mark, Reece's dad, and they probably would have been right had Cindie not mentioned Reece's outlandish ambitions to Charlie that day. It turned out that Charlie loved all things sidecars and told Cindie that if we needed any advice, we should give him a call.

A couple of weeks later we were greeted by the Prescott brothers at their barn in Warwickshire. Smiling under his Peaky Blinders-style farmer's cap, Charlie welcomed us in his proper Banbury accent (think West Country) with, "So what's the plan boys?"

"Well we're going to be the first people to ride around the world on a scooter and sidecar, Charlie, only thing is we can't get our hands on a scooter and sidecar."

"You spoke to Watsonian?"

"Yeah, it was looking to be around £10,000."

"Bloody hell! Well, if we weren't so busy, we could put one together for you."

Richard, Charlie's younger brother, popped out from inside the barn, "Well, we could probably do it, couldn't we?"

I think Charlie knew he might say that, and his eyes lit up. As did ours, because within two minutes we appeared to have a manufacturing team. We had absolutely no idea about the credibility of these two fellas or whether they really had it in their locker to build a sidecar that would take us around the world but we had zero other options and they seemed like good blokes, so we shook hands and said, "Let's do it!"

The agreement was that we would buy the bike Charlie thought was most appropriate and then they would bang a sidecar on. We had no idea how much it was going to cost us and no idea if

Charlie and Richard could actually do it, but a week later, I drove out of Metropolis Motorcycles on a brand new Honda SH300i scooter. It cost a cool £4,000 and I banged it on a credit card in case we had to give the £5,000 Flight Centre had given us to the fellas. I cruised down the motorway at 80 mph on the scooter and pulled in at the Prescotts' fully expecting to muck in and help build the sidecar, but it soon became apparent I was more getting in the way than I was helping. This was serious business. To our knowledge, nobody had ever put a sidecar on this bike before and the lads had a real task on their hands. They were planning to pull it to pieces in order to build it back up and they didn't need me kicking around, getting in the way. I was alright with that because I had a lot to do. At this point I was a one-man team.

Reece was having problems at home. A couple of days after we got back from chatting to the Prescotts I was sat in my living room when I got a knock at the door. It was Reece in full bike gear and his helmet, with a rucksack full of things. He flicked up his visor and revealed some exceptionally bloodshot, watery eyes. He'd been balling it all the way from Lambeth to Hither Green because he and Anuschka had split up. Two weeks away on the UK tour and the subsequent sponsorship from Flight Centre had made the trip seem very real. It was actually going to happen and there was a very real possibility that Reece and I would be driving off on an adventure for the best part of two years. We wouldn't be coming home in that time, we would have very little time for visits and we'd have long periods where we were completely uncontactable. Having that kind of commitment looming over a relationship is straining. Ultimately, it was too straining for Reece and Anuschka and they decided to go their separate ways.

Reece took it pretty badly. By this time, I was living back in London. I had started to lose my mind out in Sibford and managed to get a decent gig working part-time in the charity sector in the big city. Chels and I were living in a house share with Tama, his girlfriend, Laurel, and another mate called Bec. We had a spare room, so Reece bought a dodgy mattress and moved in. He spent the next couple of months getting drunk and hiding from the fact he'd split up with his first love to drive around the world in a stupid sidecar. It was a tough pill to swallow. It made things tougher for me too because things were getting real and we had a countdown.

David at Flight Centre brought us back in and said, "We need a departure date." After learning about our success with the pro sidecar manufacturers he offered to provide us with the cash we needed to get there. This was brilliant. We wanted to keep Flight Centre happy, so we just set an arbitrary date ASAP: the 21st October 2017. Wonderful! From the outside we were looking great: we had a date set, a sidecar being built and a major corporate sponsor on board. Behind the scenes, we were a mess.

We had six months until departure, and nothing was prepared. Reece was festering in a pity cave with a broken heart, while I was spending long nights either staring at an endless list of tasks or trying to convince Chels not to follow Anuschka's lead and jump ship, too. Meanwhile, we had the Prescott brothers, who could have been the Chuckle brothers for all we knew, potentially spending the only money we had on a barn-built hunk of junk, and time was ticking away fast. In less than six months we would still need to plan which way to go, buy all the kit we would need, work out how to tell the stories so that we might actually achieve something, find out how not to die in all of the places we'd be going, learn how to drive a sidecar and somehow get clued up on mechanics. It was a challenging time.

– 2 –

"IF YOU ARE TAKEN HOSTAGE, THERE'S A CHANCE YOU COULD BE RAPED, IT'S NOT A SEXUAL THING, IT'S A DOMINANCE THING."

Throughout the start of 2017, I was in full Colonel Sanders mode. Although Flight Centre had pledged a huge amount of support, it was nowhere near enough to get us around the world. If we wanted to make it through the toughest places on the planet, we'd need to be well equipped and if we wanted to film it to a good standard, we'd need good camera kit too. That stuff costs a lot of money. You can spend tens of thousands of pounds equipping two blokes with all the gear, especially if you have no idea what you really need.

I spent my days and nights either working or trying to get sponsorship. I'd apply for grants, ring companies, email off to request kit and just try and get any support I could find. I had very limited success, most people weren't as keen as Chris Spinks. Fortunately, it didn't take Reece long to drag himself off the pavement and he was doing the same. Plus, I never really had to worry about Chels. We were going to miss each other, but she had her own plans to travel and see the world. She wanted to travel to far-flung places, buy rare and bespoke products from local artisans and then sell them online. She did it. It now exists as www.higgler.shop and it's awesome, check it out. So, all was fine at home and at least we were tackling this massive to-do list as a team. Plus, the manufacturing arm of the team was more than pulling its weight.

It wasn't long before the fellas had rustled up an outfit. My parents drove us over to take our first look at the sidecar when it was finished, and it was a thing of beauty. A bright, shiny Flight Centre red. It had a rally car seat in it and a theme park-style bar in front to hold on to. There was a secret compartment behind the chair so we could hide our valuables, too (Charlie was a bit pissed off with us when we announced to the world that it was there in our first vlog). The lads had constructed the sidecar in just a few weeks in their evenings and they had done a wonderful job, we had lucked out. They certainly weren't the Chuckle brothers. There were no modifications to the bike except they had upgraded the rear suspension to help with the balance. The suspension was donated by the legendary Hagon Shocks. It's said, "They take the load from the road," and they really did. They were about the only thing on the rig that didn't break at all.

We took it for an exceptionally tentative first spin, as we were very nervous to drive it. So nervous in fact that we later ended up taking it to shows on the back of Reece's dad's pickup. How ridiculous is that? We were taking it to shows to promote the fact we were going to drive it around the world, but we were too scared to ride it to the show. It was a sign of just how underprepared we were.

Charlie, Richard, and the rest of their team, including Malcolm Kew, really had done a wonderful job. That made me a little nervous. I was kind of hoping they would have banged something together out of old bits of metal they found lying around but this thing looked like the real deal. It looked too good. It looked expensive.

After the last test drive and the last bit of tinkering with the fellas, I went to pick up the sidecar from Richard's house and asked him that big question.

"Richard, thanks so much for all of your help, mate! It's just perfect. How much do we owe you for all the parts and all of your time?"

To which he replied, "Ahhh, I don't want your money, boy!"

"What, come on? I've got to give you something, at least for the parts!"

"No, I'm just pleased to see a couple of lads your age, out trying to do something with their time, rather than sitting in, glued to the telly!"

Unbelievable. I was completely taken aback. I asked a couple more times to give him something, but he wasn't interested. We knew the lads were doing us a solid and it wouldn't be as pricey as Watsonian but not even letting us pay for the parts was just completely unexpected. The Prescotts and their team didn't do it to associate a brand, get a bit of marketing or for any personal gain. They just did it because they thought it was a good thing to do. As simple as that. We wanted to go on this trip to prove that the world is full of great people and we didn't have to go far to start collecting the evidence we needed. Before I left, I promised to take good care of it and Richard said, "Well, she's built to break and I'm sure she will. I don't know how far you'll get but you'll just have to suck it and see!" That advice, "suck it and see," became somewhat of a trip motto from then on.

So, we were looking good. We had corporate backing, a beauty of a sidecar, Barclaycard had paid for the bike (we still owe them for that) and we had £5,000 sat in the company account to buy kit with. I say company, I mean it literally. We decided to set up the project as a community interest company (CIC) under the name, "As Seen From The Sidecar." The project name was never really right but we didn't have time to mess around with it, so it just stuck, but registering as a CIC meant two things. Firstly, we could collect money to be distributed at a later stage to the charities we would support but all funds raised would be legally tied to the fight against modern slavery; secondly, it meant we were eligible for other streams of funding, such as start-up grants.

It just so happened that in the summer of 2017 Honda released the Honda Engine Room Champions for Change competition. It was a £5,000 start-up grant to be awarded to a company that wanted to make a change in society. We couldn't believe it. We'd been trying to get through to Honda for months but with no luck and this would be the perfect angle. Surely, we could win—we were hoping to change the world using a Honda machine! We made a dodgy video explaining our idea, in which I chucked a banana at Reece, uploaded it and won the public vote. It was incredible. We had been grinding it out so much on the phones and emails and then £5,000 landed on our lap from a little public vote. It was quite funny really. I think that Honda was probably a bit annoyed we won at the time because they just gave us the money and buried it. There was no announcement, nobody who voted would have known that we had won. They didn't want to back the trip because they were thinking what everyone else was thinking: it can't be done!

Slowly, though, it was getting done and we were starting to convince people that we were at least going to leave. A couple more companies started to get behind us, too. Devitt Insurance promised to sponsor our insurance wherever they could and, most importantly, a company called Survival Wisdom agreed to get us expedition-ready.

We first went down to see the Survival Wisdom guys in April of 2017. I had been on a bit of a holiday down to Cornwall in 2016 and had been walking around the incredible Mount Edgcumbe estate where I passed a bloke giving a little talk about a rowing boat. The bloke was a guy called Richard Pyshorn and he was talking about how his team had provided survival training for a group of women who became the first all-female team to row the Pacific. I was blown away by the story and later watched their documentary on Netflix, "Losing Sight of Shore." It's unbelievable; watch it. I thought at the time, "If I ever get this thing off the ground, I'm going to get that guy on the team," so I reached out to Richard and gave him an irresistible offer:

"Can you give me a crapload of your time and expertise for free just because we're trying to do a good thing, even though there's a strong chance we will fail and potentially damage your company's reputation?"

Richard replied with an instant yes. What a guy. He sent us a kit list and said turn up on these dates and we will put you through your paces.

We turned up to Plymouth on the Megabus with a massive rucksack full of nothing practical and went to meet Richard. He introduced us to one of his trainers, Jason, and explained the company's background. It turned out they were all ex-military and had made careers out of training the toughest of the tough. Jason had delivered survival training to the SAS and Richard had been at the top of the game when it comes to coping with being captured by the enemy. They were the real deal. After all of the intros Richard told us he wanted us to kick off the session by talking Jase through all of what we had planned. We told Jase that we had a scooter and sidecar being built and even though we'd never driven one before we wanted to take it down the length of Africa, up through the Americas and then drive it home from far east Russia. We told him that this would mean taking it through some of the world's toughest environments: through the Sahara, over the Andes and back through a Siberian winter.

Jason already knew all of this of course. He's the kind of bloke that does his homework, he just wanted to hear it from the horse's mouth. He told us that he admired our courage, but he thought it was one of the biggest challenges he'd ever heard of. He said, "Usually with stuff like this you've got one kind of environment to prepare for, cold, hot, jungle etc., but you fellas have got to prepare for them all!" We knew that, but he really knew it. He'd been to these environments and knew how bloody miserable and potentially deadly they could be. We hadn't. We were incredibly naïve. But that naivety was probably the only reason it happened. I certainly wouldn't be quite so bold, knowing what I know now.

Over the course of the weekend Jase took us through the ins and outs of the kinds of environments we would face. He showed us how to set up a camp, how to start a fire and how to stay warm at night without a sleeping bag. That last bit wasn't in the plan. Reece and I had both not thought to bring a sleeping bag to an outdoor, overnight course (I hope you're starting to understand the level of idiocy you're dealing with here). The next day Richard took us through some first aid stuff. He taught us what a tourniquet was and explained why we needed to buy Quick Clot but most importantly he took us through some mental preparation stuff. We talked about the kinds of stress and strains we would get from doing this kind of thing. We talked about some of the situations that could unfold and how we should deal with them. He taught us how to stay calm in high pressure environments.

How to weigh up your decisions by "counting your lemons" and using your "Spidey senses." Basically, he taught us how to stay alive when stuff turns south.

He also took us through some hostage scenarios and explained what it would be like if we were to be taken and how we should deal with it. He said stuff like, "If you are captured, there's a chance you could be raped, it's not a sexual thing, it's a dominance thing." We struggled to contain our nervous laughter. This wasn't a joke though, he was serious. So much so that Jase gave us a bollocking halfway through for not taking notes. Well, not so much a bollocking, it was worse than that: one of those glaring stares, the kind that makes the hairs on the back of your neck stand up. I don't think I've ever found a pen quicker.

The fellas weren't convinced by us at all and told us we needed to come back for another weekend. A few months later we did exactly that and drove the sidecar down there. It was our first real ride out on the rig, and it went pretty smoothly. We managed to clock something like 75 mph going downhill on the M5 and I even had my first nap in the sidecar. This was before we had a seat belt or a screen, so I was flying along the motorway sat in the open, in a rally seat, napping at 75 mph.

It was probably that day that we realised how much fun driving a sidecar is. A sidecar outfit in the UK is registered as a solo motorcycle which is completely absurd because you may as well be riding a penny farthing. They are that different. If you're any good at riding a motorcycle you more or less control it by leaning one way or the other whereas a sidecar is almost fully controlled by the accelerator. Want to go right? Ease off the accelerator and let the sidecar swing you 'round. Want to go left? Pile on the mustard and overtake the seat. As simple as that. However, always remember that too many beans and you'll lift the chair, too heavy on the brakes and you'll lift your back wheel.

Fortunately, we eased into it slowly and on that trip down to Cornwall we were steering the rig like it was a ship, with no danger of lifting anything. We pulled into the Survival Wisdom HQ and Richard was really impressed with what we had brought along. He said the only modification he would make would be to fit a screen to add some protection so after another weekend of going through emergency procedures, lighting fires and learning how not to die, we returned home and had a local guy weld on that monstrosity of a roof. It was a bit dodgy but by this time we were only a few weeks away from departure so we needed a quick fix.

So, logistically we were more or less set. We had a sidecar, we had an idea of what to take, where to go and how not to die, plus we had a few grand in the account from the Flight Centre sponsorship and the Honda Engine Room winnings. What we didn't have was a clear idea of how we would tell the stories and how we would raise money and awareness for the fight against modern slavery. We decided that as well as telling the stories of everyday people we met on the road, we would arrange to meet up with a charity which was fighting modern slavery in every country we passed through and tell their story too.

To kick off this idea we met up with a UK anti-slavery charity called Unseen. Unseen is based in Bristol, so we first dropped in there, stinking of bonfire, on the way back from the survival training. We met with Kate Garbers, co-founder of Unseen, and Hannah Young, their Head of Fundraising. By this point we had done a fair bit of research about Unseen's work and slavery in general, but it was pretty humbling to hear just how big an issue modern slavery is, directly from the people who are trying to end it. At this point, Unseen was an organisation with around ten to twenty full-time heads, and they had a primary goal of ending modern slavery. Full stop. Not modern slavery in Bristol, not modern slavery in the South West, not the UK, they wanted to end it the world over.

Modern slavery and human trafficking globally are more profitable annually than Apple, Samsung, Toyota, Microsoft, and Facebook combined, totaling around US$150 billion in 2017. There are estimated to be 40.3 million people enslaved worldwide, three times the amount there was at the time of the trans-Atlantic slave trade. It's in every country on earth and it's underground; it's quite literally *unseen*. Just let those stats sink in for a minute . . . 40.3 million people. The size of the issue is just completely unfathomable. Impossible to imagine, let alone change. Yet, sat in front of us were two people who were saying, deadpan, cold-faced, outright serious, "We're going to end it." That left us completely inspired and wholly confident we could chalk off our little challenge. We've been back to visit them since our return and they've now got over 70 people working at Unseen. Their positive attitude is completely infectious. It's no surprise they're growing so rapidly. I think Kate and Hannah are right, I think they probably will end it.

We told them about our project and how we thought the key to counteracting the scaremongering in the news was by creating a more personally connected world. We thought that we could also apply that idea to modern slavery. Statistically, we all enslave at least ten people a year through the products we buy and the services we use. If we knew those people personally, there's no way we would do it. So, we figured if we could make the issue more personal it would be a good start. The best way of forging personal connections is, of course, by meeting people so Hannah and Kate agreed to see if any of the survivors they support would be up for talking to us. A few weeks later we found ourselves in a community kitchen with a guy called Mo (not his real name). Mo had agreed to talk to us and to tell us his story. We wanted to hear Mo's whole story. Not just his modern slavery story. We wanted to find out who he really was and convey that, at the same time as learning about the ordeal he had been through.

We lucked out with Mo because what made Mo, Mo was a passion for cooking. Hannah arranged for us to meet up in a community kitchen and to cook a curry. At first Mo was a fairly reserved kind of guy and, being kind of nerdy and awkward ourselves, it was polite handshakes and smiles all 'round. Then we got around to the cooking.   In true "Ready. Steady. Cook." fashion, Mo turned out his bag with a grin that would rival Ainsley's himself. From this point on he was a different a kind of guy. He was completely at home in the kitchen. Dicing, chopping, shaking, stirring, Mo controlled the kitchen like no man you've ever seen. He did it with such certainty and flair, it was like watching a true pro at work.

Mo uses cooking as a form of escape. He loves to cook and said that when he cooks, he feels like he's singing and dancing. We chatted to him for a couple of hours while he magnificently constructed a slow cooked lamb curry complete with fried aubergine and pilau rice. Mo told us all about himself. All about what he did in his spare time but mainly about how much he loved to cook and how his dream was to one day open a restaurant of his own. The curry was genuinely out of this world and when Mo does finally open his restaurant, I'll be the first through the door.

Mo also talked to us about his life and how he had come to be living in a safe house in the South West with Unseen. Originally from Myanmar, Mo's family had to flee to Bangladesh when he was just six. They were refugees, forced to run from the persecution of the Myanmar Military, who were described by the UN as carrying out ethnic cleansing in the country. Mo's salvation in Bangladesh was short lived, as he and his family were tossed into a refugee camp which he describes as a prison camp. He told us of the awful conditions people in the camp suffered, which included forced labour, a lack of food and even torture. Anyone who tried to leave was shot, but at age fourteen, Mo decided it was worth the risk and fled the camp.

He made it out, but after being forced to flee the camp Mo found himself in Bangladesh illegally. Being there illegally made life hard. It meant that he had no official identification to use to get good work. But being the charismatic, quick-witted guy that he is, Mo managed to hustle his way through life in Bangladesh and by his twenties he was living a decent life and making good money as a model. Still though, Mo was living there illegally and constantly looking over his shoulder. Being there without identification also meant that Mo had been unable to go back to the camp and see his family, whom he had left behind. If he went back without official identification, he would be at risk of being deported back to Myanmar or thrown back into the camp he had escaped.

One-day Mo got an offer. An offer too good to refuse: good work and a passport, a British one. Two people approached Mo and told him how nice people were in the UK and that in the UK they would accept him as a migrant and give him a British passport. How could he resist? That passport would be official documentation and his ticket to getting back to find his family.

Mo committed to going to the UK.

After a month in the back of a lorry (he had no idea it was so far), Mo was trafficked into slavery, working first in a household as a domestic servant and then in a kitchen in London. He wasn't paid for his work and was just given food to survive. He was completely trapped. Eventually, Mo escaped the kitchen but then ended up being enslaved on building sites in other parts of London. Finally, someone put him in touch with Unseen, who pulled him out of slavery and put him up in their safe house.

When we met, Mo was waiting for his paperwork to come through so he could finally get that UK passport. He's now got what he was after and has left Unseen's support network to start a new life. Hearing Mo's story firsthand gave us a deeper understanding of the issue. It made those horrendous facts jump off the page and come to life. Mo's story was just horrific. His life had been governed by people abusing his vulnerability, a constant flow of traffickers taking Mo's freedom and keeping it for themselves, profiting from his suffering. We were just so shocked that people could do such terrible things to other people and, worse still, we couldn't pass it off as just really bad luck for Mo, because there were another 40.3 million people out there with a similar story to tell. This experience just made us more certain that we had to succeed in this challenge and that we had to do anything we could to inspire action against modern slavery.

The summer of 2017 passed in a flash. Before we knew it, it was September 30th, my birthday, and there were only three weeks left to go. Reece's mum, Debbie, and step-dad Marc had arranged a fundraiser for us at their local village hall that night. It was just a gig night but a good one. Reece's cousin Mark Stanley (voice of an angel) and his band, The Epics, performed. Reece's family ran the bar and my parents served out fish and chips from their chip van. We raised about £1,000 through ticket sales, food and a raffle, but we also landed another corporate sponsor. We were offering up the chance to name the sidecar for a cool £2,500. We didn't think anyone would ever actually go for it but thought it was worth a go. Incredibly, it was purchased that night for a sale rate of £2,000 by a guy called Munya Mukatini. He named it Kuishi na Kuishi after a sustainable pig farm he was planning to set up in Tanzania. Just completely random, you couldn't dream it up. Munya was Reece's brother's mate and had just come to support. Kuishi na Kuishi means something along the lines of "live well" in Swahili. Although we were hoping for a more run-of-the-mill name, maybe Barry or something, we thought a name that meant "live well" was quite apt and it stuck!

Reece's parents' neighbours Luigi and Jan decided that their company, the Gazeboshop, would like to sponsor too and they offered £1,000 worth of backing. It was pretty humbling to get the support of these two additional companies. It really was great to see that they just believed in the same things the trip stood for. It was a good job too, because despite our efforts at impersonating Colonel Sanders, we hadn't had any luck with getting sponsors, so we were left with no option but to buy all of the expensive kit. By this time, we had moved back to our parents' places in Banbury and were working full time on preparing for the trip. We still had zero gear so over the next couple of weeks we just went on one giant shopping spree. We still had to buy everything, including all of the first aid stuff the survival guys had advised. Chels actually caught me ordering a couple of tourniquets online, which made for an awkward conversation.

"What's a tourniquet then?" asked Chels.

"Well, if we have a big crash in the middle of nowhere and we can't stop the bleeding on one of our limbs, you just slip that over it and tighten it up."

"What? Are you serious?" Chels replied in a very worried tone.

I reassuringly replied with, "Yeah, yeah it's okay though because you just lose the limb and not your life. Don't worry about it."

Chels burst into tears. She had been very understanding about the whole project but the idea of us preparing to lose a limb was just too much to hear. I don't blame her really. We look back at it and laugh now but at the time it was really getting too much. I'd completely ripped us away from our life in London for the project and this wasn't the first, or the last time, it brought Chels to tears. Making her upset like that was terrible, not just because I love the girl but because of who she is. She's completely the kindest, most loving person you could ever meet and making her cry makes you feel like you're kicking a kitten.

It wasn't just Chels crying either. Reece and I were weeping at the stack of receipts we were piling up. We spent thousands and thousands of pounds over those last few weeks, all stacked up on credit cards so we would still have the cash from our corporate backing to get us around the world. We went to the Motorcycle Megastore in Swindon and walked out with about £3,000 worth of kit. It sounds a lot, but this stuff is important. We knew we would be living in our helmets for the next couple of years, so we didn't cheap out on them plus we had to get boots, riding gear, intercoms, a sat nav, the full works.

On the 19th October, we found ourselves stood in my parent's dining room with kit absolutely everywhere. There was motorcycle gear, camping gear, first aid kit, emergency rations, tools and, of course, loads of camera kit. Just as we thought there couldn't be anymore, the doorbell rang. Our sleeping bags had finally arrived. They were massive. We'd opted for some really warm ones, but we'd got it horribly wrong. They took up about as much space as the rest of our kit combined. There was no way we could take them, and they'd have to go back.

We were getting pretty stressed. Well, I say getting pretty stressed, we had been pretty stressed for a while and now we were getting really stressed. On the surface we were both quite relaxed, but signs were starting to show. In the past, if I've been a little bit stressed, I'd end up getting the odd mouth ulcer, just a little one, but by the 19th October, I had Bonjela coming out of my ears and could barely open my mouth. In usual circumstances we would have just admitted we weren't ready and pushed back our departure, but we couldn't do that because we had made an almighty song and dance about leaving. We had arranged our London-to-Paris Rally Against Modern Slavery.

It turned out that the week we were departing was Anti-Slavery week so we teamed up with Unseen to put on an event that would tie in with their "Let's Nail It" campaign, which was targeting slavery in nail bars. The idea was that we would get as many people as possible together to leave in convoy from London's Ace Café to drive through to Paris, all with their index and middle fingernails painted yellow, performing a two-finger salute in the face of modern slavery. Amazingly, Eurotunnel had sponsored it, so the event had done quite well, and we were expecting sixty people to turn up on Saturday 21st October to ride with us to Paris. We would be setting off from Ace at 8 a.m., which meant setting off from Banbury on the 20th.

At the same time, the trip had started to attract a bit of local media attention and that night we went live on drive time with Howard Bentham from Radio Oxford. We told Howard all about what we were doing and how we were planning to set off in the morning but after the best part of two years of planning we still didn't have a sleeping bag. That night, Reece went back home to his mum's place and I went off to sleep in my own bed for what would be the last time in a very long time.

I didn't get much sleep at all, but I didn't need it either. It felt like I was just running off adrenaline constantly. Before I knew it, Reece was back over at my gaff and we were getting the bike packed up to go. Chels was taking public transport to meet us in London so she set off early. I remember seeing her walk off down the road to the bus stop and thinking how nuts it was that we wouldn't be back in this house together for potentially a couple of years. Chels had been running our press office at the time and had been responsible for getting us on the radio. That morning she'd had a call from BBC Oxford News and booked us in for a recorded interview for their social media channels.

We had also arranged to do some tours of London by sidecar to raise some more money for the charities. Suddenly we were up against it. We had to pack the sidecar, drive to the BBC interview, drive on to London, do two tours of London by Sidecar, crack on again to the Ace Café and be ready for the morning departure. We'd never packed the sidecar before and it turned out to be a lot harder than we imagined. We spent ages trying to tie our spare tyres on but just couldn't work it out. Eventually, my dad had to take over and he drilled a hole through our roof and made a kind of vise thing that would screw down onto the tyres, keeping them stuck on. It worked well enough to get going and we set sail for London.

We left the house in a rushed kind of fashion. No pictures or anything. There's no footage. It was just, "Must dash Mum, we're going to be late," and we sped off into the distance. We did the interview quickly at Bicester and pushed on to London. I did the first tour of London by Sidecar which had been bought by Emily Holzhausen, who was part of the Carers UK crew, whom I had worked with in the six months building up to the trip. Without their support and advice, it would have taken a lot longer to get the project off the ground. I took Emily's mum for a quick spin around all of the sites in London and said a final goodbye to the Carers UK team. Meanwhile Reece had been trying to get us some travel insurance sorted. Yeah, we hadn't done that either. It had looked for a while like we were going to get it sponsored but they dropped out last minute.

If you don't get travel insurance sorted before you leave, then you're done for. You can get it once you're on the road but it's much harder to do and it costs an absolute fortune. We managed to get ours done at 17:05 on that Friday night. The place shut at 17:00 but amazingly someone stayed on to push it through for us. It cost £2,000 but it had to be done and we were so relieved to get it locked in at the last minute. Next, Reece took the sidecar off me and took our mate Cathal on the other tour of London. For him that meant sitting in traffic on the North Circular up to the Ace Café. Meanwhile, I met up with Chels and we were tasked with getting the last bits. Nothing too big, just the small matter of getting the things we would sleep in most nights for the next eighteen months or so.

We found a sports shop in Covent Garden and snapped up a couple of bags. We then took a stroll back up through China Town, grabbed a BBQ pork bun for dinner, and jumped on the Northern Line headed for Ace Café. Everyone was already there and by this point it was around 8 p.m. We decided to check into the Travelodge first and then head down but we went to the wrong one and got lost.

Chels and I finally made it to the Ace at about 10 p.m., completely stressed and worn out. We grabbed a pint and ended up sitting in the Travelodge bar nattering with friends until 2 a.m. I didn't feel tired at all. I had just turned on my adrenaline tap and it wasn't going off. After another pint, we finally went off to sleep for what would be the last time on British soil for a long time.

–3–

"I REMEMBER LOOKING AROUND AND JUST THINKING '*FUCKING HELL THIS IS INSANE.*"

Six a.m. alarm rang. I woke up in an instant and just lay there for a few minutes. A part of me just didn't want to get up and turn that light on. Turning it on meant leaving for real. It meant setting off from the UK on a scooter and sidecar, driving off in one direction and driving back in from the other, having gone around the entire planet. That was one part of me. The other was just absolutely buzzing with excitement. Today, after all this bloody faffing, after the stress, after the tubes and tubes of Bonjela, we were finally doing it. I rolled over, packed my things, and got going. We were at Ace Café for 7 a.m. and people started to pour in straight away. All of our family and friends, old work colleagues, and bikers who had heard about the trip were there, seemingly everybody we knew and more.

I set up a little registration desk by the front door and started ticking off people as they came. The first on the scene was a girl called Gemma. She was a real character. Gemma reached out to us as soon as she heard of the event. She was a passionate volunteer event steward (who knew that was a thing?) and in a two-minute conversation, told us how she loves organising rallies and would be happy to lead the charge to Paris with the proper convoy lights and everything. She also said, "Lads, quick tip for you, when you're shitting in the wild, hold onto a tree." So, she was a somewhat sporadic fountain of practical knowledge but a real asset for the team.

Next to walk in was Gerry. Gerry's an Irish guy who lives on the road. Classes himself as a Minimalist Motorcycle Vagabond. He lives on his bike and loves to travel. Gerry found us when we were down promoting the ride at the Ace Café's Brighton Burnout. He took a flyer off Reece, read it and, in his ever-excited Irish voice, said, "You're doing what? You're going around the world on that thing! My word, give me those flyers." He then proceeded to spend the next hour or so working the stand and trying to get people in to hear what we had planned. It turned out the ride out coincided with his birthday and he'd been wanting to plan something for it, so he signed up there and then. The man is a legend.

After Gerry came Bob or, as he's best known, Bob the Bear. Bob is one of these brilliant characters who does something quirky, just because it's quirky. Bob drives a Ural sidecar outfit and has built his very own life-size teddy bear as a passenger. He made it at the time of the Queen's Golden Jubilee. He now dresses up in a full bear costume and, from time to time, just races around London putting a smile on people's faces. Another complete legend. Next in was Roger, or Roger Redbeard as he's more widely known. He too, drives a Ural outfit. He had found us at the Overland Event and hadn't signed up to come to Paris but had just driven down from Birmingham to wave us off. There were a load more people who turned up to wave us off including some of the Carers UK team, lots of friends and our web guy turned good pal, Todd Specht. Todd found out about our project really early and offered to do all of our website stuff for nothing. He does it for a living and is a real pro, he's donated what would normally be thousands of pounds worth of web development just because he believes in the same things the project stands for.

Mark Wilsmore (a.k.a. the Face of the Ace) and Vasilis, their main man for organising all events, gave all participants a sausage sarnie on the house as they entered, but there was barely any time to wolf it down. Before we knew it, it had passed 8 a.m. and we needed to crack on. We got all of the bikes in together for a big final picture and then geared up to set off. I was in the driving seat, so I grabbed Kuishi's reins, sounded the horn a few times, got a chorus of horns back and pulled out of the car park. A guy called Tamas raced past me on his motorbike and turned on his steward lights. He and Gemma would be top-and-tailing the group all the way to Paris.

The next thing we knew, we were on the North Circular heading around London. It was a glorious morning, a bit chilly with the sun only just piercing through the clouds. We were racing along at the front of the pack. Every turn we made or any time we needed to change lanes, there was no need to indicate or look because either the steward crew were holding the traffic, or the motorcyclists were riding in formation behind us. It felt like we were in a royal convoy.

We made great progress, got around London and headed south for the tunnel. Around halfway there the weather turned, and it tipped it down. England was giving us a final taste of what she was made of, something to remember her by. In the rush at the Ace I'd forgotten to don my waterproof trousers too, so I was drenched.

Gemma met us at the entrance to the terminal. "All trains delayed, lads. Severe weather in France." Great, I thought, I can pay a final visit to the home of the Whopper and dry off before leaving the UK. We were only an hour or so delayed and before we knew it, we were back in the rig and queuing to get on the train. It was absolutely hammering it down and we were sat there getting sodden. That was until we spotted a little tea stand by the entrance. We went over just to get out of the rain but after hearing what we had planned, the ladies running it gave us our last proper brew on the house.

Going down into the tunnel was a bit of a weird feeling. There was just so much nervous anticipation. We knew this was it. Say goodbye to UK soil, we were off to see the world! The atmosphere on the train was great. Everyone seemed to have the same excited buzz about them. I think it might have had something to do with the weather. If there's anything that will get a bunch of Brits buzzed off their collective tits, it's a weather warning.

We arrived at Calais, pulled out on the other side of the road, and sure enough the weather was atrocious. Really, really strong winds and fairly heavy rain. The idea was to meet in the first garage, but we lost a couple of people who cheesed it off onto the continent. All of the bikers were still with us, though, and we were huddling in the shelter of the garage where we considered calling the whole thing off. The weather really was that bad and it just didn't seem safe for the guys on two wheels to continue. Plus, we obviously had no insurance to run an event like this so if anyone was seriously injured, we'd be returning in a couple of years to a stern word from the boys in blue. Reece and I were mainly okay in Kuishi, the third wheel meant we weren't going to tip over in the wind but for the bikers it seemed genuinely dodgy. A couple of bikers did decide to call it a day there. The rest of us thought, "Ahh it'll be alright," and we cracked on.

As we pressed on, the wind didn't get any better and, at times, we were driving straight into it. With the screen and the tower of tyres on top, we had an absolute crapload of drag. At one point we were getting about 40 mph full throttle. We were rinsing the fuel, too, and were having to pull in at every fuel station we passed. Eventually, at around 7 p.m. we pulled into the campsite in Paris. We'd lost Bob the Bear somewhere and most of the cars had gone ahead to start their holidays rather than following us at 40 mph. With us still were a couple on Lambrettas, Gerry, Gemma, and Andy Barnes. Andy was an absolute hero that day and managed to keep up the whole way, despite being absolutely battered around on his tiny 125cc bike.

We had arranged for everyone to meet for a celebratory dinner in a little biker hangout called La Forge. They were mates of the Ace Café and had promised everyone a three-course dinner for £20 a head. We got there and it was only a cheese toastie. It was a very cool place, though. It was basically a really expensive bike garage for commuters, but the bikes were left on display. The sidecar got put up next to them for the night and everyone settled into an evening celebrating the success of the rally. Halfway through the evening my brother Lee and his then-fiancée, Charlotte, pulled us aside to show us a video he had put together with the help of Chels. It was good luck messages from all of our friends and family. They were hilarious. The funniest of all was the message from Reece's mum. Chels had asked her to record the video "landscape" so it would fit with the others. Deb sent a portrait video of her in a field with a nice landscape in the background. Brilliant.

We spent the evening drinking beers and hanging out. There were so many people there that I ended up doing that thing where you don't really talk to anyone. We partied late but the following morning there was no time to rest, as we had planned a ride out with the guys from La Forge. A group of French bikers turned out to give us the most incredible tour of the city. Bikers and cars were welcome to join, and we took in the sights before the city woke up. We did the standard shot in front of the Eiffel Tower, took a drive past the Arc de Triomphe and scooted to the top of the city to look over the most incredible views from the Sacré-Cœur Basilica. Bob had a spare bear costume with him (of course), so Chels dressed up as a bear and got to ride pillion with him. It was brilliant. After the ride, we waved goodbye to many. Gerry had originally planned to explore France but because of the weather he said, "I'm going to head north with the bear." After we had said goodbye to a load of friends, we had a couple of hours to take stock before we went to meet with our first charity of the trip, Utopia 56.

We had got in touch with Ivan of Utopia 56 sometime before we had set off. We wanted to learn a little bit about the ongoing migrant crisis in Europe as it had been what had originally inspired us to start the project. We had initially wanted to visit the Calais Jungle but in the time it had taken us to plan the trip, the Jungle had been shut down. On the surface you could be forgiven for thinking the shutting down of the Jungle would be a good thing, maybe there wasn't a need for it anymore? Ivan told us that wasn't the case at all and that in fact all of the people who had been stranded there were now just on the streets somewhere in Europe, most of them on the streets of Paris. Ivan told us that Utopia 56 estimated there to be something like 3,000 people living on the streets in Paris, many of them refugees. He told us that if we really wanted to understand the issue, we should come back at night-time and visit the humanitarian aid centre they work at. We thought that was a great idea and agreed to meet his colleague Fred the following night.

We went back to meet family and friends for a final night of goodbyes before waving them off the following morning. There was a steady line of goodbyes that all went fine until it was time to wave off our parents. Reece's went first. He balled it. He was a blubbering mess, I had never seen a face quite so puffy, that was until I turned to my left and saw Chelsea's. Her cheeks had puffed up so much that they were pressing against her glasses and actual puddles of tears were forming. Chels wasn't leaving, she was just crying at everyone else crying. Before we knew it, Reece's parents were driving off. Mine followed shortly after. I got a little choked up but didn't really cry, that's not to say there was a lack of tears though. My mum was balling it and I looked around to find both Chels and Reece, once again, in a blubbering mess. It was sad, to be fair, it would be unlikely that we would see them again for at least a year.

Eventually, the dust settled, and it was just me, Reece, Chels and Chelsea's mate Abby left. Chels and Abby had decided that they would drive south with us and keep us company for the first couple of days. They would treat it as a bit of a holiday, take in the Alps and give us a hand with filming, etc. We spent the day hanging out at the campsite and recovering from the weekend. There was no more adrenaline pumping and we were all absolutely knackered. Before we knew it, it was 19:00 and time to go and visit Utopia 56. We took a potter into the centre of Paris, the girls headed to a bar while we jumped on the metro and took a twenty-minute train to an area called Port de la Chappelle.

It was a miserable October evening. There was a piercing cold rain and a heavy wind that made it uncomfortable just to be stood outside. We walked down from the metro station to where we were supposed to be meeting Fred. We didn't have an exact address and couldn't find it at first, then we turned a corner and realised why we didn't need a door number. Poking out between a couple of derelict looking buildings was an almighty, fluorescent, emergency dome. It looked like it had come straight off the set of *The Day After Tomorrow* or some other Hollywood blockbuster. We walked up to the front gate, passing a long queue of inadequately clad people trying to get in. Fred spotted us immediately; we stood out like a sore thumb because we had proper clothes.

Fred took us through the gate, into the registration area, and asked us to wait while he sorted something out. I remember looking around and just thinking, "Fucking hell this is insane." Twenty minutes ago, we had been at the Eiffel Tower arranging what bar to meet the girls in and now we were stood in a real-life disaster movie. We were surrounded by complete desperation. It was incredibly bleak. It was a dark night, but the blisteringly bright emergency lighting showed fear on the faces of almost everybody present.

Fred was running around the place trying to arrange things and instructing other volunteers. The queue of people was mainly made up of guys in their twenties. We managed to have a chat to a few of them. They had come from all over. Some of them had been hopping from migrant camp to migrant camp all the way from West Africa. We asked one guy if he would share his stories on camera, but he refused because he had spoken to the press at a camp in Italy and had been beaten up by officials as a warning not to do it again. Fred explained to us that this centre had been set up by the UN and was supposed to provide short-term relief for no longer than ten days, just for male refugees. There were other camps elsewhere for women and children. Fred said that Utopia 56 was just there to help run the camp because it is so understaffed. His main job was to manage the queue of people and help those who couldn't get in, which, on this occasion, was everyone. The camp was full and only people who had been found on the street in the day were allowed to come in. All of the guys in the queue were advised to just look "elsewhere." Fred knew, of course, that there wasn't an elsewhere and what he was really having to say was, "Find a doorstep somewhere."

It was really a very desperate situation and hard to watch unfold. It was even worse when the families turned up. After we had been at the camp for a little while, I looked over at a smaller registration tent. The zip was undone, and poking through the entrance were two tiny legs. They belonged to somebody who couldn't have been more than three or four. They were just swinging back and forth not quite able to touch the ground below.

I asked Fred about the situation for those in the tent and he said they weren't allowed to stay in the camp, but Utopia had arranged a system whereby volunteers would put families up for a night or two if there was really nowhere else to go. On this occasion though, all of the volunteers already had a family to look after, so Fred was forced to hand a guy a pop-up tent and show him on a map where the closest city park was. They had a couple of blankets, too, and that was it. A normal family of four, in soaking wet clothes, given a couple of blankets, a pop-up tent and told where the closest bit of grass was. We camped that night with proper kit and it was cold. I can't imagine just how bad it must have been for them. The cold, but also the fear.

Imagine being pitched up in a dark corner of an inner-city park with your toddler and young child, with just a blanket to keep warm and absolutely no idea what tomorrow will bring. Now imagine you wake up and somebody comes to the tent and says to you, "Hey man, this is horrendous you can't live like this. I can get you a UK passport and proper job. You can leave your family with my friends and you'll be able to send money back to them until you can afford to send them over. Sound good?" Would you take the offer? Surely you would consider it. It would have to be better than risking it in the park, freezing cold already and with winter on the horizon. Many people do take it, hand over their passports, get in the back of a lorry and leave their families, hoping for a job but ending up trapped in a life of slavery.

It was an unbelievable situation, and more so because we were in Paris. It was France, for Christ's sake, twenty minutes away from those fancy restaurants outside of the Eiffel Tower. We were not in war-torn Sudan yet, this shouldn't be happening. People shouldn't have been queuing for an emergency dome a stone's throw away from the bloody Louvre. It was ridiculous. It made us realise just how ridiculous it all is. We went back to meet Chels and Abby after a couple of hours at the camp. It was one of the most surreal experiences of my life. I got on the Metro and it felt like I was being transported back to another world. It was tough to look at my world the same way. The Eiffel Tower was genuinely mesmerising when it was all lit up that night, but we couldn't sit there watching it without thinking about those people stood out in the rain just twenty minutes away. Looking back, I feel like we should have done something there and then. Paid for a family to go to a hotel or something, but at the time the situation just completely overwhelmed me. I had never seen anything like it before and I just felt like a completely helpless fly on the wall in somebody else's real-life nightmare. We added Utopia 56 onto the list of the charities we would raise for and then the following morning we left Paris and continued our journey to Cape Town.

The first day we decided we would just get through the rest of France ASAP. Not because we didn't like France, but we'd been here before and wanted to get down to the Alps to experience something new. We jumped on the toll roads and, despite some pretty bleak weather, we managed to keep at around 50 mph. It all went rather swimmingly and before we knew it, we had made it to Dijon, the home of mustard. The only delay we had was that Reece had dropped his £100 Gore-Tex rain jacket on our exhaust and burnt a hole in it but to add salt to the wound, he had burnt it through the pocket and scorched our receipt for the toll road so we had to pay the maximum as a penalty, a cool twenty euros.

We spent the following couple of days making our way through the Alps. They were incredible. Just immense view after immense view. We knew it would be good, but we weren't prepared for the relentless beauty that unfolded. Wonderful winding stretches of tarmac through steep valleys with snow-capped peaks above and in the distance. Before we knew it, we had made it to Ace Café Lucerne where we pulled in for a spot of lunch, having made it from Ace to Ace. The following morning, we took on the biggest challenge the sidecar had come across so far, the Gotthard Pass. The pass snakes its way up to just over 2,000 metres above sea level and we had never even really been up a steep hill on the sidecar, let alone taken on a proper mountain. Fortunately, the road surface was immaculate and Kuishi took it in stride. In the end it was Reece and I who slowed down the journey, as we had to stop every ten minutes or so to warm up our hands on the exhaust. It was absolutely freezing and for the first time we found ourselves scooting past snow to the top of a mountain, moaning about the cold.

At the top we were rewarded with some sensational views and we made the most of them by diving into a little coffee shop and enjoying the view from the warm, while tucking into a bar of Toblerone and proper coffee. Posh coffees and Swiss chocolate wouldn't be our normal expedition protocol but while Chels and Abby were here, we still had the excuse for the odd treat. We flew down the mountain a lot quicker than we got up it and pulled into Lake Como that evening.

Lake Como was where we would say goodbye to Chels and Abby. We had a day of exploring the local area and then the following morning, the girls drove off from the Airbnb we had been staying in. It was really quite sad; Chels and I both had a bit of a teary goodbye before we left our bedroom that morning. We got it out of the system so that we could both look hard as nails when Reece inevitably rolled the camera as she drove off. Then, they were gone, and we were well and truly on our own. We were properly off on our expedition.

– 4 –

"HEY MATE, DO LAKES HAVE TIDES?"

We spent a couple more days in Como, sorting our kit out, before pressing on towards Cape Town. The next part of the journey was going to be incredible. We planned to take in the Italian lakes, head up past Venice, and stretch out towards Lake Bled in Slovenia. But the first few days were a massive letdown. It wasn't the serene picture postcard experience I was expecting. We had managed to get stuck on a boring, straight road out to the Adriatic Sea and all we came across were suicidal Italian motorists who genuinely seemed intent on ending our trip as soon as they could. After a couple of days of dodging dangerous potholes and hostile Fiat Pandas, we found ourselves in Chioggia, a little town just down the road from Venice.

It was an incredibly romantic place. It was just like Venice but without the hordes of tourists. We took a little potter around and for some reason Reece found himself thinking back to Anuschka. He stalked her Instagram account to see how she was getting on without him and found that she was doing quite fine, in fact she was on holiday with her new boyfriend. Here Reece was, with his idiotic school mate, on their stupid scooter and sidecar, in one of the most romantic places on the planet, while his first love was off in some far-flung beach resort enjoying the company of her new fella. And, to make matters worse, the new guy had an absolute corker of a beard, something Reece had always wanted but never managed to muster. I think Reece really started to question what the hell he was doing with his life. I said I'd cheer him up and I made him his favourite tea, sausage and mash. It seemed to work; it really doesn't take much to lift Reece's spirits.

The following morning, we pressed on to Lake Bled and decided to take the Vrsic Pass through Triglav National Park. If you've not been, go. It's incredible. It was one of the most unexpected and beautiful pieces of road we drove on throughout the whole trip. The cobbled pass that takes you over the top of the Julian Alps is one of those stretches of road that you get to and think, "How on earth did they put this here?" Well, I gave it a google and they got it there with the help of 10,000 Russian prisoners of war in 1915 and the road is now formally called Russian Road to honour those who constructed it. It was used to fuel the front line during World War I and, in October 2017, it was used by Reece as a quiet place to scoot through, listening to David Gray in his helmet, while shedding a few tears at just how bad a mistake he had made. Oh well, all's fair in love and war, I guess.

That evening, we arrived into Lake Bled after dark and were welcomed with open arms by a lady called Silka. We had contacted Silka through Couchsurfing and she had offered to put us up for the night free of charge. She was a lovely lady and suggested that we stayed a couple of nights so that we could meet her brother, Simon, who spoke great English and would love to hang out. The following evening, we found ourselves in the bar of a local ice hockey rink with Silka and Simon. It turned out that Simon was actually an English teacher and he was Slovenia's number one Bruce Springsteen fan. He was such a fan of Bruce's work that he had managed to land the gig of translating *Born to Run,* Bruce's autobiography, into Slovenian.

Simon offered for us to stay at this cabin in the mountains a little further down the road in a place called Kranj. He said we could stay as long as we liked and that if we had the time, we could come into his school and talk about modern slavery and our trip. We bit his hand off at the idea for two reasons. Firstly, we needed somewhere to stay for a few days so we could just take stock. Everything had been such a rush that we hadn't even unboxed some of our kit. Most importantly though, it was a great chance to spread the message about modern slavery and human trafficking. We had hoped to visit an anti-slavery charity in every country we passed through on the trip, but we hadn't managed to set up any in Switzerland, Italy or Slovenia. We figured we could maybe do them on the way home, but it was really starting to come to light that it would be harder to find these organisations than we had previously anticipated. Although the main goal of the trip was to champion the kindness of strangers, we had told a lot of people back home that we were going to use the trip to shine a light on the issue of modern slavery, but it had been two weeks since the London-to-Paris rally and we had barely mentioned the issue since. It had been really weighing on our minds so getting the chance to share the message in the school was great.

We left late from Bled after exploring the area a bit and found ourselves heading for Simon's cabin in the mountains after dark. It was pouring down with rain too, and to make matters worse the only directions we had were what Simon had scribbled down on the back of a serviette the night before. After winding up mountain roads for some time, we found a log cabin that looked like it must be the one. We rummaged around in the wet and through the dark until we eventually found the key, confirming that we were in the right place. On entry we found an immaculately kept cabin with a basement full of beer. We were relieved but not completely relaxed. It suddenly dawned on us that we were out in the middle of nowhere, we had no phone signal, no Wi-Fi and nobody knew where we were, except of course Simon, whom we had met in a bar, and his sister, Silka, whom we had found on the internet. We looked around the place again, I peered out the window of the dining room and about six feet away I could see a cross glimmering in the moonlight which I assumed to be marking a grave of some description. I hoped it didn't mark the graves of the last scooter and sidecar duo to come across Silka and Simon.

We woke up in the morning to huge relief that Simon and Silka were indeed good people and not opportunistic murderers as we had semi-convinced ourselves the night before. See, told you the world was a good place. Simon met us as planned at his school and we spoke to two different groups about modern slavery. Everyone in the classroom was surprised to hear that slavery still exists, including the teachers. We weren't surprised to hear that they had never heard of the issue though. The Global Slavery Index estimates that there are about 5,000 people living in slavery in Slovenia but just as in the UK they go unseen and most people don't know they exist at all. Awareness has improved dramatically in the UK over the past couple of years, but when we were originally planning this trip modern slavery was a completely alien concept to most people. In fact, before we left I was trying to find places to put fundraising pots for the charities and a local pub landlord actually kicked me out, told me that I was a fraud and that nobody would be stupid enough to believe that slavery still existed. So, we cut the kids some slack when they struggled to get their heads around it.

The school visit was great, and they gave us some lunch too, which to our delight was the most fantastic sausage and mash. Things were really looking up for Reece. After a few more nights, we eventually left Simon's cabin and cracked on further south. We trundled through a rainy Slovenia until we reached the Adriatic Sea once again and hit the glorious Croatian coastline. We had arranged to stay with Rod Young, from 3 Wheels Better, whom we had approached to build the sidecar about a year prior. He had ended up moving to Croatia and he was a couple of days south in a little town called Karin, near Zadar. For those two days we were given absolutely fantastic driving conditions. Rod later informed us that he actually knows the guy who worked on designing the Croatian coastal road and he was a biker. You can believe it, too. The road twists and turns around the rocky cliffs at the same time as dipping down and soaring up like a roller coaster. You get so close to the water that at times it feels like you could just lean out and scoop up the sea as you scoot along.

I had only ever met Rod once for a quick cup of tea and had never met his wife Cheryl but we were welcomed into their home as if we had been lifelong friends. It was our first experience of the level of hospitality that the international biker community assumes as standard. We had planned to stay for a couple of nights so that Rod could put us through our paces and teach us a thing or two about scooter and sidecar maintenance. Fortunately for us though, the Bura struck. The Bura is a devilish wind that batters the Croatian coastline from time to time. The locals are all pretty clear that if you go out in the Bura, you *will* die. We thought we'd probably be okay, but it was pretty blustery, so we extended our stay at sidecar camp and ended up in Karin for four nights.

I think Rod was pretty surprised we had got as far as we had, we knew nothing about maintenance whatsoever. We had done a little bit of a course with a local mechanic back home, but we were still completely clueless. Rod's first port of call was to repack the rig so that we weren't having three tyres' worth of drag on top. After that he took us through everything we needed to monitor and maintain on our travels. We spent those days just trying to soak up as much info as we could at the same time as wallowing in the luxury that was a nice house and incredible food.

Eventually, we left Rod and Cheryl to head further south. We continued along the coast, passing by the tourist town of Split and we stopped to check out the magnificent waterfalls at Krka National Park. We were staying in Airbnbs almost every night. Out of season and out of town, the Airbnbs were around £7 a night total, £3.50 each. Even on our shoestring budget that made sense, even if it was just so we could get Wi-Fi to keep up the social media side of things. It's amazing how much time and effort it takes to run the social media for a trip like this. We really wanted to grow our audience because the whole project was about getting the stories out there but that really is easier said than done.

Our average day would involve getting on the road as early as possible but by the time we had packed all the stuff, the best we could hope for was usually 8 a.m. Then we would rack up eight to ten hours of riding before pulling into a random Airbnb and sitting down to work. Usually I would draft a Facebook and Instagram post while Reece would sort out the footage and start putting together our weekly video update. Then we would send updates to our sponsors, contact anti-slavery charities further down the road, or share content in groups on Facebook in order to reach new people. By the time we had done all that and had some noodles or a chocolate spread sandwich we would be completely zonked and either bang a movie on Netflix or buy the cheapest beer we could find and have a game of chess.

Although that daily routine would be fairly standard for the next year or so, we were keen to have some real adventure. We pulled out our Splash Map and decided that instead of continuing along the coast to Dubrovnik we would turn left and head for Bosnia and Herzegovina, that sounded far more adventurous! Bosnia was completely different to anywhere we had been so far. Well, to be honest, it just wasn't as well off as anywhere we had been so far. The border for Bosnia was an old-school big stick blocking the road. The guy in control of the stick, the border guard, tried to act all stern and scary, but we weren't having any of it, we were both distracted by an absolute corker of a sunset.

Everyone who rides a motorbike knows that good sunsets are a mixed blessing. You can't help but stop to take that gorgeous picture but in reality, you should be cheesing it as fast as you can in order to get where you need to be before the sun does eventually set. Driving at night can be dangerous, mainly because animals tend to jump out of the bushes and in Bosnia and Herzegovina that animal could be anything from a rabbit to a wolf. Yes, a real-life wolf, they have a few hundred of them.

We stayed the night in Mostar and pressed on again. We had run out of emails to recommend each other with on Airbnb so we decided it was time for our first-ever wild camp. After a long day on the road the sun was again beginning to set so it was time to find a decent place to stop. We were driving along through non-descript Bosnian countryside and could have probably got away with pulling in anywhere. We were pretty nervous though, we'd never camped anywhere that wasn't full of Europeans walking around in flip-flops, farting, as they washed up their disgusting pots and pans in the same piss-stinking sink that you're supposed to brush your teeth in. Sorry, I'm a bit touchy about that.

As we scooted along, we noticed a little lay-by that seemed to be hidden quite well. Perfect! Close to the road but well out of sight so we shouldn't have any problems with any passing nasties. We whipped the bike around and headed back for it but, as we turned in, we found ourselves in a field of rubbish, namely used nappies. It was absolutely vile. We got back on the bike and continued on in search of a better spot. Eventually we came to a big lake and there was a little track running down to it. Brilliant! Thank heavens we didn't pitch up at Camp Nappy. It didn't look like there was anyone around for miles but as we got to the bottom of the track a tiny village of no more than five or six houses emerged.

There was an elderly lady out tending to the cows and the mooing was the only sound you could hear. Ahead of us we could see a big, dried-out lakebed with a decent lake still in the middle, all set against the backdrop of some pretty cool mountains. It was glorious. We don't speak any Bosnian, so we showed the lady our tent and asked her through miming if it was okay if we pitched up by her lake. She gestured for us to crack on and we proceeded to the shore.

As we got onto the lakebed, the track turned into thick mud and we were pushing the limits of the rig. Eventually we found a place dry enough to pitch the tent, so we got it up and popped the kettle on. Now this was it. The adventure we were looking for! There was no Facebook tonight, no sign of an email, we were out in the middle of the Bosnian countryside, camping by a lake and we were loving it.

In the middle of the lake there was an old church on an island. It looked beautiful when we arrived but as the night grew darker, it began to look more and more creepy. We looked around and I had a sudden realisation of what I was doing. I was camping in the bloody Bosnian wilds, watching out for ghosts and waiting for the wolves to take me. This was too much adventure. What I would do to hear the snore of a German man coming from a caravan parked a few yards down the road.

Reece was feeling the same. We told each other to stop being so stupid and agreed that the best thing to do was just get in the tent, get our heads down and get out of there pronto in the morning. Sensible stuff. I headed into the tent first and just as I was getting into my sleeping bag Reece said, "Hey mate, do lakes have tides? Only, that one looks a lot closer than before."

"No, don't be so stupid," I retorted, in a kind of "I've got a geography degree don't you know" tone. "Only the absolutely massive ones, that thing's just a bit bigger than a pond."

"Well it does look closer, mate."

"Oh, for heaven's sake, let me take a look," I said as I disapprovingly got out of my sleeping bag. "Christ, it does look closer doesn't it!"

Balls. What had we done? It all began to make sense. We did drive through thick wet mud to get here and somehow this bloody thing must be tidal. I began cursing the day that I switched to Human Geography. I was racking my brain for an explanation as to how the lake could be getting closer. I reasoned that it couldn't have its own tide because that's literally just the Great Lakes, and we were a good fifty miles or so from the coast so it couldn't be part of an estuary or anything like that.

"No, we must just be going nuts, it can't be getting closer, let's go back to bed," I said.

We both got into our sleeping bags and lay silently for a minute.

"Mate, I'm not being funny, but you can hear it lapping up against the bloody shore!" Reece said.

"Christ you can as well!" Jeez. How? It made no sense. We decided we'd hang tight for ten minutes and then get out to see if it was any closer. While we were waiting, the lapping of the waves wasn't the only thing we could hear. Footsteps. Rustling. Running.

"Jesus Christ mate, what is that?" I said to Reece.

"I don't know but it's flipping creepy!" Reece replied.

"Right, well let's just get out there and find out who or what it is and if they, or it, are taking a dip a couple of yards away or not."

Thankfully, there were no ghosts or ghouls waiting for us as we undid the tent, but we were no clearer on the lake situation. We simply couldn't tell. The water was only about fifty feet away but it was impossible to judge if it was closer or not. We agreed to have another look in half an hour. No clarification then either, so we did it again, and again. Eventually we ended up getting our heads down for half an hour and setting an alarm. Not that we needed it because we were both still weighing up in our minds if the noises we could hear where ghosts, wolves, or perhaps Simon and Silka playing the long game and they were finally going to do us in.

I woke up the following morning and felt the floor beneath me. "Mate, excellent news we're not floating!" I said to Reece.

The lake was in exactly the same position it had been when we arrived. There were no ghosts in the cold light of day, the wolves were off on the other side of the country where they always were, and Simon and Silka were still talking about Springsteen somewhere in Slovenia. Wonderful. We got packed up and headed off towards our next country, Montenegro.

Montenegro is absolutely knock-out beautiful. It's one of those places that as you drive through you can't help but sing the theme tune to *Jurassic Park*. We were genuinely going along with "Do, do-do do, do-do, do-do, do doo," on repeat. As you get towards Lake Skadar, the roads snake right up through mountains and you find yourself peeping through thick green forest to see the turquoise colours of the lake below. Reece was enjoying the ride; he was at the handlebars, throwing Kuishi into the bends and loving every minute. That was until I tried probably the most dangerous prank of my life. I leaned out of the sidecar and tapped Reece on his right shoulder, that old classic! He jolted to the right and screamed through his headset as he looked over his shoulder. Nothing there! "Argh you prick! You scared the shit out of me!" Reece clearly hadn't shaken off the heebie-jeebies from the night before and I'd given him quite the fright. I was in complete hysterics; he had jumped out of his skin and was genuinely angry about it. I was pleased as punch, I had pulled off a top-draw, back-to-basics, prank.

Reece was still on edge and after the fiasco of the night before we'd had enough adventure, so we decided to book ourselves into a £7 Airbnb. It was completely in the middle of nowhere and as usual we had messed around too long and arrived there after dark. We couldn't find the place and had no internet or phone signal to contact the owner, so we ended up following the coordinates to a random couple of houses at the top of a big hill and just started knocking on doors. Eventually an elderly guy came out, we showed him the address on the phone, and he smiled and gave us a thumbs-up.

"Wait. Owner come soon," said the guy in very broken English but far less broken than our Montenegrin would have been. It was freezing, so he marched us over to a little hut to wait in the warm. It turned out the hut was a tiny bar and he cracked us open a cold one and lit a fire in one glorious swoop. We all sat around the fire and had five minutes of doing that thing:

"Mmm beer, thank you," said Reece.

"Ooo fire, nice, thank you," I said next.

"Brrrrrr," said the Montenegrin man as he pointed outside, pretending to shiver.

"Yes, cold," said Reece.

Then it was time for the animal game. He pointed out of the window and let out a "Grrr!" as he mimed a bear and then next "Hoooowlllll!"

Christ, maybe they really were wolves last night then, I thought. That was about as far as the conversation could go. We sat there in silence for a few minutes when he jumped up and excitedly put on the TV with a big smile. He was flicking through the channels until we eventually stumbled onto *Desperate Housewives*. He picked up the English in it and grinned at us, as if to say, "I've got you covered lads." Four beers and an episode and a half later, our host eventually showed up. I was a bit disappointed; Gabriel and Carlos were fighting again, and I wanted to see how it all turned out.

The Airbnb was fine, and we woke up the following morning fully refreshed and ready for adventure again. We were excited too because it was another day, another country, next stop Albania! It took us the entire day to get around the lake and into Albania. The scenery was so incredible that we had chosen to take a scenic route and jumped on a tiny road that led through the mountains around the lake. Big mistake. It was fun for the first hour or two, but seven hours of twists and turns down a single-track road later and we were desperate for a straight line. We crossed into Albania late afternoon and decided that we would try our hand at wild camping once again. The lake had worked in Bosnia and we had enjoyed the morning dip, so we thought, why change a winning team? And we headed for the shores of the Albanian side of Lake Skadar.

By the time we had got to the town of Shkoder it was getting pretty dark and to camp up by the lake we had to drive the wrong direction. Not wanting to go too far out of the way, we ended up pitching our tent on a rocky beach around two miles out of town. We were hidden down a bank from the main road, so we thought it was a pretty good place for a kind of stealth camp. I noticed that there was a little hotel a bit further up the road so I took the bike up there and agreed with the guy that I would buy a few bottles of beer if I could leave the bike locked up in the hotel car park. He was cool with it so I pottered back to the beach and we cracked open a beer to enjoy the view with gentle waves lapping up against a pebbled beach and awesome snow-capped peaks providing the backdrop. Just as we were sitting down, a small, beat-up looking car pulled up right above us and a couple of dangerous looking fellas piled out. We could see them, so they could surely see us. They stopped for a second, jumped back in their car, and then screeched around before racing off back towards town.

"Blimey, that can't be good," said Reece. "Why would they turn around there and race back to town if it had nothing to do with us?"

"I don't know mate but we're sitting bloody ducks here," I replied. We were too. We couldn't even leave, as Kuishi was locked up for the night. For Christ's sake, I thought, we're done for. The bloody Albanian mafia have just clocked us on the outskirts of their town and they'll surely be back after dark to rinse us of everything we have.

"We're snookered here," said Reece. "What are we going to do?"

"Well there's nothing we can do mate. We'll just have to suck it and see."

We sat down and slowly watched the sun disappear over the mountains while we enjoyed a couple of beers. As darkness fell, the noises of the night before started to appear again. We sat outside our tent just looking for what might be out there and every now and again we shot a beam of light in the direction of a rustle. Then Reece pointed out a silhouette scurrying along by the water. "It's a cat, mate," I said.

"No, too big for a cat," replied Reece.

"Well a dog then."

"No, it doesn't move like a dog," said Reece.

"Well light the bloody thing up then, mate!"

He did and, sure enough, in the beam was neither a dog nor a cat but a very scared, embarrassed-looking fox, stood on its tip-toes. Genuinely on its tip toes. It moved off sideways, keeping its eyes firmly on us while it crept into the darkness. We both burst out laughing. We'd never seen anything like it. It was such a creep. We decided it had all got a bit nuts out on the beach and we were knackered anyway so turned in to get our heads down. It wasn't long before we were asleep but just as quickly, we were rudely awakened.

Sniff, sniff, sniff, sniff, sniff.

"Mate!! There's something sniffing my head!" exclaimed Reece.

"Jesus Christ," I replied. "Do you think it's a wolf?"

"Well it's a whole bloody pack if it is mate!"

We were surrounded. There was sniffing coming from all around the tent and frantic running around. We sat in the middle of the tent for a minute or two, completely bricking it.

Finally, the noises seemed to die down so we decided to get up and see if we could see what was out there. Reece stumbled out first in his pants and I followed close behind in mine. Reece armed with a torch and me with our camping knife. Nothing there. Then suddenly, something shot off to our left. Reece lit it up. A scraggly looking dog. Thank heavens! He panned the light across the bushes and there were about six or seven sets of eyes looking back at us. A pack of stray dogs could clearly smell the beans we'd rustled up for tea and they wanted in.

Relieved we weren't going to get eaten, we got back in the tent and got back to bed. We were just getting off to sleep when the tent lit up for a second. A car screeched to a stop and loud music started blaring out.

"Holy shit, it's the fellas from earlier. They're back!" I frantically said. Once again, we stumbled out of the tent but this time we left our weapons behind. We didn't want to be seen and we weren't planning on butchering anybody.

"Christ, it really is them!" There was a small car parked in exactly the same spot the other one had turned around from.

"My word, we really are snookered here," said Reece. "What shall we do now?"

"Well, I reckon we should put some bloody jeans on for a start, mate."

We got dressed and started to ponder what the hell we should do. There would be no reason that someone would come out here. It's the middle of nowhere, and this exact spot, too. Why here if not to come and mug us? We waited for about ten minutes before we decided we would have to go and take a closer look. Creeping slowly up through the scraggly, dog-infested bushes, we were able to see that there were five lads sat in the car. We waited and watched them for a minute but couldn't really see. What were they doing out here? Planning their attack, we expected. Waiting to make sure we were definitely asleep so they could join the dogs and start sniffing around.

"Bollocks to it mate, let's just go and say hi," I said.

"Are you nuts? They'll have your guts for garters if you go over there," replied a worried Reece.

"Well they're going to have them anyway if that's their intention. Let just find out one way or another and see what they're made of."

So off we marched. We crept up out of the bushes and confidently knocked on their window. They completely shat themselves. Here they were, five teenage lads just trying to smoke a joint out by the lake and a couple of British headcases have jumped out the bushes at them. They had no idea we were there at all. After they realised we weren't the police and were completely harmless, they burst into laughter and offered us a puff. We passed them up on it but had a nice chat. They said they would take us into town for a party if we liked but we didn't fancy leaving the tent on its Todd, so politely declined again. We had a nice five- or ten-minute chat before one of the guys gave us his number and said to let him know if we needed any help while we were in town. What a lovely bunch. We finally went back down to bed and got a good night's sleep safe in the knowledge that the guys were looking out for us.

The following morning, we took a refreshing dip in the icy cold lake, before pressing on to Tirana where we once again booked a cheap Airbnb and decided to take stock. This time we were taking stock because we had been on the road for a month already and it wasn't all going exactly to plan. We had hoped to visit a charity fighting modern slavery in every country we passed through and we'd had no luck since France. Not for lack of trying. We sent hundreds of emails to potential organisations but it either wasn't appropriate, not the right time or the right organisation didn't exist. It wasn't just us who were getting annoyed about it either. There was a general feeling from a few people back home that, "They're just on a bloody jolly." One friend actually messaged us and said, "Lads where's the modern slavery stuff, you look like you're just on holiday." It was seemingly what everyone was feeling.

The problem was that we were in between a rock and a hard place. We weren't having the best time because we were so stressed about not producing the right content and at the same time we had to do posts that looked like we were having the best time because we were sponsored by a travel agent. We were barely going to post, "In Split today, can't tell you what it's like we've been sat in a dodgy Airbnb doing our emails all day!"

We had well and truly bitten off more than we could chew. Our followers were annoyed because we had got our messaging all wrong. Before we had gone, we had essentially said we're going to run the marathon for the British Heart Foundation and while we're at it we'll try and find a cure for heart disease, too. It's impossible. Worse still we were making the marathon look like a bloody doddle, when in actual fact it wasn't. It was long days of tiresome repetition, muddled in with the stress of travelling and the ever-present imaginary wolves, ghosts, and ghouls.

Something had to give, and something had to change. We decided in the end that, actually, we knew we were trying to do a good thing, our moral compass was in the right place, so we just needed to focus on getting around the world and bloody enjoy it. The money raising would come when the times got really tough and if we kept reaching out to people, we'd be able to spread the message too. We decided, too, that we would have a day off. If everyone thought we were just on a jolly then you know what, we'd go on one for the day! We both withdrew £50 from our savings and went wild in Tirana. I mean, wild for us was checking out the museum before a game of ping pong and finishing the day off with a beer watching the footy but it was exactly what we needed. We left Tirana with a game plan, our heads in the right space, and energised for the road ahead.

– 5 –

"WE WERE TAKEN INTO THE BUSH AND TRAINED TO BECOME WARRIORS."

"Mate this egg is freezing!" Reece exclaimed.

"I know, mate, just eat your breakfast and let's get out of here."

And get out of there we did. The lady at our Airbnb in Tirana insisted on throwing in breakfast, but for some reason she chilled her fried eggs. Why anyone would chill a runny fried egg, I really don't know. Fortunately, it was the only thing I didn't like about her and we'd had a lovely stay, but now, it was time to press on.

Our next stop was Pogradec on the shores of the incredible Lake Ohrid. Getting there was a dangerous business though. The Albanians were as bad as the Italians at driving, but they had more tools at their disposal to be deadly with. In Italy it was just motorised vehicles you had to deal with, but here you had to handle yourself against horse and carts, too. You wouldn't think that a horse and cart would be more dangerous but because they are notably different to the motorised modes of transport, they seemed to think they should work to a different set of rules—the most dangerous of which was their habit of trotting the wrong way down the dual carriageway. Most of the time they would be in the hard shoulder, which made sense, you could hardly expect them to cheese it up the road to take the flyover, but unfortunately they would often stray onto the slow lane, as it had a better surface. Now that's a big problem. More so for us than anyone else because the driver of the horse and cart wouldn't know what we were and more often than not people expect a scooter and sidecar to go a lot slower than it does. We had a few really close shaves where we would be getting overtaken by a lorry at the same time as a horse and cart were coming at us head on. Truly deadly stuff.

We'd heard a lot about Lake Ohrid from Robin and Kim Grigsby, fellow overlanders, who had been giving us loads of tips online. As we approached it, we started to see what all the fuss was about. We arrived to the shore as the sun began to drop on a cold and clear November evening. It must have been around freezing and there was a kind of winter mist coming off the lake. The backdrop was incredible—snow-capped peaks reaching up to the pink and red sky. We scooted along the shore into Pogradec where we had booked the cheapest thing on Airbnb again, but all we had was a location on a map. We pulled up into a tiny cobbled street and Gary the Garmin, as we unimaginatively called him, said, "You have arrived at your destination." Well, we hadn't, Gary. We knocked on a few doors and nobody could speak any English or understand what was on the phone. It was beginning to look like we would just have to go back to the lake and chuck the tent up when a local guy had a brain wave.

The next thing we knew we were marching off to a house around the corner and as we got closer, we could hear American people speaking to each other. The gates flung open and we were greeted with a warm welcome from Cory and Kristine. We were very surprised to see them there as we were in a tiny, tiny town in deepest Albania. It turned out that the husband and wife duo had moved here to work with their church, and they were planning on staying. They had a bunch of other American friends over, too, and by chance it was Thanksgiving, so they were having a bit of a shindig. They could speak Albanian as well, and quickly managed to get us into our room.

It was a cosy little place just around the corner. We had an open fire and the hosts were incredibly friendly. We got in, got warmed up and then I turned to Reece and said, "Mate, we're having turkey for tea!" Reece agreed and we pottered around to the Americans' house again. I knocked on the gate.

"Oh, hey guys," said Cory. "What can I do for you?"

"Well, we just thought we'd pop around and say a huge thanks again for helping us out," replied Reece.

"Yeah and we think it's amazing that you guys are living out here doing all this great work with your church," I added.

"Yeah sure thing man, you guys wanna hear more about it? We've got wine and food in here."

"Oh, that's so kind but we don't want to put you out."

"Don't be silly, get in here!" said Cory.

And in we went. Easiest turkey dinner we'd ever earnt! It was absolutely gorgeous, and they were genuinely a really nice bunch. They were perhaps a touch overzealous with their desire to spread the word of God, but they knew a good red when they saw one, and could handle themselves in the kitchen, so they were okay with us. We left them to their evening and got our heads down early because tomorrow was going to be a big day. We were off to meet the mayor.

Vasilis, from the Ace Café, grew up in a small city called Trikala in northern Greece. He knew our project had been inspired by the European Migrant Crisis and in early 2017 Trikala had ended up in the heart of it. The town, along with many others in Greece, found itself full of people trying to make their way into northern Europe. Hundreds of refugees had arrived overnight, and the local mayor was praised for his unorthodox approach to tackling the issue, so Vasilis thought we might like to meet him. Amazingly, the mayor agreed to meet us and not only that, he offered to put us up for a couple of nights so we could explore the town. We agreed to meet him and the vice mayor at the town's Christmas market at midday.

Getting to Trikala for midday meant racking up 250 km that morning so we were on the road for sunrise. It was an incredibly cold morning, probably just below freezing, but we had packed for Africa and had very little winter riding gear. It was a gorgeous start to the day, we had picked up from where we had left it at sunset, but it was so cold that we had to swap who was riding every twenty minutes or so. After a short while, it hadn't warmed up much and we were pressing on trying to make it to the Greek border where we had agreed to stop for a coffee. I told Reece over the headset that I'd need to swap soon as my hands were becoming cold and he said, "Well you're only about 5 km from the border so may as well just make it." Thirty-five kilometers later and I was literally screaming with cold pains shooting up my fingers. He had got it horribly, horribly wrong. Eventually though we crossed into Greece. The day began to warm up a touch and we enjoyed the ride.

We pulled into Trikala at just after midday and to our delight we were welcomed by Dimitris Papastergiou, the town mayor. We exchanged some niceties before he left us in the capable hands of Giannis Kotoulas, the vice mayor. Giannis said that they would either pay for us to stay in a hotel or they could put us up at the Christmas market. We opted for the latter, it sounded like much more fun. Trikala is home to Greece's biggest Christmas market and they spend a fortune on it. We were staying behind the scenes with a couple of guys who spend three months of their year decorating the place, so you can imagine what it looks like. It was a very cool place to crash for a couple of nights. We chucked our stuff down and Giannis took us out for a tour of the city.

The first stop was to pick up a couple of bicycles, which are completely free for the public to use, and then we followed Giannis to a local restaurant where he said he'd show us proper Greek food. As you'd expect it was completely amazing: corking Greek salad, top taramasalata, and some sumptuous souvlaki. Eventually, we got chatting about the refugee crisis that had struck the town. Giannis said that one night they literally had 400 Syrian refugees walk into town. They had no idea they were coming and no idea what to do, but they knew they wanted to help. Trikala is Greece's first smart city, which means they use technology to help with the running of the place. You pay your taxes on an app and resolve complaints through it, too. There are driverless busses and sensors on streetlights to cut power usage. It's impressive stuff. More impressive, though, was the smart city's approach to the refugee crisis.

The city did the usual thing and got everyone set up in a few sports halls with camp beds and blankets, but then they went a step further. They organised for every person passing through to have access to free Wi-Fi, they set up Skype rooms that people could use for free so they could call home, and they circulated Arabic newspapers so people could feel welcome. They thought about how these people were feeling and reacted with humanity, a far cry from the situation we had found back in Paris.

We stayed in Trikala for a couple of nights and then set our sights on our finish line for the first leg of the trip, Athens. The plan was to get into Athens and ship the bike over to Alexandria. We had originally wanted to ferry-hop to Cyprus and then on to

Lebanon so we could drive around to Africa, but sadly the Sinai region of Egypt was closed for overlanders and we would have been turned away at the border. This meant that we would have to arrange for the bike to be put on a container ship and then fly to Alexandria to meet it there. We had been researching ferry options online since before we set off on the trip, but we couldn't find anything. We reasoned that it was just in Greek or something and if we went down to the port, we would soon find a boat.

So, we left the fake snow of the Christmas market behind and set off for Athens. We had managed to blag a two-bedroom, centrally located Airbnb in Athens for about £5 a night each. Manos, the owner, was just happy to see it used out of season and he loved the project. We loved Manos, too, because he owned the bakery over the road from the apartment and he welcomed us with a couple of gorgeous cakes. We scoffed them that evening while we worked away on our laptops trying to get things organised. We were relieved because we had managed to get a charity visit lined up for while we were in town. Smile of a Child, a Greek national children's charity, asked to meet us in a few days' time, the 5th December, and there was no way we would be able to get the bike on a boat that quick, so we penciled it in.

The following day we went down to the port and scooted around from open until close without finding any leads. It was pretty worrying but the place was massive so we went back the following day and eventually managed to find someone who could ship for us. The lady organising it said we could rush it onto the next boat which was on the 5th or wait for the one the following week on the 12th. We had tried so long to get a charity to talk to about modern slavery, so we opted for the 12th. I was pretty pleased with that too because it meant we would have a good bit of time in a single place in order to plan for the road ahead. Better still, it meant we would certainly be stationary for a while, so Chels bought a cheap flight and came out to visit.

Chels arrived on the 3rd December and came for a week. It was fab to see her, and we were super pleased we could get one last visit in before Reece and I took on Africa. After a few touristy bits, it was time to go and meet Smile of a Child. As the name suggests, they are a children's charity and are concerned with doing anything they can to help children in Greece. Whether it's medical care, social work or help with school, they are there to help children in any way they can. They seemed to be doing everything the Greek state should be doing but we won't get into that. One part of their work was helping victims of child trafficking and modern slavery. We sat with them and discussed the issue at length for five full hours. It was intense and eye-opening. The charity said that since the European Migrant Crisis the majority of their work had been in helping children who had washed up on the boats. They suggested the best way to get to understand the issue would be to go along to a refugee camp they work at.

We jumped at the chance and a couple of days later we found ourselves in a camp just outside the city centre. Again, just like the camp we had visited in Paris, it was no more than twenty minutes from the city's main tourist attraction, in this case the Acropolis, which we had visited the day before. The gulf between the two worlds didn't seem quite as big this time, though. I guess it was because this was a long-term camp and people had actually made their homes there. There was no emergency dome, instead it was a shipping container village. Each container was divided down the middle with a living space for a family built into each half. This essentially meant a small kitchen, bathroom, and living area where a family of four could all sleep next to each other on mattresses they put on the floor.

We walked around the camp for a little while and got to meet a few of the people living there. The kids were all particularly friendly as the Smile of a Child staff knew every single one of them by name. It was a bleak situation and although all was fine in the daytime, you could see it might have a different feeling at night. The Smile of a Child staff told us that traffickers would waltz into the camp pretending to offer people jobs and try to coerce them into slavery. They said they would do exactly the same with the children, too, and it's hard to stop. In fact, Europol states that there were 10,000 refugee children who entered Europe who could no longer be accounted for, many of whom were feared to be trapped in situations of forced labour or sexual exploitation. So, the children's safety was a genuine concern.

People in the camp were likely to be there for months on end while they tried to find a more permanent housing situation. As a result, many had started to form a kind of life there and even started their own mini businesses from the containers. We ended up buying our lunch from a lady who was serving falafel wraps out of her kitchen window. They were great. Visiting the camp was an eye-opening experience and a behind-the-scenes look at where a lot of those who get trafficked around Europe begin their fall into a life of modern slavery.

That night was date night. Weird isn't it? To switch topics like that, but I do it to show what it's like when you're on a trip like this. One minute you're visiting people stuck in crisis, the next you're trying to make sure your girlfriend has a corker of a holiday so she will come to visit again. Chels and I went to a lovely little seafood restaurant and had a cracker of a night. Meanwhile, Reece decided he would see if he could find a date for himself and downloaded Tinder. He was in luck, and ended up going out for drinks with an Italian girl called Barbara.

We spent the next few days just working away on our laptops, visiting places around Athens and eating a crapload of gyros. It was brilliant to have Chels there and for a few days it felt like we were at home again. On our request, she had even brought out some Bisto gravy, so we cooked a roast dinner and pretended to be back in our normal lives in London. But, before long, it was time for Chels to fly home. I strapped her suitcase on the back of the sidecar and whizzed her down to the airport for another teary goodbye. It was a bit more teary because I knew we wouldn't see each other for a long time, and we both knew that Reece and I were heading into Africa, a somewhat daunting prospect.

We had plenty of time to stew on it though because the boat was delayed. The port claimed that it was because of strikes and then because of weather, but ultimately it's because they don't set off until they're full. We were stuck in Greece twiddling our thumbs with nothing to do when Reece's Tinder date asked him if we wanted to come along to a storytelling workshop she was hosting in a community centre. It was a very random request, but we had nothing to do and seeing that we were on a storytelling mission, we thought we'd go along. The session was being facilitated by an Irish lady and it was mainly expats or students in the room. There were around eight to ten of us and the idea was to explore different ways of telling a story. We were just about to go into a new exercise when a lady in her fifties or sixties limped in and sat down next to me.

Her name was Click and we got paired up together for the next exercise. The task was to tell the other person a story about yourself and then they would have to tell your story as if it was their own, to the rest of the group. Click and I told each other our stories and before long, it was my turn to pretend to be Click and share her story with the group. It went something like this:

When I was a little girl, living in Zimbabwe, my parents were both brutally murdered. I, along with my siblings, became an orphan. It was a horrible, scary time, but one day a nice man gave me a book and told me to write all of my feelings down in it, every single one. I did as he said, and it helped me greatly. I had a way to channel my emotions and when I was feeling sad, I could always flick back to a happier time. From that point on I have always kept a book with my feelings. As I grew up, my country became torn apart through war. The army was coming through villages and terrorising people. Killing people, torturing people, it was too much to bear. My friend asked me to join the rebels with her and to become a guerrilla fighter. I was scared but I couldn't go on living as a civilian with the fear of the army, so I joined.

We were taken into the bush and trained to become warriors. I learnt how to fight, how to shoot a gun, and how to use my personal skills for my advantage. My main skill was my looks, I was eighteen and I was a good-looking girl. Lucky for me all of the enemy were men and they were only thinking of one thing. Once I was trained I would fight by walking right up to the enemy, flirting with them and then once they let me inside their car I would show them a bomb I had strapped to me and tell them, "Get out, leave the keys or I'll blow us all up." It worked well.

Finally, the war ended, and I was able to live a normal life. I have always loved knitting, so I began to make small things to sell. At the same time, I fell in love. I had a wonderful husband who I loved completely. We had two sets of twins together, but my husband had a dangerous job. He was a journalist and he was reporting on the atrocities of the war, somebody didn't like what he had found out and they murdered him. The police called it a car accident, but I went to the site and I saw his car covered in bullet holes. It was horrible.

I had to carry on though. My second set of twins had only just been born and the others were still young. I was a single mother who now had to provide for four young children without a good salary. Fortunately, my knitting was going well, and I was selling my products all over town. I even had a purchase from a Greek family who liked my work so much that they asked me to come over to Greece so I could study, get even better and then knit all of the products they needed. I was sad to leave my children, but I wanted to give them a better life and this was the opportunity I had been waiting for. I went to Greece.

When I arrived, they took my passport off me and said they needed it to enroll me at school. They told me that while I was waiting to go to school I could help around the house. So, I started helping. After a few days they said to me that I would be going to their friend's house to help for the day. This kept happening for weeks and eventually it became clear that I was never going to school. I was trapped. I knew they had my passport and there was nothing I could do. Every day they would have someone watching me or they would lock me in the house. I was paid nothing at all and just given enough food to survive. For two years I was a slave, until one day they lost their keys and I found them while cleaning the house. I picked up the keys, unlocked the front door and left with only the clothes on my back.

I managed to find help in Greece and eventually built a life for myself. I was able to get in touch with my children for the first time in two years and I began to send them money just as I had planned. I started to hear about other girls who were trafficked from Africa to Athens who were in the same situation I had escaped from, so I started breaking them out. Sometimes I would just break into the house and steal them away as they were too scared to leave.

I have never been back to Zimbabwe and instead I have spent my life trying to help people who ended up in my situation. I co-founded an organisation called Melissa. It helps people who come to Greece as refugees and migrants, of which there are many. They get advice and all of the children get given a bag for the road. Inside the bag there is food, a toothbrush, a blanket, some soap, but most importantly a book to write down their feelings in.

I know. I was blown away. I could not believe what I was hearing. We were trying everything we could to find stories that shine a light on modern slavery and she just walked in, and without me even asking, said, "Yeah I was a slave once." Click's story is incredibly sad, unbelievably inspiring and completely true. She's talked about it on the TED stage and there are two movies about her life.

Next, she had to tell my story and all she could say was "I'm Matt, I'm very interested in Click's story, I'm going to come and visit Click's organisation."

I was just completely shocked. We'd done our research and knew that domestic servitude was prevalent in Greece but to have someone come and tell their story like that was just completely grounding. It made it so real for us and we were more passionate than ever to get around the world and raise some decent cash for the cause. We did go to visit Click's organisation the next day and it was a sizeable operation. "Melissa" is "bee" in Greek, and the building was a hive of activity. There must have been around fifty women there, all refugees, all learning a language or getting advice on what to do next. It was incredible to see what Click had achieved. She is without a doubt the most inspiring person I have ever had the pleasure of meeting.

We spent another couple of days in Athens and devoured five or six more gyros before we finally received the news the boat had set sail. Brilliant! We were free to go and on the morning of the 16th December we finally flew to Cairo.

– 6 –

"GUYS, THIS IS A BIG PROBLEM. YOU'RE GOING TO NEED TO CALL YOUR EMBASSY."

Getting to Greece had been fairly plain sailing but as we waited to board our flight to Cairo, we were both pretty nervous. In going to Africa, we were going into the complete unknown. We had both flown to different parts of Africa on our holidays, but this was a completely different ball game. This would be a complete top-to-tail of the continent. We had planned the safest route we could find but we knew there were potential dangers we just wouldn't be able to avoid. Even in the safe countries it's not generally advisable to drive through in a big red scooter and sidecar, sticking out like a sore thumb. We had decided to take the East Coast route. This would mean our first countries would be Egypt and Sudan.

Now, our project is completely born out of a belief that no matter where you go, people are good, but when we were boarding that flight to Cairo we couldn't help but think, "Are they?" All we knew about Egypt was the recent rise in terrorism and all we knew about Sudan was the brutal war in the south that resulted in the formation of South Sudan. Would we really be okay to just drive from the top to the bottom of both countries, right across the Sahara, looking like complete plonkas in our scooter and sidecar? Well there was only one way to find out.

We touched down in Cairo on the 16th December. The city is Africa's largest metropolitan area and it's fricking barmy. The place is just full of hustle and bustle. We arrived at night and it was still buzzing. Just crossing a road on foot seemed impossible at first. There was seemingly no order to the chaos and it was every man for himself. We checked into a cheap hotel for a few nights and decided to explore the capital while we waited for our boat to cross the Med.

The following day, we took a stroll around the bazaars in Khan el-Khalili. It's a crazy experience that's not for the faint hearted. We found ourselves ducking under hooves, still attached to the legs of animals hanging from hooks above us, at the same time as staring into the eyes of cute little rabbits sat next to their friends who had already been slaughtered. We were carried through the market by the flow of the busy crowds and did all we could to evade the various dead and live animals that populated it. There were turkeys sat atop cages of chickens just waiting for the chop, and scariest of all were the geese who seemed to have some fight left in them and would let out an almighty hiss if you got too close. I had never seen anything like it. Not only was it the sights but the smells, too. They ranged from putrid meat to fresh bread to fried fish to incense to poo. We walked around for about forty minutes, completely amazed. Eventually, we took a second to look up and take in the grandeur of the 14th-century buildings towering over us. It really was an incredible experience and it seemed that aside from the addition of smart phones and a few bits of plastic, the markets in Cairo hadn't changed for centuries.

At first Cairo hits you with such a culture shock that you could be forgiven for finding it a bit much. It's just so intense. But after you've given yourself the chance to adjust to this manic city, you get taken in by its undeniable charm. The people of Cairo (and Egypt in general) are exceptionally friendly. They just want to chat. We couldn't walk down the street without having a full-blown conversation about the UK or Mohamed Salah of Liverpool FC. If you're lucky, you'll escape with a quick natter, but at least once a day you'll end up going through somebody's family tree over a cup of Turkish coffee thick with sugar. We loved it.

We stayed for five days and we didn't see one pyramid or visit a single museum. We spent most of our time queuing in the Sudanese Embassy while we tried to get our visas or chatting football with the locals in the various cafés around the city.

Next, we caught a train north to Alexandria where we would be reunited with Kuishi na Kuishi. The train cost £2 for a three-hour journey in first class. We were amazed at how good it was. Big leather seats, nice and comfy, and really fast. We couldn't believe how they could do it for so cheap. Well, it turns out that really, they can't do it that cheap, not safely anyway. The railways are in dangerous need of repair, so much so that recently a train failed to stop at the station and ploughed into a buffer. It burst into flames and twenty people lost their lives to the disaster, with forty more injured. This is a symptom of a completely negligent government who don't concern themselves too much with the safety of your average citizen.

We arrived into Alexandria as planned and met Farouk and Hassan who had agreed to host us for a few nights while we were in town. Farouk and Hassan were both about our age, both big into football, and both from working class Egyptian backgrounds. We met them on Couchsurfing and we were to stay at Farouk's gaff where he lived with all of his family. Literally, all of it. Five floors of fun. Lord knows how many kids lived there but they were very friendly. We spent the next week, including Christmas Day, living in their family home. For us it was a rare opportunity to really get to experience a different culture. Farouk's house is in a line of terraced buildings that backs a train track, that cuts through a local market, that sits next to a tuk-tuk station, that doubles as a footy pitch for the kids. The place was teeming with life twenty-four hours a day. It felt like nobody slept and certainly not the kids, who made you play a quick round of Next Goal Wins every time you left the house.

The place is amazing, but life is hard in Egypt right now. Tourism once thrived there but over recent years security concerns have sent most holiday makers elsewhere. It's had a real effect on life for almost everybody. Farouk and Hassan both dream to travel but it's hugely expensive. Both were working two jobs and all of the hours under the sun to save for expensive visas that they needed to get out of the country. When they invited us to play football, we kicked off at midnight because it was the only time people weren't working. Knowing how hard up things are for people in Egypt made the Egyptian hospitality that bit more special. We were treated daily to a mixture of strawberry milkshakes, chip butties, and falafel wraps by Farouk's family, and they were just so, so generous towards us, it was incredible.

We spent a week or so at Farouk's house. He essentially didn't work while we were there because he could make more money out of us. Not in a bad way but he was a taxi driver and we needed to get about. Even though we were only spending around a tenner a day, he was earning more with us than if he had been out doing the daily grind. We gave him a bit of cash now and again and just bought him whatever we were eating or drinking. It was like having our own tour guide and he was chuffed because he was earning while he got to hang out with us, practicing his English. Plus, he got to show us around his town which, for Farouk, was an absolute joy. He was so proud of Alexandria. He loved it. He gave us an insight into what life was really like there.

Farouk was particularly keen for us not to take pictures out of the back of his house. It was a dump. It wasn't supposed to be, but there was no rubbish collection anymore, so the litter just piled high alongside the train tracks. Farouk was embarrassed about it. It's not how they wanted to live but it's hard when the government does nothing, and if you speak out, you get locked up. Farouk and his friends were all petrified of the government. They had many friends who had been locked up just for saying the wrong thing about the wrong person at the wrong time. Farouk told us that the government is completely paranoid. So paranoid that normal people aren't even allowed to go to football matches in case they're plotting treason from the terraces. It's a tough situation. But life goes on and everyday people in Alexandria are an incredibly friendly, fun bunch.

We loved staying with Farouk and fully immersing ourselves in the culture. My favourite thing to do was trying all of the funky food. I said to Farouk one day, "Farouk, what's your favourite thing to eat?"

To which he replied with a big smile, "You really want to know?"

"Yeah, course."

"Okay, it's cow dick sandwich."

I literally spat my coffee out. I couldn't believe it.

"You want to try?" Farouk said excitedly.

"Do I want to eat a cow dick sandwich? Yeah, of course," I replied.

I was completely intrigued. This must be an ultra-delicacy. Your average cow doesn't have a penis so he must be meaning a bull's bits, in between two slices of bread. But really, how many sandwiches does a bull's bits make? A couple tops, surely? If this was normal, everyday street food, they must have fields of bulls somewhere in Egypt. We arrived at the stand and Farouk told us they were sold out. Unsurprising, I thought. "Okay, what's next best?" I said.

"We could have tit?" Farouk replied.

Three minutes later, I kid you not, we were going bite-for-bite on a cow udder sandwich. It was exactly how you'd expect it. Rubbery, bland, and worse still, stone cold. Disgusting. It got us onto a discussion about our favourite foods and I told Farouk that one of mine was a proper bacon sandwich. He looked at me worried and said "You mean pig. You eat pig!! Oh my God."

He was completely repulsed and looked at me as if to say you dirty thing. Aren't cultural differences brilliant? We all had a good laugh about how we were both so weird for eating different bits of different animals and agreed to disagree on what was nicer.

After nearly a week of waiting and just hanging out with Farouk, the boat finally arrived at Alexandria. Farouk hooked us up with a guy who said he could help us get the scooter out of the port and we all headed down there to get the process going. Farouk warned us that it would most likely take three days to get the bike through customs and it would cost a lot of money. Our first day at the port was Christmas Eve and it was very nearly one to remember.

Security is exceptionally tight at the port and you have to apply for a pass just to get into the room where you can talk to a customs agent. It takes a couple of hours to get the pass and in that time you just have to sit on a couple of benches outside of the front gate. As we were pretty bored, Reece decided he would whip out the camera and take a couple of snaps of the entrance. Big mistake. After a couple of shots, he received a tap on his shoulder from a very serious looking security guard. He took the camera off Reece and asked him to follow him to his office. The next thing we knew, there were five or six security guards surrounding us and they all seemed pretty angry. They were your usual henchmen, green army uniforms, big guns, and on a power trip.

They asked Reece to show them the pictures on the camera. He did so. They didn't like what they saw and angry sounding Egyptian words started coming from all angles. Reece and I were pretty chilled. Sure, we are international men of mystery but we weren't spying that day so there should have been no problem. That wasn't how the guys saw it. The next thing we knew, Farouk turned around and said something along the lines of, "Guys, this is a big problem. You're going to need to call your embassy." Reece went white as a ghost. It looked certain that he'd be locked up for Christmas. I started to crack up—a combination of nervous laughter and the sight of Reece visibly pooing himself at the port.

Of course, we didn't ring the embassy-eventually everyone stopped talking so loudly and we managed to get a word in. We calmly turned to the guy with the most stripes on his arm and said, "Sir this is a big misunderstanding, we are tourists and we have a silly motorbike inside the port. Let us show you." Farouk translated as we got out our phones and showed the guys a picture of the bike.

"We're driving it to Cape Town. Let us get it out and you can have a ride if you like?" He smiled a bit and then kicked off again. This went on for a couple of hours until the sergeant had filled his boring day and we were all allowed to go home ready to try again the next day, Christmas Day.

It was a funny old Christmas. I absolutely love Christmas and hate not being in the UK for it, but celebrating at Farouk's was fun. Well, I say celebrated, we just queued at the port, got the permit we should have got the day before, and then went for a beer in the evening. Beer in Egypt is a thing, by the way. All alcohol is against the law but it's easily accessible to foreigners, and Egypt even has a national beer, Stella (no relation to Stella Artois). Farouk doesn't drink alcohol because it's against his religious beliefs. This lack of pint led us on to a four-hour long conversation about religion and many other things in the world. It was a fantastic opportunity to really try and understand his point of view; what was crazy to us was that every question we tossed at Farouk he batted away with a simple answer that really made you think. I'm pretty ignorant when it comes to religion. I was hugely surprised then, when Farouk told me the story of the Garden of Eden only with different names for Adam and Eve. I had no idea that the same stories featured in other religions; neither did Farouk.

Religion is life for most people in Egypt and Farouk firmly believes that if anything bad happens to him it's because he hasn't served God correctly. When you're there you can see how easy it would be to feel like that. Farouk thought we were completely off the scale nuts for having no religion at all, but then I didn't grow up with a speaker at the end of my road that screams out the call to prayer five times a day. It was brilliant to get to understand both sides of it, and I think we all learnt a lot. I also learnt that night that a traditional cheese fondue in Egypt is served with offal and it will give you the shits.

We spent Boxing Day sat in the port before we finally got our hands on the sidecar on the 27th. It had been three full days sat in the port bribing people. We spent about £300 in bribes. How it worked was I gave the fixer about £400, he kept a cheeky hundred for himself and then passed the rest under the table at the port. Literally, under the table. I saw him do it at every desk. People say you shouldn't bribe at the ports because it keeps the system corrupt. I say a man told me if you don't bribe, we will be sat there for three weeks. I said, "Let's play ball then."

Also, I'm not sure I entirely agree with the whole don't bribe thing. Many of these guys get paid next to nothing and a few quid here and there from the odd tourist isn't the end of the world in my opinion. Yes, I'd like it if they got paid a decent wage and the whole system was honest but that's just not how it works out there. Most of them aren't getting minted, they're just trying to get by.

The next morning, we said goodbye to Farouk and Hassan (and seemingly everyone else in Alexandria) and we had our first day on the road in Africa. The rig was kitted out with Egyptian number plates and we really looked the part. Our next stop would be Cairo, specifically a little campsite on the outskirts where many overlanders plan for their journey south. It's run by Maryanne, a Canadian lady who has been farming there for years. The day's drive was very routine. It was just a quiet stretch of motorway connecting the two biggest cities in the country. We messed around long enough on the way to find ourselves arriving into Cairo just after dark.

We had done as we always had. Put a location into Gary and followed it blindly. Again, it said, "You have arrived at your destination." And again, we most certainly had not. We were in a tiny little village in a random suburb of Cairo. It was now pitch black and at first there wasn't a soul around. We pulled up, took off our helmets and started to scratch our heads. As we did so, somebody emerged from a house and just stood looking at us. We gave a little wave. Then another person came out. Then another, then another. Then the kids came. They weren't so shy and came running over screaming and laughing. Instantly they jumped in the sidecar and started pulling on anything they could get their hands on. Their parents came soon after to try and calm them down and before we knew it, we were surrounded by fifty or so people. They were so excited to have us!

Everything was going fine at first, but before long the crowd started to get over excited. Drunk people emerged too, and the situation started to escalate. A couple of guys on motorbikes arrived. They'd clearly been on something, but they could speak English and asked if they could help. We put them on the phone to Maryanne and she told them how to direct us to the farm. They asked us to follow them, so we chucked seven or eight kids off the bike and sped off blindly into the dark. We expected to almost immediately turn into the farm but ten minutes later we were still riding alongside the Nile. It was an absolutely horrific stretch of road and every 100 metres we hit a brick wall, otherwise known as an Egyptian speed bump. The bumps are ridiculously big; eventually they took their toll and ripped a bit of plastic off the underside of the scooter.

We had to pull in to take a look and found half the bike hanging off. Fortunately, it was only cosmetic, and we managed to stitch it up with some cable ties. Unfortunately, the fellas had got bored and left us alone in the dark with no idea where to go. We finally arrived to Maryanne's an hour later, completely worn out. Thankfully, she greeted us with a smile and an incredible home-cooked meal. We spent a couple of nights at Maryanne's as she managed to persuade us to go and look at some pyramids. We went to Saqqara, the oldest pyramid. I'm pleased we did. It was impressive, very old and nice to look at. I won't pretend to know anything more about it.

By the time we set off again it was New Year's Eve. After much research we had decided that we would take the coastal road via Hurghada, rather than head straight down the Nile to Aswan. The Nile road meant more traffic and more speed bumps and even though it was a lot more miles to go through the desert, to the sea, and back through the desert to the Nile, we thought it was worth it. Leaving Cairo was absolutely crazy. The traffic was horrific, and everyone was driving like the Italians (terribly). We saw a very near miss in which a pickup full of children swerved to avoid another truck. The kids very nearly flew out of the back and onto the motorway.

As we were leaving Cairo, we noticed a service station on the side of the road. It was almost as out of place as we were. We had seen nothing particularly Westernised in days and then suddenly there was a services that looked like it had been scooped up off Route 66 and plonked on the outskirts of Cairo. We went inside and walked into a glorious wall of air conditioning. We were so amazed that we bought an Americano and sat down to soak it in. What the hell was it doing here? Serving the other half of Egypt, of course. It was for the super-rich who had all moved to the area, a place called New Cairo.

In 2016, the President decided that it was too inconvenient to traipse through the congested capital city of Cairo and instead decided to use New Cairo as a place to base the government and big business. That meant that all of the workings of the government moved to the new city and anybody who wasn't completely minted couldn't afford to move with it or travel to it. The government claimed they moved it to ease congestion in the city, but many believe that it was just to make life a little easier for the rich at the expense of making life a lot tougher for your average person in Cairo. Nonetheless, we had a nice cool-down and a lovely cup of coffee before pressing on.

Riding out across the desert was awesome. There's a big stretch of tarmac that takes you straight out to the Red Sea without a single bump. It was boiling hot, but okay when you're cheesing it along and we were just amazed to be out there. I remember pulling in and just being blown away at how dry it was. We knew we were in the Sahara Desert and should have been expecting it, but we were still kind of shocked at just how exceptionally dry, sandy, and remote it was. You could look all around in any direction and there was nothing but sand and a thin line of tarmac for us to scoot on.

By lunch time we had made it to the coast. We turned south and started heading along what I can only describe as Ghost Coast. All the way along the sea there was empty hotel after empty hotel. Sometimes they would be completely finished, massive resorts with big names like the Marriott or JA Ocean, but most would just be concrete shells. There would be a break now and again but really it was like the whole coastline was getting developed and then suddenly the tourists just stopped coming.

We were flying along the coast and making good progress, enjoying our first day south of Cairo and in uncharted waters. Our plan was to make it to the tourist town of Hurghada and celebrate New Year's Eve in some dodgy bar somewhere. At around 4 p.m. we were cracking on and only around 100 km from our destination when the bike suddenly became a lot bumpier. We were on smooth tarmac, but it felt like corrugations on a rough track. Reece was at the handlebars and he pulled in on the side of the road. We were completely in the middle of nowhere. We had passed a town about 20 km back and the next one we would come to south was where we were heading.

We jumped off the bike and had a look around. It was instantly clear what the problem was: there was a mangled bit of metal hanging out of the sidecar wheel.

"Christ mate, what the hell is that?" said Reece.

"Lord knows, mate. A bearing?" I replied.

It was just a word I had heard and something we had bought back in Alexandria. We knew nothing of what a bearing did, we just had a couple of boxes that said bearing on them in the bottom of the bag. Either way, it was way above our pay grade. We didn't even know how to get the wheel off let alone change a bearing. We needed help or we would be spending New Year's Eve out in the desert.

Traffic wasn't fast flowing but a car did come past every few minutes. Not too long after we had got stuck an ambulance pulled up and the guys said they would ring the police for us who would be happy to help. Would they really? We had heard a lot of bad press about the Egyptian police from other motorcyclists. That they're annoying, they follow you, and they want money. Well about thirty minutes later a couple of really nice blokes turned up in their police truck and started trying to help. Straightaway, they clocked what the problem was and they got very excited when I showed them the bearing in our spares. As the sun set, the lads spent an hour or so getting the wheel off the bike and tried to change the bearing. Unfortunately, the old bearing had got mashed up inside the wheel and we needed a proper workshop to get it out. Finally, we admitted defeat and at about 10 p.m. we arrived into Hurghada on the back of a recovery truck. The police guys weren't at all annoying and didn't want anything from us in return for their help. They had saved our bacon, or as they might say in Egypt, they had saved our udder (surely, they don't say that).

We got to our hotel in Hurghada, grabbed a couple of bottles of Stella, and sat down. We were completely fried and absolutely knackered. We had survived our first breakdown; we had been saved by the locals and had been proven right. Even more to celebrate on New Year's Eve! After we had spent half an hour recovering, we thought we'd go and find somewhere to sing *Auld Lang Syne* and all that jazz. We popped around the corner to the local shop and asked the cashier which way it was to the main strip. They didn't have the foggiest what we were on about, but an Egyptian guy in the queue said the best spot was El Gouda and we should grab a couple of beers and join him and his friends there. We jumped at the chance and jumped in the car.

It turned out El Gouda was another town just up the road. It took us about an hour to get in. Not because it was far away but because of the queue. The police had set up checkpoints on all the roads in and everyone had to leave their IDs at the gate. We, of course, said no and they let us pass anyway on account of being foreign. We pulled into the marina at about five minutes to midnight and we were in the main square just in time for the countdown. The fireworks set off as the clock turned to midnight and they reflected back off the bay. It was quite the sight. Not really because of the fireworks, but because of the yachts. We had been teleported into the other half of Egypt and it was fricking minted. The port was absolutely choc-a-bloc with boats that must have been worth a million apiece.

We started to understand where we were and I looked down at the floor to a perfectly paved footpath. Around us were the rich kids of Egypt and to be honest it was just about the last place either of us wanted to be. We would have both much rather been somewhere that brought in the new year in a traditionally Egyptian way, rather than with a bunch of guys who had watched too much MTV *Cribs* and wanted to pretend to be in this weird fake version of Monaco. I snuck off for a second and gave Chels a quick call to wish her happy new year. She was at her neighbour's house celebrating and was still in 2017. I could barely hear her so I told her it was great in 2018 and that she would love it, before saying bye and getting back to the party.

The guys wanted to go to a club but Reece and I weren't all that keen. We had spotted our excuse, the Smugglers Inn. Yes, this place was so Westernised that it even had a traditional British pub. We told the guys we fancied sinking one in there before hitting the dance floor. It was spot on to be fair. You literally wouldn't have known you were in a different country. Most of the time British pubs abroad are cheap copies but this place was exactly as if we had walked into our local boozer back home. It even had all those weird little trinkets and ornaments you get. The bar man said,

"Alright lads, what can I get ya?" and there were two blokes talking about Brexit at the bar. No really, there genuinely were. We had driven all the way here into the middle of the Sahara and, somehow, we had ended up with the kind of New Year's Eve you'd expect in a shit pub in Slough or somewhere like that.

We told the bloke he'd got Remainers all wrong, nailed a couple of pints of Guinness and finally gave in to the Egyptian guys who took us to a glowstick party. It was crap. Really crap. We had a bit of a dance and then got a cab back to Hurghada. As we got back, I got a call from Chels, "Happy New Year!!" England had caught up. I think she thought I had taken some kind of drugs when I told her I had spent the night drinking Guinness and discussing Brexit with a bloke called Steve, in the middle of the Sahara. I don't blame her really.

We spent the entirety of the following day fixing the sidecar. We couldn't work out why it wouldn't go back together. We were getting completely furious with it. Just so frustrated. We tried every single combination of spacers and bearings, but it just wouldn't work. Then at about 5 p.m., around six hours after it should have been fixed, I found another part in my pocket. I think Reece nearly had a breakdown. The next morning, we drove back to where we broke down and turned back around, to then drive back to where we had set off from. We had committed to driving around the world on a scooter and sidecar, not a scooter, sidecar, and recovery truck, and we were planning to cover every inch. Then finally, on the 3rd of January we started making progress again.

We scooted through the desert to the town of Luxor, where we stayed with a charity called Animal Care Egypt (ACE). A British lady who worked there had been following our journey on the Ace Café Facebook page and had invited us to stay. It was a great place to explore from. Then we pressed on south again to Aswan.

On the way to Aswan we passed a police checkpoint. We told the fellas there that we were heading to Cape Town, to which they replied, "Okay, we come with you!" A bold move. We pressed on in convoy once again, pleased we had the support crew we'd always wanted, but after about twenty minutes of pushing 47-48 mph the fellas got bored and headed to Cape Town without us.

Police escorts were a fairly common thing throughout our time in Egypt. The government is just petrified of what any attack on a tourist would do to the country's economy, so they try to keep you wrapped up in cotton wool. Some overlanders hate it; we thought it was fun. Plus, they were a useful bunch. As we arrived at another checkpoint on the outskirts of Aswan, the guys pointed out that our back tyre was as flat as a pancake. Incredibly, we had planned for that and had a plug kit with us. The lads let us plug our electric pump into their pickup and we had it back up thirty minutes later.

We arrived in Aswan at about six or seven and I can honestly say it was one of my least favourite places of the whole trip. You get a lot of people hassling you, wanting to sell you stuff. That doesn't really bother me but what does bother me is that the place is filthy, too. Apart from the odd pocket of tourist wealth, with the big hotels, the town is just completely and utterly run down. It's well and truly on its knees. We were staying on a budget so checked into one of the cheapest hotels. This hotel was the birthplace of our "no crawling" rule. From that point on we decided that places could be dirty, but it had to be dead for us to sleep there. We were fairly used to staying in not-so-nice places, but it was another level. It wasn't just the filth that got me riled up, either. The place seemed to have none of the charm that we loved Egypt for. There was no character and the people there were just fed up. You could see why: the stark disparities between the rich and the poor were clear for everyone to see when the luxury cruise boats docked along the river. I don't think we saw a single Westerner in town, but we could see them all sat atop their cruise boats, waltzing around in bikinis and swimmers, sipping piña coladas in a country where that just isn't cool. Obviously, that goes on in other places in Egypt, but at least the locals get jobs and the opportunity to sell a postcard. Here they just get to watch as a bunch of foreigners cruise into the centre of the city, disrespect their culture, and cruise off again. To me, it seemed to be the ultimate insult.

Aswan is the exit point for most overlanders when they leave Egypt. You can jump on a boat and spend a couple of days cruising up the Nile and across Lake Nasser. The boat is a far cry from the cruise ships though. It's supposedly overcrowded and pretty ghastly. We decided that we would take the other option, a new road down to Abu Simbel, where we could get a short local ferry over the lake and into Sudan. We had heard that you were supposed to leave in a convoy with all of the truckers at certain times of day because the road wasn't safe, but we couldn't work out where it went from, so just braved it alone. It all went completely fine and we rocked up into the town at about four in the afternoon. We had heard that people had been allowed to camp in the car park of the incredible Abu Simbel temples, so we thought we'd give that a go, too.

It was a fantastic idea. There's a police checkpoint right next door so we let them know we were staying and they said we were very welcome. There's no alcohol allowed in Sudan and the security at the border is really tight, so we drank a drop of whiskey somebody had given us before we left. It was an awesome place to camp; we didn't bother with the tent, instead just slung out our sleeping bags on a bench and got our heads down.

In the morning we grabbed a cup of coffee from the local café and sat to watch the sunrise over the temples. It was an incredible location. The temples were relocated to the site in 1969, as the construction of the Aswan High Dam and the subsequent flooding of the Nasser Valley would have drowned the monuments. It's incredible to think that they actually managed to move them, they are absolutely ginormous. I think it's a bit of a shame they did get moved though, because it turns out the other plan was to build a kind of dome around the monuments to create underwater viewing stations, how cool would that have been?

After a mooch around the monuments, we grabbed some breakfast and headed to the port. It was a tiny little bay which just had the one boat and five or six lorries queuing up to get on it. We queued behind them, boarded the boat, and set sail for Sudan.

− 7 −

"GET IT OFF, GET IT OFF, GET IT OFF!"

Sailing across Lake Nasser heading for Sudan was one of the coolest things I've ever done. Not many overlanders take that route so it was completely authentic. The local guys were really excited to have us, and the captain even invited us onto the top deck for tea. There we were, sailing across this lake, sipping sweet Egyptian tea with the crew, while looking back over the incredible Abu Simbel temples and looking forward to our next country, Sudan. This was adventure.

Well actually there's about another twenty-five miles of brand-new tarmac to Sudan but it's best not to let that get in the way of a good story. We drove the twenty-five miles and went from the best part of overlanding to the worst, the paperwork. We knew we'd need a fixer to get out of Egypt but we'd heard getting into Sudan was quite a lot simpler. It wasn't. We paid the fixer and got out of Egypt within an hour or so, and as we drove into Sudan a man came up to us and said in perfect English, "Hey guys, I can help you get into Sudan, no problem."

"No thanks," I replied. "We'll be fine on our own."

"No, you won't," he said, laughing.

He was right. Eight hours later we finally admitted defeat and got him to help us get out. It was becoming ever more likely that we would be camping at the border for the night and we were just so desperate to get out of there. It had been a day of aimlessly getting sent from one office to another. The fixer dude helped us out in less than thirty minutes. I like to think that meant we had done most of the stuff, but it probably didn't. We gave him £15 which he was chuffed with, and we were able to press on to the town of Wadi Halfa as the sun disappeared into the desert. We arrived into the town, splashed out on a £7 hotel room, chucked our stuff down, and went searching for food.

In the town centre, there was no street lighting at all but instead the place was lit up with super-bright LED lights hovering over the shops and food stalls. All of the food stalls were identical, and they were all selling exactly the same thing: bones, with bits of meat attached to them, fried over hot coals in a giant silver pan. Served with super-hot chili sauce and loads of bread, it was absolute paradise. We were so hungry that we slammed through half a kilo each; it was exactly what the doctor ordered. About an hour later we were full with mutton, bread, and regret. It was just so greasy that it sent us over the edge, and we passed out in our dodgy hotel room feeling pretty disgusting.

The following morning, we set about getting some supplies to keep us alive on our journey through the desert. You don't really have to plan where to go in Sudan, there's essentially one road south, you can take it all the way to Khartoum, or you can veer off to the east to the Port of Sudan. It's not complicated at all, but you do need to be prepared. There's not much there and aside from the odd village and occasional town, it's just you and the sand all the way to the capital. We thought that was great fun and planned to camp all the way there. We were well equipped for the road, too. My travel diary reads that we picked up: 1 x small jam, 2 x yoghurts, 6 x bananas, 8 x rolls (hot dog style), and 2 x tins of tuna. A winning, Sahara-tackling combination. After about twenty minutes on the road, we realised that carrying yoghurts at 35°C wasn't a great idea so pulled over and tucked in.

We spent the next few hours heading down a big piece of tarmac running parallel with the Nile. It was more remote than Egypt, and there was less traffic and certainly fewer police. Generally though, it was pretty similar but with one notable difference. Dead cows. They were everywhere. Every couple of miles there would be another, just lying on the side of the road soaking up the desert sun, slowly but surely turning to leather. They stank. It turned out that it's a pretty regular occurrence for cows to die of heat exhaustion in the back of trucks and when discovered they just get turfed out. Nasty business.

After a full day of scooting south, we turned off the road at about 4 p.m. to find somewhere to camp. We pulled up to the banks of the Nile and bumped into a farmer. The meeting broke into a game of charades and we tried to mime that we would like to set up camp there. He nodded, smiled, and offered us a date by way of a welcome.

It was an absolutely gorgeous spot: palm trees, sand dunes, and the Nile gently flowing through it all, giving life to everything around. Although, just as we had got everything set up, another farmer came along and started his own game of charades. He was acting as a crocodile and laughing a lot. It was a pretty easy one to guess and we decided that we wouldn't go for a dip in the river. The farmer also offered for us to come and stay at his house but we had just set up camp so politely declined. Instead, we lit a fire, put the kettle on and sat down to enjoy the incredible sunset, and then the stars above. All we could hear were distant sounds of the farmers singing as they worked the land around us. It was one hell of a place for a camp.

The following day we made incredible progress down empty roads through the blistering, intense heat of the desert. Stopping only to fill the tank and glug some water, we rotated who was at the handlebars and who was napping in the sidecar. The napping wasn't because we were tired but because the intense heat and pure nothingness of the landscape subdued us into a doze. Eventually we made it to Dongola where we pulled in for lunch. Dongola is a bit more of a proper town and it had all sorts of luxuries, the most important of which was a fridge. We inhaled two or three cold Cokes each and had another whopping helping of bread and meat; this time it was chicken. While we were sipping away, a couple of the local guys were checking out the sidecar and noticed something we hadn't: the rear tyre had worn completely through and all the metal wire was hanging out.

We had absolutely no idea how to change a tyre, so we started trawling through our manual. It told us nothing. After about an hour of trying to do it ourselves with no progress whatsoever, we let the Sudanese guys have their turn. They were a little less delicate than us and in seemingly no time at all they had whipped off the exhaust and the swinging arm, pulled the wheel off and changed the tyre. Getting it back together was a whole different story. It turned out they had sheared two bolts while removing the exhaust and lost a couple more in the process. The next thing I knew I was sitting on the back of this guy's little motorbike and racing off down sand roads to get the other half of the bolt out. I was clinging onto the bike with one hand and our exhaust with the other while we steamed it along. It was petrifying. Fortunately, I managed to convince him to let me ride us back, although in hindsight that was probably more dangerous as I was used to three wheels! After a few hours, the fellas managed to bodge it back together and we drove out into the desert for another camp in the wild.

The next couple of days were a similar story of driving through extreme heat and camping in the wild but they were interrupted with some bizarre meetings, the first of which was slap-bang in the middle of nowhere. We were driving down an incredibly long stretch of tarmac with nothing but sand all around, when a weirdly shaped object started coming towards us. As it got closer and closer, we started to think we were hallucinating. It looked just like a sidecar outfit. Fortunately, we hadn't gone crackers and it actually was a Ural sidecar outfit with a German couple in it. Both of us took a double take and screeched to a halt on opposite sides of the road. We stopped for pictures and to exchange notes on the road ahead. The couple told us that we should look out for a British girl riding a Honda motorcycle north. We pressed on to Karima and sure enough, as we lived and breathed, Steph Jeavons appeared on her little 250cc, Rhonda the Honda. We were completely star-struck. We had been following Steph's progress around the world for the last couple of years and absolutely never expected to actually bump into her.

Steph arrived just as we were driving around a car park, trying to work out what was wrong with our bike. It was making another funny sound. Steph had a listen and said she had no idea what it was because she didn't know much about how to fix bikes. We couldn't believe that, Steph was just about to get home as the first Brit to ride on all seven continents, how could you do that without being able to repair your bike? At the time, we thought it was good news for us; if Steph could achieve everything she had on Rhonda and not know how to repair her, then surely we could whip our sidecar around the world, no problem. Looking back though, maybe Steph could have fixed it and just thought, "I need to get away from these weirdos." I wouldn't blame her. We must have looked completely off the scale nuts. From her point of view the situation was that there are two weird-looking British blokes, driving around in circles, in a random Sudanese town, on a bright red scooter and sidecar, they look a mess, they completely stink and when you say hi they turn around and go completely fan girl on you as if they'd just bumped into David Beckham. I'd have been running for the hills.

We screwed our exhaust back together and headed out for the desert again to look for somewhere to camp. Bizarrely, we couldn't find anywhere at all. Each time we thought we'd cracked it, a guy would come out and point for us to move on. Our search for somewhere went on for hours and just as it turned completely dark, we found a garage to pull into and reassess. We thought we might be able to stay at the garage but the guys there said that wouldn't be an option either. At about 8 p.m. we decided we would just drive off road in the dark and camp where nobody could see us, then get up early and get out of there. The only problem was that when we got onto the sand, we could see tyre tracks everywhere. Now, we didn't know the area at all and the last thing we wanted to do was camp up and have a local guy crash through our tent in his pickup at 3 a.m. We pressed on into the sand, looking for somewhere with a bit of protection.

I was driving at this point and could see what looked like a good place so I drove down a small mound to check it out. Big mistake. It turned out to be a kind of sand pit and we were instantly stuck. We spent an hour trying to push and pull it out of the sand but to no avail. Eventually, I decided that I would take a walk and try to find some board or something to get a bit of traction. I said to Reece that I'd be two minutes. About thirty minutes later, I came over the top of the mound, riding on the mud guard of a farmer's tractor. Reece was both relieved and absolutely furious. I had wanted to run back and tell him that I had found a tractor, but I couldn't because the farmer didn't want to help me. I couldn't risk letting the farmer go so I just had to stand and offer him things for thirty minutes until he'd help. All the while I left Reece in the desert wondering where I was. The tractor easily pulled us out of the sand, so we pitched the tent up bang opposite the garage and fell asleep, completely worn out.

We woke up the following morning and pressed on to Khartoum. We had arranged to stay there for a couple of nights with Izzy, a girl from London, and a French dude called Simon. We had randomly found them on the Couchsurfing app and we were both intrigued to find out what they were doing living in the capital of Sudan and excited for the prospect of maybe getting some home comforts in the house of some Westerners. The thing we were most excited for was a shower. We arrived to their house and were greeted by Simon. We exchanged some niceties before we said, "Dude, we've been camping in the desert for a week, we must stink. Any chance we can use your shower?"

To which he replied, "No, sorry guys, no water today." That was the reality of living in a decent flat in Sudan—running water is not a guarantee. We chucked on some deodorant and went with Simon to meet Izzy at their friend's party. It was in a penthouse flat and was the home of an embassy worker. We had walked into a party in London and were instantly handed a damn cold beer. Sudan really is a no-alcohol zone, but not for these expats. They fill their cases with the stuff when they fly over knowing that they won't get checked and it won't be hard for them to talk their way out of it if they do.

We grooved the night away and, the following morning, found ourselves very hungover in a long queue at the Ethiopian embassy. We had tried to get our Ethiopian visas when we were killing time in Cairo, but they said we had to do it in Khartoum and we knew that was bad news. All of the forums online said it can take ages and they weren't wrong. That first day we queued politely until early afternoon, when it shut for the day and they asked us to come back after the weekend. No big deal, we were quite happy to have some time off to enjoy Khartoum. Izzy and Simon showed us around on the Saturday. We took a tour of some of the sights and went for a cup of traditional coffee on one of the boats that line the Nile. They slice fresh ginger into really small strong coffees—it knocks your socks off and is absolutely gorgeous. Then we went to the Greek Club for a swim; it's just a little sports centre that was originally for Greek embassy workers but now anyone can get in if they've got a couple of quid (literally £2). We had a Greek salad, a bit of a swim, and a nice relax on the sunbeds. Finally, a chance to really enjoy the searing sunshine.

On the Sunday we went to meet up with Mohamed from the Sudanese bikers club. Steph had put us in touch, and we were really intrigued to meet the guys from the club. They were a lovely bunch, clearly minted by Sudanese standards because they asked to meet us at a nice hotel, and they wouldn't let us pay for the burgers we ordered. It took us a few more days to get our visas but we were lucky enough to keep getting great opportunities to explore the capital. The following day we queued at the embassy, got the process going and then hung out with the bikers at their weekly meet-up. There were loads of massive bikes you don't expect to see in Sudan— KTMs, BMWs, etc. Just the kind of stuff you'd expect to see at a bike meet in the UK. This was a bit more exciting though because the guys were into doing tricks on their bikes, big wheelies and the kind of endo I did on my bike test. It was a good laugh.

We were invited to a Sudanese wedding while we were in town, too. It was absolutely huge, there must have been over 500 people there, and the production level was out of this world. There were cameras on cranes, and it looked like we were at the Oscars or something. The happy couple arrived together in a fancy car and their arrival was beamed onto big screens for everyone inside to see. The band, singing in Arabic, stopped playing and Ed Sheeran's *Thinking Out Loud* blared out over the speakers for the couple's entrance. How? How on earth does he do it? Ninety percent of the room couldn't even speak English, yet somehow Ed had beaten anything in Arabic to the number one spot at this random Sudanese wedding. After Ed, the bride and groom sat down in some massive throne-like chairs and watched their guests eat, as is the tradition in Sudan. Then they left. The whole thing cost them around US$30,000 and I kid you not they were there for an hour. This wasn't an exceptional wedding either, by Sudanese standards anyway. Apparently, if you can, then it's normal to save up for a similarly sized shindig. Unreal, imagine how far thirty grand gets you in Sudan!

The wedding went on long into the night, loads of dancing. Some truly crazy shapes were thrown. But not a single drop of liquor was consumed, and we woke up the following morning hangover-free. We took on our daily battle with the Ethiopian embassy before heading off in the afternoon to meet an anti-slavery organisation, the People's Legal Aid Centre Sudan (PLACE).

PLACE is about as close as you get to an anti-slavery organisation in Sudan. In a country that is estimated to be home to over 400,000 people living in slavery, Rifaat Makkawi and his team are more or less the only people trying to fight it.

Rifaat founded PLACE in 1998 in order to provide legal aid for marginalised people in Sudan. Twenty years on, PLACE now has offices all over Sudan and is a vital service for people who can't afford access to justice. As part of their work, PLACE regularly provides legal aid to victims of human trafficking and modern slavery in Sudan. We went to meet Rifaat in his office in Khartoum, where he welcomed us with the smallest, punchiest coffee I've ever come across. We sat with him for an hour or so learning about his life's work while sipping on these tiny shots of pure caffeine.

Rifaat told us that in the past five to ten years he's been presented with more and more cases of modern slavery and human trafficking. He said that maybe they just didn't know about the issue as much before but at the moment they're having people come in from all walks of life. He's supporting both Sudanese nationals and people who have been trafficked into Sudan from places like Bangladesh. He said most of the people who come to him have escaped forced labour, but he has also come across cases of forced marriage.

It's not surprising to hear that Rifaat has a lot of forced labour cases because the majority of people enslaved in Sudan are thought to be in forced labour. The Global Slavery Index estimates that just over one in every hundred people in Sudan are living in slavery. They also estimate that over two-thirds of the population are at risk of being trapped in modern slavery. High levels of poverty and low literacy rates make much of the Sudanese population especially vulnerable, so as part of their work, PLACE runs workshops in communities to educate people about their legal rights.

At the PLACE headquarters, we met with a group of Bangladeshi guys who had been told they would come to Sudan to work as tailors. In fact, they were trafficked into forced labour and paid nothing for years of work. Rifaat told us that they were tortured when they tried to escape. PLACE is now trying to prosecute the people who enslaved the group, but Rifaat didn't hold out much hope for a conviction. He said that, as always, they would try their very best but a prosecution requires the assistance of the police and the government, who are usually very reluctant to help.

He spoke to us in detail about his opinions on the government. He said that government policies were at the root of most of the problems of the people of Sudan, especially victims of modern slavery. He went as far as to say that the government actually encouraged it because it makes them money. He was serious. We told him we obviously wouldn't publish any of his thoughts on the government as we knew it could get him in big trouble, to which he replied, "Tell everyone you can. I am not scared, I am old, they can kill me if they like, I'd rather people know the truth." The "they" he was referring to was the government of Omar al-Bashir who had been running the country as a dictatorship for nearly three decades. At the time there was a warrant for al-Bashir's arrest from the International Criminal Court on the grounds of genocide and crimes against humanity.

Late in 2018, the price of bread in Sudan tripled overnight and the people decided they'd had enough. Widespread protest against al-Bashir started and continued until he was arrested by the military. He now sits behind bars, but protests continue as the people strive for a properly elected civilian government rather than the military rule that continues. Not too long ago the protests got bloody and the new military government opened fire on people protesting peacefully, so it seems there is still a ways to go until progress can be made. We know that Rifaat and his team will be protesting alongside those in the streets and have seen his name pop up in documents filed against the current government. Hopefully, Rifaat and the people of Sudan can win the battle and live in a peaceful place with democratically elected leaders. Then one day, they may have more of a chance of freeing the 400,000 people estimated to be enslaved there.

Eventually, we managed to get our visas for Ethiopia, said goodbye to our friends in Sudan, and headed south for the border. All that stood in our way of Ethiopia was around 450 miles and a couple of nights in the desert. We pressed on south and found a camping spot easily. It was just off the main road and the farmer guys were over the moon to have us. We gave them a marshmallow and exchanged Facebook details on their smart phone before pitching our tent. The people of Sudan were probably the most welcoming, helpful, peaceful people we met on the whole trip. These guys sat with us for a while and we tried to chat but the language barrier was a bit of a problem. Eventually they left us to camp out on their land and went home.

Reece was pretty pleased about this because he wasn't feeling great. He had got food poisoning. "Poor bloke," I thought. "Out in the middle of the desert and he's ended up with a serious case of the shits." About an hour later, I was sat there by the fire looking up at the incredible stars, pretty pleased it wasn't me with the food poisoning, when I fully pooed myself. It hit me like a wave. We didn't stop digging holes on that poor farmer's land until the early hours of the morning. It was truly disgusting.

We woke up feeling really run down. We'd had very little sleep, we were pretty dehydrated, and a bit dazed. I was outside the tent, packing a bag when Reece crawled out. As he stood up, I saw a shadow flash up his leg. *What was it? Surely, nothing. I'm just delusional from all of the hole digging.* As the shadow shot up his leg, Reece sat down and perched on a small sandy mound. I thought it was probably nothing but had to make sure, so I told Reece to stay still while I had a peer around. Nothing there. *But I did see something, I was sure I saw something.* I asked Reece to stand up and I had another look around.

"Reece, stay very, very still. There is a scorpion on the back of your knee."

"Oh my God, get it off, get it off, get it off, get it off, get it off!" Reece exclaimed in a very serious, worried voice.

I found a lighter and flicked it off Reece's knee and onto the sand. Reece was saved. The scorpion wasn't giving up yet, though, and every time we tried to flick it away it just kept scurrying back towards us. I think it was trying to burrow under the tent. I was scared, and rightfully so. We were 300 km from the nearest hospital, we were both exceptionally weak from the food poisoning and this potentially deadly creature was trying to join the team. We decided that we couldn't take the risk of letting it hang around, and regretfully, I bludgeoned it with our camping mallet. It was a ridiculous moment. I didn't want to do it, but at the time it felt like it was us or it. When we got some internet, we googled "scorpions" in and around that area. The first one that came up was called the Death Stalker and it was unmistakably the one that had been on the back of Reece's knee. True to its name, the Death Stalker was known for killing the young, the elderly, and the weak. Fresh off the back of food poisoning and 300 km from the nearest hospital, Reece would have been dust. It was a close shave.

We eventually got packed up and back on the road. We just had one more night's wild camping before we would be in Ethiopia and heading towards the relative civilisation of Gondar. Gondar is just a small tourist town in northern Ethiopia but after that bout of food poisoning, for us, it was the light at the end of the tunnel. We were absolutely desperate to get there. We had decided we would splash out a tenner each and get a nice bed for the night with a working toilet. Plus, reaching Ethiopia meant beer was back on the menu and my word could we do with a pint.

Feeling rank but with the finish line in our sights, we cracked on down through Sudan. It wasn't long before we made it to the town of Al Qadarif, where we filled up on fuel, had a spot of lunch and a couple of Cokes. They were heaven; ice-cold and full of sugar, exactly what we needed. It was another scorcher of a day, probably around 40°C. At Al Qadarif, we turned off the main road and our time on perfect tarmac finally came to an end. The last 150 km to the border was a horrendous stretch of road. It was just pothole after pothole. They were deep, too, and so frequent that many were unavoidable for the sidecar. We were reduced to traveling at about 15-20 mph but even at those speeds it's a bone-jarring crash when you drop into a hole that deep. We trundled down this stretch of road for about five hours and it got no better. We wondered if this was it now. If the roads would be this bad all the way through Ethiopia, maybe all the way through Africa, right to Cape Town.

Eventually, the sun started to drop so we decided it was time to pull in for that final wild camp. By this time, we had made it as far south as the outskirts of Dinder National Park and we were praying we didn't have any more run-ins with wildlife. Here, a scorpion would be the least of our worries; lions, leopards, and cheetahs aren't so easily fought off with a camping mallet. The landscape also had changed slightly. Over the past couple of days we had gone from desert sand dunes to flat sandy farmland to, now, tall grass. Just the kind of stuff you'd imagine a lion to be lurking in.

It's great for wild camping though. We pulled off down a little dirt track and pitched up in a small clearing, totally hidden from any passers-by. We were completely drained from all the food poisoning, tough riding, and extreme heat, so we put the tent up and passed out. We woke up the following morning and, to my relief, I hadn't pooed myself and there was nothing on the back of Reece's knee. Things were looking up. Today would be the day that we would make it out of Sudan and it would be an easy ride, right through to Gondar, or so we thought.

– 8 –

"OUT JUMPED A COUPLE OF BLOKES HOLDING AK47S AND A FEW MORE HOLDING MASSIVE STICKS."

After our final wild camp in Sudan, we got packed up early and we were at the border, ready and waiting for 9 a.m. It didn't take long to get through. It was a pretty relaxed place. The formalities amounted to a guy sat behind an old PC which looked like it must still be running Windows 95, taking our names down, and stamping our passports. Reece stayed outside to watch the bike, so I got both our passports stamped. The border official didn't see Reece at all. He asked where he was, and I said outside watching the bike, to which he gave me an approving nod and stamped him out.

As we entered Ethiopia the landscape changed almost instantly. For the first time since we had got to Africa there were hills, proper hills, you might even call them mountains. We started snaking up and down the valleys through lush green scenery. We were over the moon to be there, we'd had enough of the desert. As we snaked further into Ethiopia, the roads got busier and busier. There was seemingly an endless chain of crazy minibus drivers overtaking us on blind bends.

We turned around one corner and in the middle of the road was a burnt-out lorry, some kind of tanker. Overturned and laid out over both sides of the road with just enough room for a single lane of traffic to squeeze through it. The thing was literally charred black and still burning. Nobody on the scene. No sign of any authorities, seemingly nobody cared. It turned out it had been there for days and would stay there for a while longer. There was nobody around to move it. They keep it burning so people driving at night could see it in the road. Crazy.

We continued along, up and down the hills until we reached the first sizeable village. We could see the village down in the valley and we were surprised to see it was absolutely choc-a-bloc with people. What was it? A protest? A party? A normal day? We had no choice but to press on and find out. As we approached, our presence didn't go unnoticed and everyone slowly gathered around us. We slowed down to join a queue of traffic trying to get through and all around us people were chanting and jumping up and down with big sticks. The atmosphere was incredible. Different groups would come bouncing past with different chants. The groups ranged from over-excited, drunk, teenage lads in football shirts, to older members of the community dressed in full white robes bouncing up and down under the shade of their white umbrellas.

I was in the sidecar, so I whipped off my helmet and gave out a massive smile. People were confused by us and I wanted everyone to know we came in peace! It wasn't hard to get the message across and everyone was laughing, cheering and dancing along. We attracted a lot of attention and it was pretty intense. Although everyone was friendly, they were inquisitive souls and wanted to know what everything was. Trying to poke around in our bags, playing with the sat nav, trying to work out who was driving. All done in good spirit but when you're completely surrounded it can feel pretty hectic.

We eventually got out of the village and had a good laugh about it. It had been mental, but it was done, and we had a cheeky 60 km left before we were in Gondar where we would kick back with a beer and enjoy an afternoon off. We got to the top of the next hill and looked down to see an even bigger village with even more people in the streets. 'Blimey, this could be a long day," I thought. We pressed on once more and the same routine happened. Reece was still driving, and we had got stuck in a queue again. We were slowly crawling along when the traffic in front started to pull away. We were swamped from all angles.

"Reece man, what are you doing!? Floor it!" I shouted.

"I can't, mate, it's going nowhere!" He exclaimed.

He floored it again, full throttle, we didn't move. The crowd was all around us. Pushing, pulling, grabbing. We were going nowhere. I got off the bike to have a look around. There didn't seem to be anything wrong with it.

"Try it again," I shouted, trying to cut through the chanting of the crowd.

Reece floored it once more but moved nowhere. Instead, bits of metal flew out the bottom of the crankcase and smoke plumed up.

"It's done for, mate! Stop!" I shouted.

We got off and tried to push it off the road. The crowd mucked in and we started going up the hill. I said to Reece, "Why don't we try it again?" You know, turn it off and on again like a PC. Big mistake. We had no idea that bikes aren't like PCs. Turning it off and on again seized up the back wheel and now we could no longer push it. We were complete sitting ducks.

We had blocked the road on what we later found out was festival day. Not just any old festival either but Timkat festival, the biggest religious festival in Ethiopia. It wasn't long before the local bobbies showed up to find out what all the commotion was about. Their police pickup pulled up next to us and out jumped a couple of blokes holding AK47s and a few more holding massive sticks. The guys with the sticks instantly started hitting back the crowd. Properly hitting them. The crowd found it hilarious and turned it into a giant game of the Hokey Cokey. They would rush in to try and touch the sidecar and then they'd get whipped back. Then the policeman would whip another section of the crowd and they'd pour back in again. It was hilarious to see them all, messing around, and trying to wind the police up. At the same time though, the situation had got pretty serious and we really needed to get out of there.

Through a combination of pointing, charades, and a bit of English, the police soon understood that we had got into a pickle and agreed to put the rig on the back of their truck and take us to Gondar. The only way we would be able to get it on there was with brute force, so we asked the police to stop whipping the crowd back and instead to tell them to get hold of a bit of the rig and help us lift it onto the pickup. Everyone got on the sidecar side because they thought that was the heavy bit and lifted it straight up, nearly tipping it onto Reece who was the only person manning the real heavy bit, the actual bike. A mix of adrenaline and desperation for that afternoon pint meant Reece somehow got his side in the air too and the bike crashed onto the back of the truck. It didn't quite fit but we kind of strapped it down a bit with one wheel precariously perched on the edge of the truck before jumping in and holding on for dear life.

We raced out of the village and were soon storming it down winding roads at about 60 mph. We passed an overturned beer truck and just got past the thousands of bottles in the road. Apparently, it had only just happened, which was clearly true because there was beer everywhere. Around 10 km from Gondar we pulled in at the local cop shop.

"Okay, we stop here," said the driver.

"No, please can you take us just 10 km more to Gondar?" we replied.

"No, here you get off."

"Come on, it's 10 km. We'll pay you. Please just take us."

"No, you must get off here."

We looked around. We were at a prison. Well, you could call it a prison, it was more a chicken hut. Behind us were twenty to thirty guys stuffed into a barbed wire cage, held up with a few sticks.

"No chance, mate. Come on, it's only 10 km. We'll pay you whatever," I said to the driver as I got some money out and started offering. The sun was setting, and we did not want to stop here for the night.

"No, you must get off," he replied.

"Be reasonable man, come on, we're not getting off!" said Reece.

"No, you must get off!"

"No, we're not getting off!"

"Fine I'll take you back to where I picked you up!"

"Fine, we'll get off!"

We got off and the local police said we wouldn't be able to get a truck to take us to Gondar until after the festival. We'd have to stay there. No chance, we were just 10 km away from the tourist town and a genuinely comfortable place to recover from the food poisoning and subsequent stress of the breakdown. Staying at the prison would have been a tough night's kip and we had to get out of there. We got straight to flagging down trucks in the road. Nobody would help us. The police finally decided they would help us, and guys started turning up with their considerably undersized vehicles, trying to make a buck. Finally, just as it was about to turn pitch black and the fellas in the cell behind us were done making up our bed, we got a truck that just about worked, and we made it to Gondar. There were no rooms anywhere because it was festival night but after a while we found a little place called Yohannes' Guest House. We were greeted by a bloke called Keffi who was off his face on khat (a leaf that you can chew to get high) and a Swiss guy called Edward, who handed us a beer and said you look like you could use this. He was right.

We woke the next day to find the scooter in a sorry, sorry way. We posted up on Facebook about the problems and the response was pretty bad. Anyone who knew about mechanics thought this could be the end of the road for us. We had lots of messages with things like, "Fair play lads, you got a long way, unlucky," and "You did us proud boys!" It was nice of them to say so, but we took no notice and started working to get it fixed. It took us the whole of that first day just to get the crankcase cover off and, when we did, we were horrified at what we found, a crapload of melted metal. We posted it up again and Rod, Charlie, and the guys all said we had likely burnt out the clutch and we would need to rebuild it with new parts.

It took another day to get the old clutch off and for us to get to a point where we could start to unpack exactly what had gone wrong. I won't bore you with too many mechanical details but basically the clutch shoes had melted and seized onto the drum, creating an almighty mess. It meant we would need to get a whole new clutch. We started googling and hoped that we would be able to find the parts in Ethiopia somewhere. Part of the reason we had gone for a Honda was because it was a global brand and we'd find parts anywhere. That wasn't at all the case. After a day of searching the web and calling suppliers in Addis, we admitted defeat and got them ordered in the UK. Debbie, my sister, and her fiancé, Louis, sorted it out for us. Louis drove to Bristol and picked up the parts for us and then Debbie got the company she works for, Alto Energy, to post them out to us First Class (cheers guys!). Less than forty-eight hours after we said what parts we needed, they were on the plane to meet us.

In the meantime, we were adjusting to life at Yohannes' Guest House. The first night we had crashed in a room at Yohannes's place and he tried to get us to pay $50 for it because it was Timkat. The room was not worth $50 so we said no and gave him the advertised rate of $10. He was trying to swindle everyone in that way but if you had a laugh with him and said no, then he liked you for it. We ended up camping in the garden for around $5 a night after that. The guesthouse was a magnet for overlanders and there was seemingly an endless chain of adventurers. When we arrived there was already an Italian guy called Francesco who was cycling from Italy to Nairobi on a recumbent bicycle. He was hilarious but incredibly ill, with some kind of bug. We didn't see him smile for the first three days. There was a bloke called Phil who had already cycled around the world and was off on another trip, trying to cycle south to Cape Town from his home in Manchester. He'd made a good fist of it but had been struck down with back problems and was taking a couple of weeks off to try and let it recover.

Then a couple of days into our stay a Swiss guy called Pascal rolled in. He had blood trickling down his legs, a big stick across his handlebars and a slingshot tucked into his shorts. He slammed the bike down as Yohannes said, "Welcome, how was your journey?"

"Not good, terrible in fact. Something needs to be done about those kids!"

It turned out he had spent the day, and the last week, being terrorised by kids on the ride north from Addis. The kids thought it was funny to throw stones at the "*faranjis*" as they passed by.

Faranjis is what the Ethiopians call foreigners. It can be really funny because you can sometimes startle people in the street and they'll go, "*Aghh! Faranjis!*" and run off. The kids just saw the stone-throwing as a game, but Pascal didn't want to play. It was a brutal bit of fun for them. He had been peppered. We went for a beer with him that night and had a chat about it. He said he'd had enough and started to fight back. He was a really experienced cyclist and was on his way home after something like five years on the road. He said he'd been getting up to about 20 km an hour, taking both hands off the handlebars and firing back at the kids with a sling shot he had made. Then, other times when he couldn't get the speed, he would use his stick to beat them. He'd beaten so many kids that his stick was held together with tape. We explained that maybe hitting kids with sticks wasn't the answer, but he said that in Ethiopia it was, adding that the parents just found it funny and laughed at him.

The following day, more cyclists rode in, a couple named Peter and Coleen from South Africa. They were both in their 60s and were cycling from Amsterdam back down to their home in Knysna, South Africa. Next to arrive was a trio of cyclists, Jamie from the UK, his girlfriend Nia from Bulgaria, and a bloke they'd found cycling from Sweden called Richard or, as we called him, Dickie. Then arrived another cyclist called Daniel whom we had actually stopped and said hi to in Luxor. He really clocked up the miles and thanks to our lengthy stay in Khartoum, and then the breakdown, he had managed to catch us up. The final adventurer to add to the crew was an Irish guy called Brian. We had been in contact with him online for a couple of weeks and he'd been just behind us on his motorbike for a while.

There was a great buzz around the place. Everyone had so many stories to tell and it was great fun. For the first couple of days it was brilliant, we would just hang out, explore Gondar a bit, do some emails and crack on with a bit of maintenance on the bike. We were generally enjoying our time there. By the time we had been there for a week, the parts from the UK should have been with us. We had added on checking in at the post office as part of our daily routine but day after day there was nothing. Eventually we started saying goodbye to our motley crew of travelers. Brian pushed on with his motorbike, Phil gave up and flew home for treatment on his bad back, Francesco lay down and cycled out of there, Coleen and Pete pressed on south too, and Pascal loaded up his slingshot and headed north ready to assault some more children.

Jamie and Nia had managed to get parasites from a puppy that they had let sleep in their tent in Sudan, so they were stuck there trying to recover. Dickie was pleased with a break so stayed on, and Daniel had fallen for a girl called Linde who had come to volunteer with an NGO in town, so he was going nowhere. The days just kept creeping by and we still hadn't got the parts. We were becoming pretty bored and fairly frustrated. We didn't even know if we would be able to fix the bike when the parts did arrive, if they ever did arrive, that is. Then one day I got a random email from a customs agent called Michael in Addis Ababa. The parts had been with him for a week and if we could give a reason why we needed them he would send them via DHL to Gondar.

We were so relieved! By that time, it was the weekend again and nothing could be done but, safe in the knowledge that the parts were actually on their way, we were able to have a good time. On the Saturday we went out to the foothills of the Simien Mountains and walked through the rugged hills with the baboons. The scenery was absolutely incredible. If you ever get the chance to go to the Simiens, do it. The landscape is entirely populated by jagged mountains that rise and fall steeply, creating excellent trekking paths that keep views hidden and then unveil them just as you get to the top. We managed to find an absolutely fantastic place for a spot of lunch too, and enjoyed some wonderful kind of curry thing looking over the view.

Then on the Sunday we went to the Dashen brewery. Dashen is the national beer of Ethiopia; from a bottle it's okay but the stuff you get at the brewery is fantastic. A big group of us went down for the day and enjoyed some brilliant beer and some top food. I had lamb tibs. It's just bits of lamb in a nice sauce served with injera (sourdough pancakes) and hot chili sauce. Most of the time it's really dry, but that day they had chosen to serve it in this wonderful, meaty broth and it was probably one of the best meals I had on the trip.

We got pretty drunk and finished off the evening watching the Super Sunday premier league fixtures in a local bar with Yohannes. The following day there was still no sign of the parts, so we had another day of milling around and then finally, on the Tuesday, two and a half weeks after we had arrived, the parts touched down in Gondar. We got straight to it and took them up to the bike to try and put it all back together. Using slow-buffering YouTube videos and advice from Charlie and Rod on Facebook, we were able to get the bike assembled by nighttime. It had taken us a full eight or so hours but with the help of some local mechanics and Daniel, we had done it. Then just as we were about to think about starting it up, we noticed that we had three tiny rubber protector things left over. Each was smaller than a five-pence piece. We were tempted to just put them in our pocket and ignore it, but Daniel, an engineer, was pretty adamant that wasn't the answer.

We pulled up the parts guide again and located three similar looking parts on the diagram. The parts were right inside the clutch. They were probably the second thing that we should have put on. We could not believe it. We had been out pouring blood, sweat, and tears into fixing it all day and it had been for nothing. It would all have to be done again tomorrow. Finally, after some teething problems the next day, including accidentally draining the final drive oil and not tightening the driven face properly, we eventually fixed the scooter. We took it off for a spin to where we had broken down three weeks prior and drove back to Gondar with no problems at all. We had a final night at Yohannes' and sunk some pints looking over the city from Yohannes's favourite spot at the top of the town. It was an incredible view over the city and a brilliant way to end our stay in Gondar.

We were in Gondar for three full weeks and staying for that long gave us a nice insight into Ethiopian culture. With all the stone-throwing and name-calling it can feel abrasive at first, but once you get under the surface everyone is sound. They are a hilarious bunch and love to mess around, hence the stone-throwing and name-calling. Ethiopia is completely different to any other country I've ever been to. It was the only country in Africa never to be officially colonised and as a result it's managed to cling onto much of its rich culture. There are some truly notable differences about Ethiopia, the first and most important to know about is that they work on a different time to anywhere else. I'm not talking time zones, they literally start the day at a different time. So, our 7 a.m. is 1 a.m. and then it goes on from there. It makes a lot of sense if you think about it. Most people get up at about seven so why shouldn't it be the first hour of the day? Equally odd is the fact that if you're waking up at 7 a.m. and reading this in Ethiopia then you're also seven years behind. It's currently 2013 there. Barmy, right?

The other notable thing about Ethiopia is that it is by far and away the worst place we went to for people asking for money. As a *faranji* you are seen as a walking cash cow. Of course, when you get the message across that you're not completely minted and aren't able to give people money, everyone is just as friendly as anywhere else. I'm not sure why it's so bad in Ethiopia—was it the years of extreme drought, environmental degradation, and a host of other problems that killed thousands and sent millions into poverty so that the country and its people became dependent on foreign aid (and all *faranjis* are seen as deep pocket donors)? That's not to say I think foreign aid is a bad thing, I think it's absolutely necessary, I just wonder if it could have been managed so that whole generations didn't grow up seemingly dependent on hand-outs.

We left Gondar on the 9th February and headed south for Bahir Dar. Getting out of Gondar was huge for us. We had come up against our first major challenge and had overcome it. I think we both felt more confident than ever that we would actually get the thing around the world. We passed through the town of Bahir Dar early in the day and decided to just keep racking up the miles, make hay while the sun shines and all that. We ended up clocking over 400 km and made it to Debre Markos. It was a long way on those roads, no longer were we cheesing it through the desert—Ethiopia was made up of constant twists and turns.

The following day we pressed on to Addis Ababa, the capital city. It was just 300 km so ordinarily wouldn't be particularly challenging; however, this 300-km stretch of road passed straight through the Blue Nile Canyon. We had heard a bit about this enormous canyon complex when we were in Gondar; the cyclists heading south had talked about how they were dreading it. They were right. It's massive. Often likened to the Grand Canyon in the States, the Blue Nile Canyon is of similar size, stature, and, well, grandeur. After riding through wheat fields and across flat farmland all morning we suddenly came to the edge of the canyon. It was magnificent. We pulled in to appreciate the view and a few Ethiopian guys came over to shake our hands and take it in with us. They pointed out the road on the far side and you could just about see it snaking up the valley. It looked steep, even from there. The temperature was in the high 30s and we knew Kuishi could be in for a tough ride.

It was Reece's shift, so he was set to snake us down to the bottom. As is the way for most of the roads in Ethiopia, the surface ranged from perfect tarmac to decent gravel to full-on potholes. The corners were tight and with a sheer drop at the edge of the road you wouldn't want to get one wrong. Taking a left-hand turn going downhill is the toughest maneuver to make with a sidecar. It just feels uncomfortable and awkward. Taking them on the rough roads with a few hundred metres to fall the other side was more than a bit scary. To make matters worse we hadn't fixed the clutch properly and the scooter was always driving, even when you weren't on the accelerator. Needless to say, I was perched on the edge of my seat, seat belt off, ready to bail, should Reece get one wrong.

Fortunately, Reece didn't get one wrong and after about forty-five minutes of constant twists and turns we arrived at the banks of the Blue Nile. We crossed the Nile over the suspension bridge and watched the water flow underneath us, down towards Khartoum, where it would converge with the White Nile, before heading on all the way past Cairo to the Med. It's incredible to think we had been trying to make our way south through the African continent for just over six weeks and we were still driving along the same river. As always, the Nile completely changed the environment directly around it and all of a sudden we had company: baboons. We were used to dodging animals in the road, but they were usually donkeys or goats, not monkeys. It felt like we were on safari. We stopped to take some pictures before cracking on and attempting to climb out of the canyon.

As we started to snake out of the canyon, Kuishi instantly started to struggle. We were reduced to 10-15 mph, flat-out. The bike was becoming boiling hot, the temperature gauge was roasting and we had barely got started. We continued on uphill until Reece started to feel the scooter bubbling underneath him. We pulled in on the side of the road and coolant suddenly spurted out everywhere. We didn't know what that meant but we were pretty sure it was a big deal. We figured we must have burst a pipe or something, so in the searing heat we started to pull apart the entire bike. An hour later, with bits of plastic all around us, screws lost in the sand and tools everywhere, we found the overflow pipe and realised it had just boiled up and come out of there. Another hour later and we were back on the road trundling up hill. The considerable rest was just what Kuishi needed and we pulled out of the canyon no problem.

The other side of the canyon was exactly as we had expected it. More farmland, fewer baboons, more donkeys. We trundled on and continued through the tiny farming villages that lined the roads. "*Faranjis!*" I heard somebody shout as we calmly drove through a village. I looked in my mirror and there were ten to fifteen kids running towards us with stones. Little gits. I just twisted the accelerator and left them for dust. It must have been pretty scary for the guys on bicycles who couldn't do that, though.

We came to the next village but this time the kids had seen us coming from a distance and had armed themselves ready for attack. As we entered, a bombardment of poor throws came our way with none hitting us. "Beat you again," I thought. Then I looked ahead and this small child, couldn't have been more than ten, picked up an almighty boulder, about the size of a full-size football and lifted it above his head. We were driving straight for him and the road would curve around to the right where he would surely fire and hit us sideways. This was serious. A hit from a rock that size could take us out, ruin the bike, seriously hurt us, and potentially end the trip. I decided I would take matters into my own hands and instead of tracking to follow the curve, I made sure nothing was coming, crossed the carriageway and drove straight at him. A good old-fashioned game of chicken. He dropped the rock and scurried off to the side. "Oh, well-played, mate," said Reece over the intercom.

"Yeah, that'll teach him," I replied. Yes, I know I'm a loser for playing chicken with a ten-year-old boy but at least I wasn't doing a Pascal and launching rocks back at him.

We eventually dropped off the plateau and into the city of Addis Ababa, where we would be stopping for a couple of days to sort out documentation for the journey south. The next country on our list would be Kenya, where you can spot the Big Five at pretty much anytime and ten-year-old boys with stones would be the least of our worries.

– 9 –

"OH MY GOODNESS, AREN'T YOU BEAUTIFUL."

"And then there was rock-throwing . . . and people with guns . . . and everyone was going crazy. I had to get my bike and hide in somebody's house to get out of the chaos. Then somebody let me hide in the back of their car and drove me to here," exclaimed a very frantic-looking Dickie, the Swedish cyclist we had met in Gondar. He had pressed on without the rest of the guys at Yohannes' place and got caught up in the protests that had hit Ethiopia out of nowhere.

We were very surprised to see Dickie arrive when he did, as we knew the roads were all closed. There were pretty serious protests going on. The Ethiopian people were angry about the government's response to ethnic violence around the country. They were mainly peaceful demonstrations, but they were properly disruptive. Roads were ripped up and all of the country's public transport was on lockdown. Fortunately, the airport was still running, as Chels had booked to fly in to meet us in Addis. She had been in India and Sri Lanka, travelling around and getting stock for Higgler. She fancied a change and decided that she would take on her own African adventure at the same time as us. The plan was for her to use public transport all the way down to Cape Town, meet us when she could but generally just explore and see if she could find any good products for her shop.

All of our plans had been put on hold though, while we sat in the guesthouse bar in Addis waiting for the civil unrest to blow over. Dickie hadn't got the message about the protests and his story had told us we had done the right thing to sit it out in the capital rather than try to press on regardless. So we had a few days chilling in Addis—it's okay, but not my favourite city by any stretch. Just a big industrial kind of place. As is the case with most major cities in Africa, Addis showcased the huge income inequalities within the country. On our walk from the guesthouse to the main square we would pass people's homes that were made of corrugated iron sheets placed atop sticks and other bits of scrap metal. A hundred metres further on and we could look up to towering, flashy skyscrapers, home to big business and swanky inner-city flats.

The city was relatively safe but petty crime is a major problem. If you're not holding your wallet and you take a ten-minute walk through the centre of Addis, as a *faranji*, you will have lost your wallet. The usual kinds of techniques were all used on us. The most common one is when big groups of teenagers, all acting really chatty and smiley, bounce up and start touching your shoulders and giving you a big pat on the back so you don't see their mates sneak up behind and slide a hand into your pocket. Keep your hands in your pockets, smile and joke along and you're fine, but lose your cool and it could turn nasty. The other most common threat to your possessions are really small kids, so small their heads are no higher than your hip. They dip and dive their way through busy crowds just grabbing at any pocket they can. I saw one chap getting ready to put his hand in Reece's pocket, so I did the old *Meet the Fockers* eye thing and pointed at my eyes and then pointed at him. He let out a big, knowing smile and ran off into the distance.

All good fun (unless you get your wallet nicked) and there's no malice in it. The crime in Addis is mainly just chancers having a go at making a buck. That's pretty much the only kind of crime we witnessed firsthand on the whole of the continent. There's nothing to it at all but it is important to have the right attitude. Smiles get you everywhere, frowns go down badly, scowls are a terrible idea. It's okay to be assertive but never to be aggressive.

We learnt that through hearing the horror stories of the travelers who "fought back" against the stone-throwing and got royally beat up.

We were stuck in Addis for a few days, which on one hand was great because I got to have some quality time with Chels. It was Valentine's Day and although there were no candle-lit dinners and roses, it was nice just to hang out. On the other hand, it was a nightmare. We only had a month-long visa for Ethiopia and having spent three weeks in Gondar we were fast running out of time. The border was two days away without any problems and over-staying would mean a whopping fine. We spoke to the British embassy and they actually told us that we should get on a flight and do a visa run. That seemed ridiculous.

The protests hadn't officially ended but reports were that everyone had more or less gone home. Chels' next move was to head off on public transport to a town called Arba Minch, from which she would go off to explore the tribal lands of the Omo Valley and we would also pass through there en route to Moyale, the border town with Kenya. There were rumours the busses were back on, so we decided to use Chels as the guinea pig and send her off on the first bus south. If she made it, great, we would know the roads were safe and crack on. If not, the busses wouldn't leave so she would come back. The following morning, Chels and I pulled up to the bus stop in the sidecar, in the pitch black, and there was absolutely nothing going on. No busses! We asked an attendant guy if he knew of any other way of heading south today and he pointed us to a group who were planning to drive to another regional bus station and try their luck there.

Chels looked at me as if to say, "Should I do it?" and I looked at her as if to say, "They seemed like alright blokes," and she said, "Sod it," and jumped into the back of this stranger's car, heading off into the depths of a pitch-black Addis Ababa, during a time of civil unrest, on her Todd. Brave? Stupid? Trusting? Naïve? Probably all of the above. I went back to the guesthouse and got another hour's kip until first light. Just as I was getting up, Chels walked in and said all the roads really were closed, but we had been right and they were alright blokes, so much so that she had spent the morning chatting to a school teacher who dropped her off at the guesthouse so she didn't have to get a cab across town.

We had another day in Addis exploring and then the following morning we tried the same routine again. This time it would be our final chance, we had to be through the border in three days. Fortunately, this time the busses were on and Chels was off.

Reece and I followed an hour or so later and finally started making our way south. It was an easy day of smooth riding, interspersed with 20- to 30-km sections of rough maintenance tracks while the main drag was being built. We made it to Arba Minch in good time and had an evening there, taking in its incredible views. The evening was soured somewhat by a bloke who decided to reverse over the sidecar in his 4x4. "It's built to break," Richard Prescott had said. Well it hadn't, even after somebody ran it over! The indicator did fall off though, but fortunately it was one of the only things we had a spare for and knew how to fix as my brother, Lee, had fitted it for us and shown us the ropes before we left. The following morning, we set off early, left Chels to explore Ethiopia and trucked on towards Kenya. There were no teary goodbyes this time. We were planning to crisscross all the way to Cape Town so would be seeing each other a lot more than normal.

On leaving Arba Minch, we instantly started singing the *Jurassic Park* theme tune again. This time it wasn't because we were mesmerised by the views, they were okay, it was because there was a flock of what could only be described as pterodactyls scavenging in a heap of rubbish. We didn't know whether to be excited or scared, they were absolutely gigantic birds. Gross, alien-looking things, pecking their way through piles of garbage. We later googled them and they turned out to be marabou storks, aptly dubbed the "undertaker bird." Creeps!

Having survived our dinosaur safari, we arrived in to Moyale as the sun set, with one day left on our visas. We checked into a local guesthouse and tucked into our last meal before getting an early night. There wasn't much to see or do in Moyale, it was just one of those boring kind of border towns, so we ended up chilling out to a bit of TV. We were stuck with whatever Reece had downloaded on his laptop and one of those things was the complete series of Charley Boorman and Ewan McGregor's *Long Way Down*. We watched a couple of episodes and caught up to their Ethiopia stretch. It turned out back when they had taken this route there were big safety concerns for the road south of Moyale. Talk of bandits operating in the area. Fortunately for us, those concerns no longer existed because the rough track, which Charley and Ewan had taken, had been replaced by an almighty, perfect stretch of tarmac. It's much harder to be a bandit and rob trucks when they're cheesing it past you at 60 mph.

That's not to say that you're necessarily safe heading through Moyale though. Make sure you check out the local situation before you go. Just six or so months after we passed through there was a shootout between a rebel group and government forces, which claimed the lives of thirteen and injured another forty.

The following morning, we woke up safe and sound and pressed on into Kenya. It was another very easy border crossing and we were through within an hour. We had two big surprises when we arrived into Kenya: firstly, we were driving on the left, great news if you're in a sidecar because the driver can see what's coming when he's trying to overtake; secondly, everyone had a camel. There were camels everywhere. Who would have thought it! We had seen loads in Egypt and Sudan but none in Ethiopia, so we thought we had crossed the camel line, but here we were with hundreds of the things clogging up the first roundabout. We were obviously acting like excited kids because, let's face it, riding past a camel is always going to be fun. They're just so weird and exotic.

We pressed on south once more and had the town of Marsabit in our sights for the evening. As we got deeper into Kenya the temperature just kept rising and rising. Before we knew it, we were back to Sudan levels of heat and the mercury was touching 40°C. The temperature rise was due to us dropping down from the hills and into the Dida Galgalu desert. We were almost completely alone out on the road and we probably saw another car every hour or so. It was incredibly remote. The most common things we saw on that ride were dust devils: towering, swirling tunnels of dust charging across the landscape. They were a great way to ease the boredom of the road and we'd watch them grow in strength, looking like they might turn into full-on tornadoes before hitting the tarmac and losing their legs. We'd race towards them and slow down to see if we could get one to hit us, just to see what would happen. We managed it and you guessed it, it was a tiny bit windy and dusty for a split second.

We pulled into Marsabit at night and opted to check into a campsite. We were tempted to wild camp outside of town but as it was our first night in Kenya and we didn't really know much about the region, we thought it would be wise to get our legs first. We were right, the campsite owner told us that the reason there was a big fence around the place was to keep the hyenas out.

We had struck gold that night because the campsite had been hired out as a venue for some local teacher's end-of-term party. They all spoke great English and really wanted us to join in the fun, and we were very happy to. For dinner it was BBQ'd goat and chips. Completely incredible. After a full month of injera and tibs we were so excited for something different. It was a little too different when they asked if we wanted to try a bit from inside the goat's head though. We had a great night with the guys before pressing on south again towards the town of Nanyuki.

Just before Nanyuki, we caught up with Pete and Coleen, the couple from South Africa who were pedaling from Amsterdam to their home in Knysna. We had arranged to camp up with them for the night in the garden of a little chip shop called Chuckie's Chips about 10 km from the town. You could camp there for free on the condition that you had chips for tea, and we were more than happy to oblige. Pete and Coleen are an absolute inspiration. The sheer distances they were pedaling and their unrelenting positivity towards the enormity of their challenge was just great to see. Plus, they've got more than a couple of good stories and we had a cracking night catching up with them.

The stretch from Marsabit to Nanyuki was almost entirely flourishing farmlands. The rolling hills of the region made it feel like we were back in the Cotswolds apart from the fact everything was much bigger. The fields were absolutely huge, we had driven into a colonial past in which massive estates were owned by white guys who had inherited them from their fathers and their fathers before them. It's a touchy subject and something I don't know too much about, but it does feel odd to drive from the north into what feels like massive British farms, with British farm shops attached and British-looking people cruising around in big Land Cruisers, while Kenyans wait by the roadside ready to be picked up for work. Needless to say, we enjoyed the British-style farm shop at Chuckie's and had a cracking Americano, with a wonderful view of Mount Kenya, before saying our goodbyes to Pete and Coleen and heading south once again.

As we left Nanyuki, we stopped for a bit of breakfast outside the sign for the equator. It's one of those things that you don't really think about, but when we arrived at that little yellow sign, I couldn't help but think, "Blimey, we've driven a scooter and sidecar to the equator." The sign roughly marks the halfway point on the Cairo-to-Cape Town route, so we were in good spirits and excited to take on the second half. We were in even better spirits because the people of Kenya were exceptionally friendly, and I mean exceptionally friendly. As we were pulling out of Nanyuki, we were flagged down by a local policeman stood by the roadside.

"Here we go again mate, get the papers out," Reece groaned from the handlebars.

We pulled up to the side, lifted up our visors and the policeman said, "Oh my goodness aren't you beautiful!" Well that was new!

"Thank you, sir, what a kind thing to say!" replied a beaming Reece, with whom flattery seems to get you everywhere.

"This is truly magnificent, and where will you go?" asked the policeman.

"Nairobi, today, Cape Town eventually," I said.

"Oh, how wonderful. I wish you a very safe journey!"

And he waved us on. It kept happening all day. Policemen just flagging us down only to shower us in compliments. Stuff like "Aren't you a sight to behold," and "Oh, how lovely you are." It was hilarious. The fellas were just interested and wanted a chat, but they had all learnt a very formal or old-fashioned version of English at school. It completely made our day. We just started acting the same back with stuff like, "You're not too bad yourself," or, "What a wonderful hat you have." It was a lot of fun. Kenya is great if you're an ignorant Brit who can't speak any other languages like me. Most people speak English, even though there are sixty-eight separate languages in the country. Almost everyone will learn Swahili at primary school, if they haven't been speaking it already, and then they will eventually learn and get taught in English if they can afford to stay in school long enough.

We arrived into Nairobi nice and early and should have been at our campsite, Jungle Junction, by 2 p.m. but the capital had other plans. It was gridlocked. Bumper-to-bumper traffic in every direction. It was searingly hot and, with no wind, the sidecar was turning into a greenhouse. Worse still the pollution from the queuing busses and lorries was coming straight into the cab and choking me as I sat there. Enough was enough and I whipped off my helmet to try and breathe. It worked and I was able to appreciate the place for a minute. I looked up to see rundown-looking tower blocks, discoloured by the pollution from the traffic below. In their shadows, stalls had popped up, selling everything from the latest Manchester United shirt to grilled goat skewers, cooked over hot coals there and then.

We pressed on and hit the ring road, headed for our campsite just outside of town. As we merged onto Nairobi's equivalent of the M25, we could see giraffes grazing in the fields to our left. It was our first giraffe of the trip and as you can imagine we were jumping with excitement yet again. We arrived at Jungle Junction just in time for tea. It's a magnet for overlanders exploring the continent in all kinds of weird and wonderful ways and everyone stops off there to do maintenance and restock for the journey north or south.

Chels was there when we arrived, having explored Ethiopia and then jumped on a short flight from Addis. We had arranged to stay there for a few nights as we had managed to link up with a modern slavery charity in the city, an organisation called HAART Kenya. We went to meet them the following day to learn a little bit about what they do and how modern slavery exists in the region.

We had been put in touch with HAART through Freedom United, an umbrella network based out of the States, which tries to support anti-slavery initiatives around the world. It was their support that the guys at HAART wanted to talk to us about the most. We met with Sophie and Michael who both work to support victims of modern slavery and human trafficking in various ways.

Michael explained to us that there are estimated to be around 188,000 people enslaved in Kenya but helping those people wasn't their only problem. He said the biggest problem they have is that Nairobi acts as a crossroads and a major trafficking hot spot. He said that they support people from other nations who have been trafficked into the country but also try to help Kenyan nationals who have been trafficked out. Just the week before, he had been on the phone trying to repatriate a group of Kenyan women who ended up in slavery in Syria but since the war had broken out there, they had been hiding out in a bombed-out building, awaiting rescue.

Sophie went on to explain that although getting these women back from Syria, freeing people enslaved in Kenya and stopping people getting moved through the capital is great, it is just as important to work out how to help them afterwards. She gave us an example of a twelve-year old girl they had rescued from forced prostitution within the city. Once out of her situation of slavery, the girl had been placed in a government-funded safe house, but it turned out it wasn't safe at all and the girl had been repeatedly sexually assaulted by a care worker at the house. In response, the HAART team wrote to Freedom United, who organised a crowdfunder and raised enough money for HAART to open their very own safe house within the city. The girl was eventually moved to their safe house and given a chance at recovery. Sophie said there's an anonymous way to complain in the house and the only complaints they have had so far are teenagers who want to watch TV shows that they're not old enough for.

The safe house has surely been a success and HAART is in a position to help people much in the same way Unseen does in the UK. It's a start but that's all it is and the team have got one hell of a task ahead. We asked Sophie what inspires her to do it, how does she keep motivated to work tirelessly against such massive odds? She replied, "I do it because I'm a survivor of trafficking. So, for me it's not work, it's very, very personal and that sometimes rubs people up the wrong way. I'm going to mess with you, if you mess with victims of trafficking." She talked a little bit about her story, but it didn't seem right to ask more. We didn't really need to, the passion in which she said "*I'm going to mess with you, if you mess with victims of trafficking*" certainly gave us the answer to our question. We added HAART to the list of charities we would support and went back to Jungle Junction to get ready for the journey south.

To get ready, all we had to do was pick up a spare set of tyres and carry out some minor maintenance. Rod had shown us how to do a service of the bike so I got straight on it, changed the oil, checked the fluid levels, tightened up all of the bolts holding the sidecar on and then I had a go at checking the condition of the spark plug. Easy stuff, a bit fiddly, but easy. I placed the socket over the top of the plug but instead of locking on the nut it caught the plug itself and snapped the porcelain protection. We didn't carry a spare spark plug on account of the fact that we didn't know what one did before we left. The guys at Jungle Junction said we would have to wait for one to be shipped in. Absolutely no chance! We were not planning on another Gondar episode. We spent the next two days scouring the city's bike shops, trying to find some kind of replacement and a few tyres, too. We had no luck with either.

Well, we weren't waiting again so we decided that we might have more luck in Dar es Salaam, the next big city, and that we should just crack on to there. We super-glued the spark plug, covered it in electrical tape and drove out of Jungle Junction to groans of, "They'll be back this evening." Well, we weren't, we were in Moshi by the evening. Tanzania!

– 10 –

"OH MY GOD, MATE, THAT'S A FRICKING HIPPO!"

The ride into Tanzania was super easy and really quite enjoyable. At the border we picked up a loaf of bread and a couple of packs of crisps before pulling into a lay-by in the foothills of Mount Longido for a spot of lunch. It was exceptionally quiet and a lovely spot to enjoy a crisp sarnie, and we were completely on our own in the Tanzanian countryside. After about five minutes, we were surprised to see a group of women come out from the surrounding forest. In full tribal wear, the ladies were stood for a while sizing us up. We let out a big hello with an over-the-top wave and probably a creepy smile. It worked and they approached us. The first lady knew a few words of English and said, "My name is," as she approached, to which I responded with, "Matt," and extended my hand for a handshake. She shook it and then they just sort of stood for a minute, observing us. "Would you like some lunch, girls?" Reece enthusiastically asked, while offering them some bread.

"Yes, you must," I added, holding the pack of crisps we'd got at the border. The first lady took a slice off Reece and then came to me at the crisp station. She peered into the packet, sizing it up to see what it was and then carefully and slowly went to put her hand in. She stopped and decided against it. I got one out and offered it to her as if to say, "It's fine really, dig in!" Again, she peered around my hand a bit before taking it off me. Then she proceeded to study it for a minute and eventually bit the end. A smile lit up on her face. "Nice?" I asked. It must have been, because a minute later she asked again and took the whole pack, which had me and Reece in stitches. The greedy goose! Before we knew it we had been fully hustled out of lunch. It's a good job we'd managed to wolf down a sarnie before they had arrived, as the ladies pottered off back to the forest with the rest of the loaf and the whole bag of crisps. It was an awesome experience, it really seemed like they had never had crisps before. They were so intrigued by them. We'd only bought them about five miles up the road.

After we left the girls for lunch we pressed on south through the town of Arusha and on to the foothills of Mount Kilimanjaro. Just as we were approaching the town of Moshi, we could see Kilimanjaro's great snowy peak poking through the top of the clouds. Chels had beaten us there by bus and we decided to explore the area for a couple of days. We didn't fancy climbing the mountain but instead took a dip in the nearby hot springs. They were incredible and we spent the entire day just hanging out, enjoying the crystal clear, cool water.

Next, we headed on south towards Dar es Salaam. We overnighted on the way in the town of Korogwe and managed to tune in to the Arsenal fixture with a couple of the local lads. They were big Arsenal fans, but they were saying that they would not be supporting Arsenal until they started acting like Arsenal again. Reece hit back and said that they should always support their team through the good times and the bad, but they completely disagreed. They tried to explain their view with a somewhat questionable analogy and said, "It's just like with girlfriends and wives, if they stop acting how you like them to, it's okay to see another at the same time but they are still your girlfriend or wife." In the end we all agreed that Arsene Wenger should go but agreed to disagree on the wife, girlfriend thing.

The following day we were met in Dar es Salaam by Munya Mutikani, the guy who had named the sidecar "Kuishi na Kuishi." He had offered to put us up for a while, help us get ready for the journey south and show us his new farm. We were of course very excited to see the place the scooter was named after so we jumped at the chance. First though, Munya thought it would be fun for us to check out Zanzibar, the Spice Island, the birthplace of Freddie Mercury and the home of people with exceptionally big doors (they're huge and very elaborate). We took the ferry out there and stayed for the night at Munya's friend's holiday home. It was incredible. Anybody who still thought we were just on a jolly was dead right, this place was completely gorgeous. Unrivalled sunsets, crystal clear waters, and white sandy beaches.

The following day we returned to Dar and started our search for the spark plug and tyres we so desperately needed. Again, no luck and Munya agreed that we would be very unlikely to find them. Amazingly though, Munya had a friend flying in from London Gatwick in a couple of days' time. He said if we could get someone to meet them at the airport with a spark plug, they could bring it over and we could meet them at the airport in Dar to get it. Incredibly, my old pal John Hore offered to take up the challenge, grabbed the part and then drove through a snowy West Sussex at 5 a.m. to give it to the person flying in. Thank you, John! Reece and I picked it up at the other end and managed to change it no problems for the ride south.

Before that though, we were off to see the farm. Munya and his dad are from the UK and have no ties at all to Tanzania but they saw an opportunity and wanted to do something crazy. They realised that nobody was really farming pigs in the country and that they had an opportunity to set up the industry with a standard of healthy, free-range, sustainably reared pork. Having never farmed before, they bought a plot of land outside of Dar and started to turn it into a pig farm. We arrived there and it was still in the very early stages, just a shipping container in the middle of the bush. Nothing around at all. We spent the day helping to make bricks with the team and looking at plans for the site.

To celebrate the occasion of us being there the team decided we would cook a goat for dinner. I was surprised to see it turn up alive. At first the goat was really kicking off but once the guys got it tied up, it relaxed. Then it just stood there alive for a few hours while we all waited for dinner time. About 4 p.m. and it was time to start preparing the food. Of course, on this occasion, preparing meant slaughtering. I made a point of watching and being involved. I'd never really seen anything that I've eaten killed in front of me before, so I thought it was important not to shy away from the harsh reality. I had nothing to do with the killing itself, the guys took care of that. Two of them held the goat down while the others slit its throat. Of course, blood started spurting out onto the floor and after a few gruesome seconds the goat was dead. It was a horrible thing to watch and really, really intense. As the guy put the knife to the goat's throat I could feel mine tighten too and it made my skin crawl to watch it get so brutally murdered for the sake of a meal.

We left it for a while to let it stop twitching, and then the guys hung it up ready to be skinned. I asked to have a go. I didn't really want to, but I thought that if I'm eating the thing, I should be able to handle the butchering. I grabbed the knife and pulled the skin tight before running it alongside the meat. It came off pretty easy at first and then I slipped and took out a chunk of flesh. I felt the knife go in and it sent shivers up my spine as it did. I don't know why, I guess I was still seeing the cute little goat in the field and not the BBQ'd goat I had cut into many times before. The guys took over because they could see I was going to screw it up and I went back to help with the rest of the preparations. We ate the goat alongside *ugali*, a porridge made of cornmeal, and I thought it wasn't worth it. I would have been happy with a couple of vegetables or something. I realised then that if we all prepared our own food from start to finish that I would naturally be a vegetarian. I would also never eat *ugali*, which is hands-down the worst food the world has to offer. Looks like mash-potatoes, tastes liked fluffed-up dust. Truly vile stuff.

We left the farm the following day and got ready to head south once again. I remember thinking at the time that Munya may have bitten off more than he could chew. Having never farmed before, it was a seemingly humongous challenge, but he has done it and now runs a fully functioning pig farm with a view to opening eco-lodges too. From Munya's we tracked southwest towards the town of Iringa. Originally, we thought we might be able to ride all the way through to Iringa, a big 480-km day, but in the end, we barely covered half that distance.

All was going very smoothly, and we made great progress from Dar es Salaam all the way to the Mikumi National Park. Then we saw a zebra. All bets were off. There was no way we were rushing to Iringa, we were suddenly on safari! We pulled in to watch for a while and take some pictures before continuing on. Two minutes later and we stumbled on a herd of antelope. Two minutes after and it was giraffes. Giraffes! Right by the roadside, we couldn't believe it. We knew these animals existed here, but we really weren't expecting to bump into a bloody giraffe. We spent all day driving exceptionally slowly and keeping our eyes peeled for the wildlife. By sunset, we had only made it halfway to Iringa so pulled into a local campsite.

The following day was more of the same, slow riding and wildlife watching. We pulled into Iringa in the early afternoon and checked into a little guesthouse where we jumped online to find a message from Brian, the Irish guy on a motorbike we'd met in Gondar. It read, "Alright lads, where are you? You know, like, I've just arrived at Iringa, if you know what I mean." It was unbelievable. Not only did Brian type in an Irish accent, but he happened to be in the same town as us. We met up at first light the following morning to continue our ride south together. We pressed on to Mbeya with no troubles whatsoever before riding our final day in Tanzania and heading to the border for Malawi.

If you're Irish you basically never buy a visa. Everyone loves the Irish, so when we arrived at the Malawian border Brian just waltzed straight through. For us Brits though, it was a different story. We could buy a transit visa with which we'd have to be out of Malawi in a few days, just enough time to transit, or we could buy a full visa and stay for as long as a month. The transit was around US$50 and the full visa was at least double that. We wanted to make our way along Lake Malawi and spend some time exploring, so a few days wasn't going to cut it. We had heard that cyclists had previously gone through and pleaded that they were only transiting but the transit would take a long time as they only had a bicycle, which got us thinking, maybe we could pull that one.

I was in charge of all things paperwork as the scooter is registered in my name, so I went up to the border official and said,

"Hello, I will need a two-week transit visa please as my scooter is exceptionally slow."

The border guard looked at me as if to say, "Pull the other one mate, it's a motorbike." But then he said, "How fast does it go?" I couldn't believe it; he was considering it.

"Um, 10 mph uphill and as fast as you can make it downhill."

"No, it's a motorbike," he replied.

"Yes, but a very bad one," I said.

He laughed and then escalated me to the general. The next thing I knew I was sat on a little chair outside the general's office, feeling like I was back at school waiting for the head teacher. He invited me in and asked why I needed so long to transit. I could and probably should have backed down, but instead I said, "It only goes 10 mph, I would have to drive day and night. Come on, I'll take you for a ride if you like." Blimey, why had I done that? I was bluffing the bloody general over $50. He didn't look at all like the kind of guy you should tell porkies to. He paused for a minute and then laughed before he said, "That won't be necessary," and stamped me in on a two-week transit. I don't know what I'd have done if he'd said, "Yes, take me for a spin!"

We slowly pulled away from the Malawi border point before speeding off towards the magnificent Lake Malawi. As we got to the shores of the lake, the landscape changed fantastically. It went from rolling hills full of shrub land to steep banks packed full of dense forest. We spent the entire day twisting our way up and down the hills that line the lake. As we slowly climbed the hills, we would see monkeys swinging through the trees and an ever more frustrated Brian in our mirror, who was beginning to think we really did need a two-week transit visa, both equally as entertaining as the other.

Eventually, after a 400-km day we pulled into a pitch black Nkhata Bay where we had planned to take a couple of days to explore the lake. Chels was already there when we arrived, having taken a monster bus from Dar. The following morning, I went to do a couple of maintenance checks on the bikes with Brian. It was quickly clear that there was work to be done. Our rear scooter tyre had completely worn through again and the tyre wall was showing just as it had in Sudan. This was a big problem; we had failed to find any spares in Nairobi or Dar so we weren't going to find one in Nkhata Bay. Our only hope was that our spare front tyre would fit the rear wheel. They were the same size rim but the profile and width differed.

Fortunately, Brian had brought tyre irons, so we got to work and started changing it. It took us a while but after a couple of hours we managed to get the old tyre off. Getting the new one on was impossible, though. It was too small anyway so it would be a struggle with the right tools, but for us to do it with Brian's tyre irons would be impossible. We decided we'd have to go and search for a garage of some sort in the town. There was nothing, no luck whatsoever. We were just about to give up when a local guy in his 20s came up and said, "Hey guys, can I help you with something?"

"Um, maybe, we really need to get this tyre on this wheel but can't do it ourselves," I replied.

"Okay, jump in and I'll take you there."

The next thing we knew we were racing off to the other side of town in his car. The guy's name was Dustin and he told us that he grew up here in Nkhata Bay but now lives with his wife and kids in Slovenia. We pulled into a workshop and got the tyre on, no problems. Unfortunately, the mechanic had lent his air compressor to a friend so they could use it to spray paint a car on the other side of town. No problem for us, Dustin drove us straight over there and asked him if we could borrow it quickly. Two minutes later we had a useable tyre. I asked him after if we owed him anything for all of his time or for fuel, for ferrying us around. To which he replied, "No, this is Africa, we help each other out!"

Dustin set the precedent for the rest of Malawi and it is easy to see how it bagged the title, "The Heart of Africa." Everyone is incredibly friendly there; they are throughout the whole of East Africa but I think it is probably fair to say the smiles were just that bit bigger in Malawi. We stayed at Nkhata Bay for four or five nights. We needed to do some planning for the road ahead and there's no better way to do some research than swinging in a hammock next to Lake Malawi.

Holiday season was in full swing because when we eventually did leave Lake Malawi it was to set sail for Zambia. We scooted inland from Nkhata Bay and went straight to South Luangwa National Park. Pete and Coleen had told us that you could stay in incredible tented safari lodges for very little money and get the chance to see the Big Five. We jumped at the chance and drove straight there. With Brian cracking the whip we were able to rack up 520 km in a day to make it to the lodge. We'd probably just about driven that far before, but only on straight desert roads. This was twisting and turning on country roads through the forest. Equally, we had a border crossing to contend with and that can take a fair chunk of your day too. We set off at first light but by the time we were approaching the national park it was pitch black.

Driving at night on a scooter and sidecar is never smart but driving at night into a game reserve in the pitch black is just plain stupid. By the time it was dark we still had around 50 km to go. We should have stopped at the nearest place, but we pressed on blindly. Almost literally, it was impossible to see. The light from oncoming vehicles hitting the scratches on our visors meant we could see nothing at all with the visors down, so we had to drive visor-up. Driving visor-up is a big problem in this part of the world because there are just thousands of insects buzzing around and some feel like they're the size of birds. You just had to accept that you were going to get flies in your eyes, it was going to hurt and there was nothing you could do about it. I remember thinking at the time how ridiculous it was that a fly would go in my eye and I would think, "Ahh, I'll get it later." I mean when else would you ever say that about a fly in your eye? With big riding gloves on there was just no alternative.

We pressed on and with our eyes full of flies we were just one or two kilometres away from making it to the camp. The road had turned from tarmac to rough track and we were in the middle of the game reserve. We were careful not to hit any potholes too hard because if we were to break down here, we'd be waiting to find out who would come to help us first, the local people or the local lions. We were crawling along at no more than 10 mph and Brian even slower. He had a broken rear shock and was feeling every bump. With Reece and I out in front, we drove around a bend and suddenly our headlights lit up an almighty beast blocking the entire road. "Oh my God, mate, that's a fricking hippo," exclaimed Reece over the intercom.

"I know mate. Look at the size of the thing!" I replied.

We were both bricking it. The hippopotamus is Africa's most deadly large mammal, responsible for over 500 deaths a year. It's responsible for more deaths than lions, leopards, crocodile or any other of Africa's deadly creatures. We knew all that and here we were staring one right in the face. Its bulbous, bloated torso was twice the size of our scooter and sidecar. We couldn't drive past it and the road was too narrow to just whip around and head back. We just had to stay very still and wait to see what it was going to do. It turned its head to look at us, took a second and then let out a massive, disapproving huff before walking off into the bush. Brian came around the corner just as it left and we all cheesed it to the campsite as quickly as possible. We had survived.

We arrived at the reception and told them of our encounter with one of Africa's most deadly creatures. The guy running it, Ken, laughed and said, "You mean those things?" and pointed at a couple grazing in the garden. He went on to tell us they're just mega territorial and only dangerous in the water. If you catch them on land, you're fine, so much so that he and his friends often play a game in which they run up and slap them on the bum! No wonder they eat people when they get the chance, if you're doing that, I thought.

We had two nights at the camp, and it was absolutely awesome. We saw elephants, lions, buffalo, the full works. It cost about US$50 a day each so, for us, it was a big dent out of our personal savings, but we figured it was worth it. When else do you get to see a lion? After South Luangwa we pressed on and racked up a monstrous 586 km to Lusaka. It was more than we'd ever ridden but it was a cracking road all the way there so it was a fairly comfortable day. We took an extra night again in Lusaka to hunt for tyres once more but again we couldn't find anything that would fit.

After Lusaka we trucked on to the incredible Victoria Falls. Chels and Brian joined us by bus as Brian left his bike back in Lusaka so his rear shock could get repaired. You can see the falls from either the Zambia or Zimbabwe side. We decided we'd check out the Zambia side first and then decide on the Zimbabwe one after. We ended up going to both because once you've seen Victoria Falls you will want to see it from every angle humanly possible. It's one of those big attractions about which you think, "Will it really live up to the hype?" Well, the answer is yes. Yes it will.

As you enter the park you can hear the roar of the falls and when you eventually see them it's just staggering. You can never get a full view of the whole thing, you need a helicopter for that, but our first look was from far enough way that we could see the full extent of the falls from top to bottom. We were looking at it from the opposite side of the ridge and when you peer over the edge all you can see is a cloud of spray rising up to the series of rainbows that sit all the way along the gorge. We did a walk around the full extent of it and got absolutely drenched. They've got bridges that take you within what feels like touching distance of the water. The spray is completely unrelenting and it's as if there's a constant bucket of water being chucked on you. It's just a really cool national park, too. As we walked back through the forest from the furthest viewpoint, our path was blocked by a couple of warthogs who seemed to think they owned the place. We stood and watched them for a few minutes and eventually plucked up the courage to walk past them. They gave us a little bit of room but were clearly very used to the tourists.

It was St. Paddy's Day, which was fitting as it was our last night with Brian for a little while. He had to go to get his bike and fancied a different route to Cape Town than the one we were taking. Our next country would be Zimbabwe and the following day we took a whole day just to cross the border. The reason we took the whole day is not because of all the paperwork like in Sudan but because of the view. The Zambia-to-Zimbabwe border crossing must be the best border crossing in the world. The famous Victoria Falls Bridge was the brainchild of a guy called Cecil Rhodes who wanted to build a bridge in which "the trains, as they passed, would catch the spray of the falls." Well, he got it done and you really can feel the spray of the falls from the bridge. It was a truly brilliant idea, unlike most of his other ideas; he was a strong believer of colonisation and basically believed that the

British were doing a favour to anyone they invaded. He's put down in history as a pretty grotesque white supremacist but to be fair to the bloke, he had some good thoughts around bridges.

We eventually managed to drag ourselves off the bridge, and entered Zimbabwe. It would be our penultimate country on the African continent and, despite the breakdowns, the scorpions and the hippos it was starting to look like we might actually make it to Cape Town.

– 11 –

"AND TELL ME, DO YOU LIKE AVOCADO PEARS?"

"Oh my word, mate, this Head and Shoulders is £12," exclaimed Reece.

It was our first day in Zimbabwe and we popped to the shops to pick up some supplies. Shampoo was off the menu. In fact, any import of any kind was off the menu on account of the Zimbabwean economy being completely scuppered. We were stuck with the stuff they made in country and on this occasion that meant an old school bar of soap. I hate the stuff but there was no way we were paying £12 for Head and Shoulders. The high prices in the shops weren't the only thing that surprised us about the economy in Zimbabwe; the biggest shock was that there was no money available. Literally none. Since the Zimbabwean dollar had crashed, they had been using the US dollar and that had completely run out. There was none left in the cash machines anywhere. The only way you could withdraw money was if you had a specific kind of Zimbabwean bank account but most people didn't do that, instead they paid for everything using their phones. You had to be a Zimbabwean national to do that too, so we had no choice but to head back to Zambia to get some cash.

Fortunately, the border guards let us pop our heads back through to withdraw a load of Zambian Kwacha which we could then exchange for dollars back in Zimbabwe. We got terrible exchange rates but at least we could afford to feast our eyes on the falls one last time. I appreciate that after three days of exploring the falls, I might be starting to sound like somewhat of a falls fanatic, but it really is that good. I could have stayed for longer. Eventually, we did leave the falls, though, and started heading south towards South Africa.

The first day's riding through Zimbabwe was 200 km of riding on a strip of tarmac through non-stop forest. We pulled into camp for the night at a little campsite just on the outskirts of Hwange National Park and we realised that we were sitting on the edge of a national park that's the same size as Northern Ireland. We were the only people staying at the campsite that night but that's not to say it wasn't busy, the place was choc-a-bloc with monkeys. They were into absolutely everything and I'm sure one of them was pretending to ride the scooter at one point.

After Hwange, we pressed on south again, but we were making terrible progress. All of a sudden, we were reduced to riding at 30-40 mph tops. The bike was overheating. It was a hot day but nothing Kuishi hadn't handled before. Something was certainly wrong. We checked the fluid levels and they were fine so we were flat out of ideas as to what it could be. We had no choice, we just kept scooting. After around twelve hours of crawling along, we had passed through the town of Bulawayo, where we met Chels for lunch, and made it to a guesthouse in the absolute middle of nowhere. We had seen it on iOverlander earlier in the day and thought it was about the limit of how far we could get so we went for it. By this time, we were just pushing to get to South Africa as fast as possible so we could get some new tyres and start thinking about hitting the first major milestone of the challenge, making it to Cape Town.

We pulled up the location on iOverlander and found that we were in the right place. We really were completely in the middle of nowhere, there was just this singular house and nothing else around. It was pitch black and had a pretty creepy feel about it. We decided that one of us should stay with the bike and one go and knock on the door to see if we were in the right place. The next thing I knew I was pottering up to the front door of this massive house. As I approached, I saw that the door had a little sign on it saying "Guesthouse," so I knew we were in the right place. I opened the door and all of a sudden, I was in a British pub! Just as with the pub in Egypt, this one was the real deal. All of the weird trinkets, odd kind of towel beer mat thing on the bar and a Brit stood behind it. Well he wasn't a Brit, he was Zimbabwean, but he had British ancestry and had spent half his life living in the UK.

I asked him if they had room for us to stay the night. He said, "Yeah it's $20 per person for the rooms or you can stick your tent up in the garden for $10."

"Okay nice one, we'll go with the tent, thanks!"

As easy as that. We had some beans and bread in the garden before popping our heads in the bar to sink a pint and do some social media updates. Before we knew it, we were in deep conversation with the barman. He was talking about England and how much he preferred it here in Zimbabwe. We were just generally having a pretty good chat. Somehow, we got onto the issue of race and racism in Zim, something we were interested to hear about but not a conversation we could contribute much to, having no knowledge and zero experience ourselves. The barman calmly said, "It's got out of hand you know, the other day I had a fella in here. He comes in looking like he owns the place and says, 'One room please.'

"'Okay sir, $20,' I told him. Then he went and got his wife, so I said, 'Sorry, it's $40 for the two of you.'

"'Argh this is because we're black isn't it?' he replied. The cheek of it. 'Of course not, that's just the price,' I told him."

By this point, the barman was going red in the face and getting visibly angry, just reflecting on it before he had an outburst and said very loudly, "So I told him again, I said, 'Listen here you fucking Kaffir, the price is the fucking price, take it or leave it!'"

He smiled afterwards expecting us to just laugh along but we were genuinely shocked. We both just sort of sat there for a minute in silence. He worked out we were less than impressed and started trying to make excuses. It was too late though; he'd got the wrong audience. We sat there genuinely stunned. The level of anger and hate in his outburst was just remarkable. I don't think I've ever been that angry about something in my entire life and all it took to ignite this explosive burst of racism was somebody questioning whether he was, in fact, a racist. Well, I'm sure the guy got his answer.

We went to bed pretty soon after and I think that was one of the first nights I lay there questioning what I had experienced so far. Is the world a great place full of great people? Or do strangers just always help us because we're two white guys? I wondered what this experience would be like if I was black or, in fact, if any of me was different to what I am. What would it be like if I was a girl or if I was gay? Would strangers still be quite so friendly? As a white British man with a good education, it's impossible to escape privilege in life, maybe people being nice was just another privilege that I have?

In the morning the owner of the place came over to chat to us. He asked about the rig and if we had any problems. "Yeah as it happens, it's been overheating and we can't go more than thirty." I told him.

"Well I've spent the last twenty-five years cooling things down as a fridge mechanic. Want me to take a look at it?"

"Oh wow, yeah that would be amazing! Thanks!"

He got straight to work, and it didn't take him long to fix the problem. The radiator was completely full of grit, sand and horrible gunky stuff. By the time he had identified the problem his wife came outside and said, "Breakfast is ready, boys!"

They had laid on a full English for us.

"Okay cool, I'll get mine later, you boys go on inside, have your food and I'll have this ready for you to ride off with."

We couldn't believe it. We told the lady we didn't actually order anything, but she said it was on the house. We tucked in and came back out to a sparkling clean radiator.

"Blimey, that's amazing, thanks! What do we owe you?"

"Oh, nothing boys, just happy to help! Let us know if it works!"

And it did work. Before we knew it, we were hurtling towards the South Africa border at 50 mph with Kuishi's temperature sitting just where it should be. It was a weird experience at the guesthouse and an insight into the complexities of society in this part of the world. I've chosen to leave the names of the places and people out of that story on account of the fact I wouldn't want to recommend a bar run by a racist but it would be unfair to paint the owners with the same brush and I wouldn't want to damage the reputation of their business, especially as they were so helpful.

We were at the border for South Africa in no time at all and before we knew it, we were crossing into our last country on the African continent, South Africa. Our first stop was to be Polokwane, the closest big town. We were hoping that we might well be able to find our ever-elusive tyres there. We were well on our way and riding fast towards Polokwane when the scooter suddenly jolted to the right.

"Christ mate, what the hell was that?" I said to Reece over the intercom.

"I've no idea!"

We put it down to a freak incident and then it suddenly happened again, another almighty jolt which nearly threw us into the oncoming traffic.

"What are you doing? You idiot!" I exclaimed.

"It's not me mate, there's something wrong!"

We pulled in and had a good look around but there was nothing wrong with the bike. Reece suggested we swap so I could see what it felt like and sure enough, two minutes later, another massive jolt. Then two minutes after that, another one. Then they started get more and more frequent. One after another. It soon became clear that the scooter was in fact losing power and the sidecar was trying to overtake it.

We pulled into a local garage and posted on Facebook for advice. Everyone thought the same thing: dirty fuel. It was blocking the pump and momentarily starving the engine. There was only one way to fix it, buy a pipe, siphon out the fuel, give the tank a clean and put some new stuff in. Unfortunately, there was no pipe for sale at the garage but one of the attendants was particularly keen to help. He noticed that we had an overflow pipe that ran the length of the scooter, so he grabbed that, popped it in the tank and started sucking on it. It worked and all of the fuel was flying out. He had done us a huge favour, there was no way we would have worked that out. With the new clean fuel, the bike was running great so we were able to crack on south.

The following day we arrived at Polokwane. We went straight to the Honda dealership and we were hugely relieved to hear that they could get the tyres for us. They'd be ordered in and ready for the morning. We went to a Burger King over the road to grab some Wi-Fi so we could find somewhere to stay and to our surprise we had an email from the guys at Flight Centre. A little while back we had told them that if they ever fancied promoting a particular place or wanted us to check out say, some five-star safari lodge while we were in South Africa, they should just let us know. Well incredibly they did, and they'd penciled us in for two nights at a luxury lodge in a private game reserve run by a company called Thornybush.

Chels was supposed to be meeting us in Johannesburg, where she was planning on hiring a car and driving the last leg with us through to Cape Town. She wasn't going to miss this, though, and the following day, while we got the tyres changed on Kuishi, she hired a car and drove up to meet us. I thought she would be fine but I was a bit worried, as Chels is historically a horrendous driver. Fortunately, she made it to Polokwane safe and sound. We had a new set of tyres, Chels had made it in the hire car and all was looking good, ready for our ride to Kruger National Park the following day. Chels decided that she'd like to go and do some shopping that night and Reece and I had a bit of work to do so we left her to it. At about 8 p.m. I received a message on my phone from Chels, "Matt, I've crashed. I'm on 1% battery, here's my location."

The location came through just in time. It was bizarre though. It was on a tiny road twenty minutes outside of town, nowhere near the shopping centre or the motel we were in. We were seriously worried. How could she be that far out of town? We jumped in the sidecar and started riding towards the location. We turned off the main road and onto a gravel track.

"Mate this isn't right," I said to Reece. "There's no way she'd be stupid enough to drive down here in the pitch black on her own, in South Africa."

But we had to press on, what choice did we have? I honestly thought it could be a set-up or something. Were we riding into an ambush ready to get mugged? After ten minutes of riding down this random road we saw a car in the ditch, almost upside down. Chels was out on the road stood next to it just waiting. She really had driven out here and crashed. We were all laughing but I was furious. How could she be so stupid? You just don't drive in places like this on your own at night but if you do you certainly don't check your phone when you're going along and plough into the ditch at 40 mph!

It was an absolute miracle the car hadn't overturned. Chels said she had looked down at her phone for directions and then all of a sudden, she was bumping up and down on an angle through thick grass. Fortunately, there was no damage to the car whatsoever. Around thirty yards further down the road there was a drainage tunnel and a brick wall. If she had checked her phone a split second later, she would have had a run-in with a wall, in the middle of nowhere, on her own and things may have turned out very different. I jumped in the car and tried to drive it out, but it was going nowhere. The sidecar certainly didn't have the mustard to pull it out either, so we ended up calling for help. A recovery truck turned up about forty minutes later and pulled it out. Zero damage, not even a scratch. The only cost was $50 for the pull. A very, very lucky escape.

The following day we trucked on to Thornybush, Reece and I leading the way and Chels just behind in the car. We would have both loved to take turns in the air-conditioned car, listening to music and chilling out but then we wouldn't have gone around the world in a scooter and sidecar. We arrived to the lodge and drove through a gate where we were warned that we were in Big Five territory and could bump into a lion or a leopard at any point. We were so deep into Big Five territory that just the week before we arrived, a leopard had been in pursuit of an antelope and had chucked it into a wall in the reception of the hotel, destroying a framed map that was there and, I'm sure, scaring the crap out of the receptionists.

We stayed at the camp for two nights and it was like nothing I've ever experienced. Complete and utter luxury. We went on four game drives and saw all of the Big Five and they were just as incredible as you might imagine. To give you an idea of how luxurious this place was, I spent one afternoon in my bath on the balcony of my private luxury tent, sipping on complimentary sherry, watching a herd of antelope graze no more than ten yards away.

It was a completely incredible experience and if you ever want to go on a once-in-a-lifetime mega, mega holiday then go there. Soon though, it was time to leave luxury behind and whip out our not-so-luxurious tents. We were now chasing down Cape Town. We camped up the following night at a place called Hippo Waterside lodge. We had left the luxury behind but not the wildlife and, in the morning, we were able to sit and sip coffee watching a family of hippos wallow in the river. Next, we pressed on to a place called Kestell and stayed in another campsite that was run by a lady with award-winning jam. Unlimited jam and toast were included in the price for your tent pitch and it was top stuff. After trying every kind of jam imaginable, we waddled out to our sidecar to pack up for the road ahead and found, for the first time, that it was broken.

The front fixing had snapped in half. The lady who ran the campsite was able to point us in the direction of a welder though, and he tacked it up no problem. A quick fix! Next, we pushed on towards the town of Zastron where we camped up for the night before pressing on again to the town of Graaff-Reinet. The roads were long and straight and the views were humongous. The landscape was so flat that anytime we got to the top of a hill we could see for miles in any direction. Just as impressive as the land were the big African skies and they seemed to extend on forever.

On the drive from Graaff-Reinet we pulled into a small town for a spot of breakfast. There was one café and it was absolutely full of the bikers. They were fully clad in leathers, had big Harleys and lots of tattoos. They were the real deal, a proper biker gang. We pulled our outfit up next to theirs, walked in and sat down next to them. To our surprise we couldn't understand a word they were saying, they were all speaking Afrikaans! I thought that was one of those pretend languages, you know, like Latin or something, but turns out it's real. They could speak English too, though, and they turned to us and said, "Where you come from on that, eh?"

"London," we replied.

"Yeah you're from London but where have you driven from?" the guy said back.

"Yeah London, we've been at it nearly six months."

"Wow are you serious? You've got balls."

He then proceeded to tell the whole café how big our balls were. "Can we get you something? A beer maybe?"

"No, we're good with the coffee thanks." It was 10 a.m. They were all three or four pints deep.

"Alright but you've got to have some whiskey."

One of the guys came over and took out a shot glass that was chained to the top pocket of his leather vest. He pulled out his hip flask and filled a shot for us. They weren't the kind of guys I wanted to say no to twice, so I took it off him and took the shot, as did Reece. We both got big cheers. It appeared we were part of the gang.

After a few more cups of coffee we decided we were sober enough to take on the final ride down to the coast where we would meet the South Atlantic in Plettenburg Bay. You can get to Plettenburg Bay by taking a fairly boring stretch of tarmac or the more adventurous Prince Alfred pass. The pass is a mud road that winds through the mountains and provides some truly brilliant views. With thick mud and big potholes, it was probably the wrong choice but how could we resist? It was a brilliant stretch of road, though, and well worth getting muddy for. We just about made it through and arrived to Plettenburg Bay early evening.

From Plettenburg Bay it would be an easy ride along South Africa's Garden Route, all the way to Cape Town. Our first stop was to be Knysna where we were planning to stay at Pete and Coleen's house with their good friends turned house sitters, Renton and Irene. We had planned to stay for a few nights as we wanted to explore Knysna and also get the opportunity to fix the sidecar properly. The quick job that we got done up in Kestell broke almost instantly so we needed to find a proper repair shop.

Renton and Irene were very happy to have us stay with them. They were both in their 80s and Irene had only just recovered from major heart surgery, but nothing was too much trouble. One of the first things she said to us was, "Tell me, do you like avocado pears?" in her soft English voice. They were planning on doing all the cooking and we were treated like kings. We tried to help out and after three nights of sponging they finally let us buy them a pack of fish and chips as a thank you. They were exceptionally generous and hilariously good company. Neither was ever short of a story and we spent one night drinking wine, eating cheese and hearing about what it had been like to live and work in South Africa over the past fifty or so years.

Pete and Coleen arranged for us to go for a beer with some of their friends in town and they were super helpful, too. One of them put us in touch with a local guy named Gavin who was able to do a proper repair on the sidecar. Gavin took the rig off our hands for the whole day and did a proper job. At the end of it, I asked him how much we owed him and he wouldn't take a penny. He said that he was just happy he could help us get around the world. If you're ever in Knysna and you need someone handy with a welder then look him up, his company is called Phoenix Customs.

After Gavin had got us fixed up, we said goodbye to Renton and Irene and hit the road, headed west for Cape Town. We overnighted in Mossel Bay before pressing on once more for Stellenbosch, which is only about 30 km north of Cape Town. Stellenbosch is famous for its vineyards and we had agreed to meet back up with Brian and all spend a day or two exploring them. Reece had decided it was time to celebrate and instead of us all going to a campsite or booking a cheap Airbnb he wanted us to head to a youth hostel that was renowned for fun. The place was an absolute dive and Reece got absolutely bitten to crap by bed bugs, so I actually did find it pretty fun. We had a great time exploring the vineyards though. It's a fantastic way to spend the day. The views are just incredible and you're constantly being topped up with top quality wine for not that much money.

Eventually, we dragged ourselves away from the vino and on the 8th of April we finally arrived into Cape Town. After nineteen countries, 12,000 miles and plenty of challenges we had made it from London to Cape Town. The next part of our plan was to ship the bike to South America and, as with Greece, we had found it impossible to make plans in advance. Eventually, we realised that our only option would be to fly the bike. It would be considerably cheaper to send it by ship but it would take at least ninety days before we'd get it out of the port in South America. Air freight, on the other hand, could all be done in as little as two weeks. We agreed that we would go as quickly as possible. The delay in Greece proved to us that if you have an opportunity to ship the bike you should take it.

At first the quote to fly the bike via air freight was nearly £10,000. That was just completely ludicrous. There was no way we could do it. We kept ringing around though and we eventually found an option that would cost us only £4,000 if we road freighted the bike to Johannesburg and then flew it on to Santiago, Chile via Sao Paulo in Brazil. It wasn't what we necessarily wanted to do but it would have to do. At £4,000 though, it was going to cost us about £300 more than all of the money we physically had left in the world. We started thinking outside the box and since the price was calculated on size, we decided to chop off the roof of the sidecar and pack it into the rig. One lethal sweep of an angle grinder saved us £500. We could physically pay for the shipping. South America was on the cards and even better, Kuishi was now a convertible!

We still had around ten days left to kill before the bike was set to fly though, which we were quite pleased about. It gave us lots of time to plan for South America, explore Cape Town and best of all visit a charity fighting modern slavery in South Africa. Just as in Greece we had been very lucky to get a central Airbnb for next to no money; unfortunately, this one wasn't run by a baker, but it still gave us a great base to explore from. We had a few days exploring the city and the surrounding area first. It was a great place to visit. We took a stroll up to Lion's Head and marveled at the view as the sun set over the city. We went for a swim down at one of the city's many beaches, took a stroll around the V&A Wharf and even took a jaunt out to see the penguins at Boulders Beach.

Every time we went to a new place, we would race along inner-city highways and if we weren't careful we could be completely blind to the townships we drove past. You could say the same for the whole of South Africa actually, certainly the whole of the Garden Route. For every pocket of wealth, for every very English-looking town with paved streets and lots of well-off white people, there is a township. Usually of similar size in land area to the pocket of wealth it feeds, the township will be full of two to three times the number of people and they are predominantly black. I guess it's a kind of leftover from apartheid and I found it pretty hard to ignore. I found it really hard to get my head around at first and I was trying to work out why on earth South Africa was still like this. How could it be that in 2018 there was still such a clear divide in the country and there were such huge, apparent inequalities laid bare for everyone to see?

Then I was speaking to a British guy in a bar one night and I realised that the only thing I was really struggling to get my head around was that it was so apparent and that the inequality was in your face. It wasn't the injustice itself that caught me off guard, it was the fact that it wasn't hidden. I can't remember the name of the guy I met but he said to me that in his opinion, South Africa is the healthiest place to live on the planet. He meant that if you want to be rich there you have to accept the fact that, in the way the world currently works, your relatively extreme wealth is built on the backs of the poor and comes at their expense. Here in South Africa, the people whom you feed off, to be wealthy, are right on your doorstep and you have to live with that, whereas, in the UK, we have hidden them away. I think he's probably right.

The following day we went to meet A21 South Africa, an organisation fighting modern slavery and human trafficking in the country. It's thought that nearly 50 percent of the population is at risk of being trafficked into modern slavery in South Africa, and A21 is one of a handful of organisations trying to bring that percentage down. There are currently estimated to be around 288,000 people living in slavery in the country and they are trapped in all kinds of places. From fishing trawlers, to nail bars, to brothels, to people's houses, there is pretty much no part of South African life that doesn't include modern slavery, much like every other country we travelled through.

We met with Cornel, and her job at A21 was to reach people with the message that modern slavery exists and to give them the knowledge to avoid slipping into it. Cornel's main role within that was creating A-teams, what A21 calls its network of "modern abolitionists," people who are prepared to do something to try and stop slavery within their community. They exist all over South Africa and, in fact, all over the world. The idea is that you commit to making a difference in your community and Cornel and the team equip you with the tools to do that. Usually that exists as information to be distributed on how to spot the signs and who to call if you're concerned about modern slavery.

One of Cornel's big areas of focus was developing A-teams all over the African continent. The idea is to educate people at the start of the pipeline, so they don't end up getting trafficked out of their home country. She gave us an example and told us that a pretty common story is that kids in West Africa are often approached while playing football in their towns and told that they have what it takes to make it as professional footballers. Traffickers pose as football scouts for South African football clubs and young teenagers travel to South Africa in the hope of trials but end up trapped in slavery. As someone who grew up dreaming of being the next Paul Scholes, that was a story that really struck a chord with me. I could imagine that I would have been screaming at my parents to let me go and if I had grown up in West Africa, in a community where the only way out of poverty might be football, I could imagine that my parents would have let me. A21's idea is to establish A-teams in these communities who warn people of these kinds of risks.

Another of A21's ideas for their A-teams is to encourage them to help raise money for the fight in any way they can. This could be the usual stuff like running a bake sale or hosting a gig night, right through to what Cornel does, which is donate a percentage of her business's profit to A21. Cornel runs a surf school on the weekend and a percentage of what you pay goes to fighting modern slavery in South Africa. This means you can quite literally surf against slavery. I thought that was a brilliant idea and we were chuffed she'd thought it up because it meant we had an excuse to have a lesson.

The three of us all went the following day and got absolutely battered by the waves for an hour or so. Chels was nailing it, Reece stood up and I was completely useless but it was huge amounts of fun and all for a good cause. We told Cornel we would add A21 onto the list of charities we would raise money for, and I guess became part of the A-team.

After we had been surfing, Cornel dropped us at the airport because it was time for Chels to fly on. She was heading to Jamaica, to live with her grandma for a month or so and do some more Higgler stuff. We weren't planning to meet up again for another few months, which meant there were more teary eyes at the airport. It had been nice to get some proper time with her though. We'd seen each other a lot more than expected in Africa and the night before she left, we even got to go on a date. We sunk a cocktail while watching the sunset at the beach before grabbing some dinner, loads of drinks and finally ending up in a Karaoke bar where we perfectly nailed *Stan* by Eminem.

We stumbled out of the Karaoke place in the early hours of the morning and the street was still alive. There were people everywhere and a bunch of guys came past, cheering and having a great laugh. They all surrounded us and started celebrating about something. It was all very confusing but being royally drunk we joined in. As soon as they left, I realised they had taken my phone with them. A textbook maneuver! "Oh well," I thought. "That's what you buy insurance for." I turned around and Chels was chasing them up the street! She had been so scared about "gangs" in South Africa that she had been locking her car doors at traffic lights, yet when she actually found one, she turned to them and said, "Come on, let's have it!" It was quite hilarious. Eventually, I managed to talk her down, it was a good job too, she was absolutely raging, and those fellas would have been dust.

It was sad to see Chels fly off and I would certainly miss her, but I was excited too because it meant we would be flying the following day and heading to South America for the start of a brand new adventure, heading north to Alaska!

– 12 –

"WE WERE GASPING FOR AIR THAT JUST WASN'T THERE."

We arrived into Santiago on the 18th of April having left South Africa on the 16th. It was a fifty-hour trip. Turns out it's a pretty awkward route to fly. Amazingly, Flight Centre sponsored the flights for us again, so we still had a couple of hundred quid to take on the Americas, but that really was all we had. Fortunately, we had both taken out massive credit cards while we still had jobs and decided that we would just crack on and rack up loads of debt. We're smart like that. We needed it, too, because we would be holing up in Santiago for some time. In a hugely ironic turn of events, the lorry that was carrying our sidecar to Johannesburg broke down and Kuishi missed its flight. We couldn't believe it. We only put it on the lorry because we weren't sure if we would break down and end up missing the flight ourselves. Turns out we should have risked it.

It meant delays and it ended up taking a month to air freight the bike from Cape Town to Santiago. In that time, we managed to get a good chance to plan for the journey north and explore the Chilean capital. When originally planning the trip, we had decided that we would like to drive to Anchorage, Alaska, and ship the bike to Chukotka, Russia. That was looking ever less likely. We would need to be out of Russia before winter or we would end up facing temperatures as low as −40°C and we both agreed that would be impossible in the sidecar. We decided then that we would instead make it to Alaska and aim to ship to Singapore and drive home that way. That gave us a bit more time and meant we would just need to be out of Alaska before deepest, darkest winter in about six months.

So, we had just less than half a year to make it from Santiago to Alaska. This would be done in two stages, one stretch to Cartagena, Colombia, and then the other from Panama City north to Alaska. We would have to ship between Panama and Colombia because there is an impenetrable stretch of forest between the two called the Darien Gap. It's proper rainforest and it's historically riddled with rebel groups and drug-runners. Some crazy people have taken it on and at the time of writing, our friends Spencer and Cathy were about to head into it on their motorbike. I wish them all the best, but it's certainly no place for a scooter and sidecar.

The most direct route to Cartagena was to go up through Chile, into Bolivia, through Peru, across Ecuador and up the spine of Colombia. That sounded pretty good to us, so we drew a rough line on our map and the planning was done. We ended up in Santiago for a little over two weeks and, in that time, we barely got to grips with the place at all. Not being able to speak Spanish was a real problem. It was still a lot of fun, but it was proving to be impossible to understand the place as we had tried to do in the other countries we passed through. We still managed to get a good understanding of empanadas, cervezas and the Chileans' love of football.

We barely met anybody the whole time we were there, but we did get the chance to chat to a Swiss guy who had just ridden his Africa Twin on the same route we were hoping to take north. He gave us some pointers on where to go and where to avoid, but his main piece of advice was to take on the Lagunas Route from Chile into Bolivia. He had said it was this incredible dirt-road mountain pass that cut off hundreds of kilometres and was full of amazing sights. He had just ridden through and said it's a tough ride but, "You'll be fine!" We figured that was all the research we needed so we decided to take it on if we ever managed to get out of Santiago.

Eventually, the bike did arrive and, unlike Cairo, it was very easy to get out of customs, all done in a day. We spent another day doing some repairs and reattaching our roof before scooting out of Santiago the following morning. That first day we racked up a whopping 500 km down a long straight highway and we were loving being on the road. The rest was exactly what the bike needed and we were flying along. At that pace we'd make it to Alaska no problem.

Our second day on the road was a different story. We were right along the coast and it should have been an absolute joy. We had visions of riding along the rugged coastline and tasting the local seafood as we went, but the only thing we were tasting was dirty fuel. The problems from South Africa had resurfaced but this time there was no helpful pump attendant around to save the day. Before we knew it, we were jolting off to the right every few seconds and couldn't make any progress. We decided to call it a day, pull into a guesthouse, and have a proper go at fixing it. That of course meant starting with siphoning. Learning how to siphon fuel the hard way is truly disgusting. Neither Reece nor I had ever tried siphoning, but we knew that the basic premise is to put some kind of giant straw in the tank, give it a suck, remove your mouth before the fuel gets to you, and let physics take care of the rest.

If only it was that easy! I was the first to try. I sucked on our overflow pipe and my lungs filled with toxic fumes. I coughed and spluttered before scurrying off to get water. I hadn't put the pipe in the fuel so after pushing it down a bit further, Reece had a go. He managed to get it flowing, but it was too fast for him to get out of the way and he was soon spitting petrol all over the forecourt of the nice guesthouse we had wound up in. Over the next hour and a half, we drank, spat, and occasionally siphoned our tank dry, before mopping out a load of dirt and declaring victory over the fuel problems that had stopped us in our tracks. We were unorthodox but after eight months on the road we were practically mechanics.

We set our compass north again and headed for San Pedro de Atacama the following day. The first hour or two went great and we found ourselves cruising along perfect highways through the Atacama Desert. The Atacama is an incredible place. It's the highest, driest true desert on the planet and it's completely beautiful. We were left in awe by its mighty dunes as we scooted through at a solid 50 mph. There we were, happily taking in the scenery when we were rudely brought back to reality by yet another sharp jolt to our right. A minute later and another jolt. We hadn't fixed anything. We had been drinking fuel for fun. Worse still the loss of power was so frequent that we were actually struggling to get any speed up.

We pulled in on the side of the road and whipped out a flask of tea to assess the situation with. We were out in the middle of the desert and with nobody around to help—we had to get ourselves out of trouble. We would have to try and fix it again. We figured it had worked properly for an hour or so after we swapped the fuel for clean stuff so if we did that again maybe it would work for longer. Another thirty minutes of petrol drinking and we were back cruising at 50 mph. It lasted pretty well for the rest of the day and just before sunset we pulled off the main highway, rode down a gravel track into the middle of nowhere and set up for a completely remote wild camp.

Camping in the Atacama is one of the coolest things I've ever done. It was a such a different experience to camping back in the Sahara. In Sudan, there's always someone or something around. You can always hear the singing of the nearby farmers or the call of a bird, but here it was just completely and utterly silent. Not a single sound. The stars above were great at first but clouds formed before we could see them in all their glory. It was a welcome sign to get an early night; we were spent after a hot day's riding and repairing in the desert.

The following morning, we set off once again and our fuel problems persisted. We visited a mechanic in a town, but he was none the wiser, so we just continued with our cycle of siphon, splutter, scoot, repeat until we finally arrived into the town of San Pedro de Atacama. The ride up to San Pedro was tough for the scooter. It marked the start of our ascent into the Andes and the higher we got the more the scooter struggled for breath. At around 2,500 metres above sea level, we were at full throttle, stuttering with the fuel problems, and barely getting 30 mph. The views were worth it, though. As you approach San Pedro, you drop down onto a plateau and the road, cut into the side of the sandy mountains, twists and turns its way down to the town. It has to be one of the most dramatic entrances to a town anywhere on earth.

The town itself doesn't really live up to the entrance, though. It's a centuries-old settlement, formed around an oasis, enabling indigenous people to survive in one of the harshest environments on the planet. But these days, it's just like any other tourist town you will visit, with more sand. We passed up on the opportunity to join "Happy Hour" on the strip and instead went to a French patisserie in order to get hold of a decent Wi-Fi signal. We got one, along with a £4 cup of coffee (which I moaned about for hours), and instantly posted up a call for help on our Facebook page again. Everyone agreed that we most likely just had a dirty fuel filter.

The next day we learnt what a fuel pump looked like and managed to clean the filter attached to it. The filter was completely filthy, and it seemed like our Facebook followers may have been onto something. We got everything back together, went into town to pick up some supplies, and headed off towards Bolivia via the Lagunas Route. We could have taken the long, boring way around, but we figured we would trust that guy on the Africa Twin and go for it.

The first day we did about 40 km, but we climbed about a thousand metres. It took us a solid three or four hours and by the time we set up camp we were at about 3,500 metres above sea level. The bike was really struggling for air, but it managed to keep plugging away at the steady tarmac slope. It was tough for everyone riding that way, especially the touring cyclists we rode past, and even the lorries that slalomed their way up using both sides of the road.

When we had made it to a suitable middle-of-nowhere spot, we pulled off the side of the road and camped up for the night. At 3,500 metres the altitude sickness can start to affect you, but we were okay. Pretty relaxed, we kicked back with a beer (part of the supplies we had picked up) and watched the stars. They were incredible. Temperatures soon drop at that elevation, though, and throughout the night it can get really quite cold. We woke up to a frosty tent and a chilly −5°C. A cup of coffee and a bowl of cold porridge later and we were riding for the Bolivian border, the start of the Lagunas Route proper.

The Lagunas Route isn't really a route at all. It's more just a term for a general direction—an encouraging title that describes the need to get from one side of the Eduardo Avaroa Andean Fauna National Reserve to the other. The Reserve is home to some of the most incredible natural phenomena. There's the Laguna Verde (a green lake), the Laguna Colorada (a red lake), and seemingly endless salt flats, incredible mountains, and spooky rock formations. But we were planning to miss most of it and just take the main road through the reserve. The guy from Santiago had said we would be able to get through on the main drag but anything else would be too much. The main track was about 400 km of intense washboard, but it was mainly flat. Even though it meant missing the Laguna Verde and Laguna Colorada, he suggested we should stick to that main road or we could run into trouble.

That morning we arrived at the Chilean border control at about 8 a.m.. Frozen to the core from the night before, and with the wind whipping across us, we left the last piece of tarmac behind and headed to the Bolivian checkpoint. Along with a couple of other overlanders in a 4x4, we crammed into the tiny shed that was the Bolivian passport control. Here, we expected to begin the process of clearing the bike and paying our $20 visa fee. Unfortunately, the officials had other plans.

It turned out that all foreign vehicles heading north had to report to the Bolivian customs checkpoint at the top of the reserve. It was a huge detour from the main track and, worse still, it was situated at 5,200 metres above sea level. Then the customs guys told us that we also had to pay a $50 fee each to enter the park as well as our visa fees. This completely cleared us out. In fact, we didn't even have $140 on us and we had to borrow $50 from the other overlanders and promised to pay them back on the other side. At this point, we should have turned back. We had about $5 in change in our back pockets, one big bottle of water, a

145

few bags of crisps, and a couple of bread rolls. Ahead of us lay an impassable (by scooter and sidecar) off-road track that would be made up of thick gravel and steep inclines, all at 5,000 metres above sea level. It was madness. We carried on regardless.

In fact, we did more than carry on. We decided to venture off the main track before we needed to in order to get a look at the Laguna Verde. We just couldn't resist, I mean it's a green lake. This was a terrible idea. The road was seriously thick gravel and if we didn't keep moving, we would struggle to start again. It was like a motocross track with sudden drops and steep climbs. We would floor it down the drops in order to get up the other side, often meeting the bottom of the hill with a huge crash. In order to maximise our chances of keeping the rig moving, we decided that the guy in the sidecar would hang off the side. That would enable him to jump off and push when it got slow and then jump back on, bob-sleigh style, when it got going. This technique ended in tears for Reece as he was flung off the side when I hit a big divot. Fortunately, he was wearing all of the proper gear so no serious damage, but it was quite the tumble. The lake was barely even green, so with the wind still whipping across us we hid behind a rock, drank a cup of coffee, and agreed to take the easiest possible route we could from here on in.

Another hour of tumbling along the rocky washboard track and we came to a little spot of paradise, a café situated next to some geothermal hot pools. It was a stop-off for tourists coming through, so we had a word with one of the guides who told us that we would have no problem getting to the Bolivian customs office and it takes him half an hour in his 4x4 so as long as we left an hour or two we'd be fine. Great news! We couldn't afford any proper food from the café, but we weren't going to pass on a jump in the pools. It was absolutely bliss. I just can't stress how good it was. The water was almost scalding—just bearable—and we sat in it for a good hour watching the llamas graze in the distance beneath the towering mountains. Towering mountains that we were going to have to climb.

It was probably one o'clock before we set off again and turned off the main track towards the customs office. The track pointed straight uphill. We were currently at around 4,000 metres and we would be climbing another 1,200 metres on really rough, thick gravel. The sidecar soon got stuck and we resorted to pushing the rig uphill at altitude. Altitude sickness hit us instantly. Up to this point we had been fine because we were sat down, not using much oxygen. But suddenly we were pushing the outfit uphill and it weighed a tonne (not literally, it's about a quarter of a tonne). We were gasping for air that just wasn't there. Our heads started throbbing. Dizziness hit. Both of us felt sick.

We should have turned back and taken a day to acclimatise at the pools or something, but again we pushed on regardless. The higher we got, the harder it got, and we were either pushing the rig or walking alongside it, as it carried itself up the hill. To make matters worse the track was going off in all directions. Maps.me and Gary the Garmin were no use out here. All we had was a little tourist map with a black dot on it, given to us by the border officials. We just kept going, hoping we were going the right way. It was the wrong thing to do but we got lucky and at about 6 p.m. we rolled into the Bolivian customs checkpoint. Amazingly, the officials were still there, and they got us processed pronto. They didn't seem to be surprised whatsoever that two English blokes on a scooter and sidecar had made it to their ridiculously remote office, and just treated it like an everyday occurrence.

By this time the sun had started to set. We probably should have asked to sleep in the waiting room but instead we pointed the rig downhill and headed towards the Laguna Colorada, which thanks to our detour was now en route. We were feeling really beat up, absolutely worn out, and with killer headaches. We would have been happy to just sling the tent up and get some rest, but we were freezing cold and it was set to drop to around −15°C that night. We pulled over and spotted on the iOverlander app that there were a couple of houses lined along the far side of the lake. Other overlanders had stopped there with the local people for a couple of dollars for the night. It was the wrong side of the lake for us but if there was half a chance of getting inside, we had to go for it. I took the bars and decided that I was going to just storm it as fast as I could downhill until we got to the house.

The track was really rough, and the bike was getting constantly battered. I was battling to keep it upright as we flew down the hill.

The vibrations from the rough road were ripping through my arms but fortunately my fingers felt no pain; I had lost any feeling in them thanks to the cold. After about an hour the sun was nearly set, and the sky turned a dark red. As it did, we approached the Laguna Colorada. The water was as red as the sky and apart from a small lip of dark mountains my entire surroundings were glowing all different shades of red. It was the most incredible thing I have ever seen. A sense of euphoria came over me and I was no longer desperate to get down. I could have continued riding along that lake all night if the sun would have stayed where it was.

Just as it turned pitch black, we pulled up to the house we were heading for. We knocked on the front door and to our amazement a young girl opened it. She couldn't have been more than four or five. Taking one look at us she instantly said, "No!"

We replied with a calm, "Por favor, get your mum and dad."

Grandma turned up a couple of seconds later and welcomed us in. We spent our last five dollars on two beds and two bowls of piping hot soup. We were saved.

We crawled into our beds as soon as we'd eaten and, bizarrely, we watched London Has Fallen on Reece's laptop. Both still pumped full of adrenaline, we couldn't sleep but we needed something to take our minds off our headaches. Gerard Butler did a good job and I passed out just after he saved the President.

The next morning, we found ourselves on the wrong side of the lake with a long way to go but we were through the worst of it. We set off bright and early, now with absolutely zero money and just a couple packs of crisps to last us until we could get to Uyuni. We set off as the sun rose around the lake. It was still absolutely freezing, probably around −5°C. Reece started with the riding, but we were soon swapping every five minutes to warm up our hands. We had no idea of the way to Uyuni, there were no set tracks, just a general direction to head in. We decided to stick to the rough track around the lake, which worked for a little while until we found ourselves in thick sand again. It was gritty, grey sand that swamped the whole area, and picking a path through it was impossible. We were riding with one person walking alongside and pushing but even that wasn't enough, and we eventually got properly stuck. Luckily, a 4x4 passed by and we were able to flag them down and ask for a push.

We didn't see other people very often at all but every now and again a local person or a truck full of tourists would plough past. Eventually, we made it around the lake and got close enough to look at the flamingos while sipping on a cup of tea from our flask. We had made it back onto the main drag but still had a considerable way to travel. We spent the next five or six hours hammering along the washboard towards the main road. It was really starting to get the better of Kuishi, and the better of us too. It was just never-ending, and the sidecar still couldn't carry us both uphill. At one point I was at the handlebars and Reece was riding bobsleigh as we approached a pretty steep hill. He jumped off and walked behind. Two minutes later he realised that when he jumped out of the sidecar he had dropped his phone, as he did he turned back to see a 4x4 just pulling off from where we had dropped it. The guy sped past us and sped off with Reece's phone. We were fairly confident he had taken it, but we spent an hour scouring the patch where Reece had dropped it, just in case. No luck at all. We were absolutely gutted because it had all our pictures from the most incredible part of the trip so far.

So, we were beaten up by the conditions and beaten down by the thief. We still had a couple of hundred kilometres to cover on really tough ground and it was looking more and more like we'd have to camp for the night. We genuinely didn't know if we would make it out on our own at all. The sidecar was completely battered. By this point we had a massive crack in our sidecar wheel, but it was somehow still holding. At the same time, three of our five sidecar joints had cracked off and the sidecar was dragging along the floor if one of us sat in it, so we had to ride pillion for the rest of the day. With around 100 km left to go, we bumped into a couple of cyclists doing the route the other way. They were having a terrible time and asked if they were nearly done. We didn't have the heart to tell them they had at least 1,000 metres to climb and about double the distance left to go.

At about 5 p.m., after ten hours of battering ourselves, we eventually hit tarmac and, after another 100-km scoot into the night, we arrived into the Bolivian town of Uyuni having survived the Lagunas Route by the skin of our teeth. It took us the best part of three hours to do that final stretch as we were still 3,700 metres above sea level and Kuishi's top speed was 30 mph. We found a dodgy room for the night, located a cash point, and went to buy some proper food. We weren't disappointed either. I think we spent about £1.50 each and had more BBQ'd chicken and rice than any man should ever eat.

The following day we started to assess the damage. We knew we had made a big mistake but just how bad was it? Sure enough, the sidecar was hanging on by the skin of its teeth and an enormous chunk of our aluminium sidecar wheel was missing. The latter was a huge problem. It was a wonder it still had air in it as the tyre was bulging through the gap in the wheel. We spent the day rolling around town trying to find someone to fix it. Uyuni is not a big place and the likelihood of getting spare parts was zero. If we were going to ride out of there it would have to be fixed. We had almost given up hope, but after hours of searching we stumbled on a workshop that could help. It was a team of fellas that spanned three generations and they agreed to take on the challenge a couple of days later.

That was all okay with us because we were due a day off and Reece's brother Sam and his wife Jo were coming to visit. Jo is Bolivian and they had come over to see her friends and family, but it just so happened that we managed to tie it in at the same time. Apart from Chels, they were the first people we'd seen from home in just over eight months. We all had a great catch-up and with Jo being in the know, we ate the most incredible Bolivian food. The following day Sam, Jo, and Reece went off for some quality time to explore the salt flats and I stayed in town to work on the bike with the fellas.

I rocked up bright and early and we all got to work. Grandad decided to take on the most technically tough part of the fix, repairing the aluminium wheel. Everyone online agreed that we would never, ever find an aluminium welder in Uyuni but this guy wasn't fazed by the challenge at all. This left me and the father and son duo to try and do something about the broken sidecar joints. Three of the five joints had completely snapped, and it was just held on with the two at the back. This meant we had to somehow hoist the front up at the same time as properly replacing the joints. It was quite the challenge and took most of the day, but we did it. We stopped halfway through the day for almuerzo (lunch). The fellas asked me to sod off and come back later so I went into town and tucked into almuerzo for one. I had a bowl of incredible soup, followed by some kind of steak and mash, and topped off with a great cup of coffee for £2.50. It was so good, too.

After an afternoon of tinkering, the rig was fixed, and I was free to have fun, too, so I met the guys in a bar for some beers. We all decided that we would take a little tour out onto the salt flats that night, ready to watch the sunrise. It was probably the most incredible experience of my entire life. The Uyuni Salt Flats are the biggest salt flats in the world and we joined a tour that took us right into the middle of them. We got out of the car and it was absolutely freezing but nobody cared because it felt like we were in some kind of dream world. There was a thin layer of water sitting on top of the flats and it was a completely clear night, so the stars were out in all their glory. Having stargazed in some pretty special places on this trip, we were kind of spoilt, but nothing could prepare us for seeing the stars both above and below us. It was completely surreal and felt like we were just floating through outer space.

After a while the sun started to rise and a reddish pink glow appeared above the mountains. Then this massive glowing orb slowly creeped up and our surroundings were bursting with oranges and reds that seemed to mix and swirl together with the blue glow of the water. Before we knew it, the sun was fully up, and the light show had come to an end. Time to head back to Uyuni for an exceptionally strong coffee. We relaxed for the day, said goodbye to Sam and Jo, and plotted our journey north.

– 13 –

"IT WAS ALL GOOD FUN, UNTIL I FELL OFF A HORSE."

Just as we were prepping to leave Uyuni, we received a Facebook message from a guy called Oscar. He lives in La Paz and said we should stay at his place if we were planning on heading through. We of course took him up on the offer and arranged to meet. It was 520 km to La Paz, and despite it being a pretty straight, flat road, we were going slowly. We were still at nearly 4,000 metres above sea level so Kuishi didn't have enough oxygen to go more than 45 mph. We eventually pulled into the city after dark and we were lost. We had got Oscar's address wrong and we didn't have a Bolivian SIM card so couldn't contact him. In the end, we had to dive into an internet café on the outskirts of the city to get in touch.

Reece went inside to contact Oscar and I stayed outside to guard the bike. I was able to take a minute just to appreciate the place I was in. It felt like Africa again. The atmosphere was immense. We were pulled up on the side of a six-lane carriageway next to a load of other parked cars. The cars that were on the road were all driving erratically, trying to weave their way through the queues. Each vehicle was armed with its own distinctive horn and none were afraid to use it. I was stood on the path and watching a street dog drink from a muddy puddle that was a fluorescent red as it reflected the lights of the shops behind me. Next to the internet café, there was a baker's which didn't look too dissimilar to Manos' place back in Greece and, on the other side, some sleazy motel. People were muddling through everywhere and it was one of those crazy places where there's so frequently something nuts going on that the sidecar just blends in. Nobody even noticed I was there.

Reece came and he'd been given the name of a road to follow. Oscar was going to set off in the other direction and meet us en route. The road took us to the edge of the crater that La Paz sits in and the city looked incredible all lit up. We made our way downhill in the dark and after about twenty minutes we heard someone sound their horn loads and shout from the opposite direction. They spun around and a red convertible Ford Mustang pulled up next to us. "Hey guys!! It's me, Oscar!" he shouted.

Oscar waved for us to follow him and we started making our way to his place. It turned out his place was back up towards the top of the crater. We had been going in the right direction though, as the only access was via a gravel track that led from the bottom. As we started to weave our way up, the road seemed to get steeper and steeper. At 3,000 metres above sea level, Kuishi was still starved of oxygen and we couldn't get any traction on the gritty track. We were crawling uphill at what must have been 7 or 8 mph —just enough for one person to stand on the sidecar and then push when it got tough. We got to a flat bit and Oscar pointed at his house just a few hundred metres further up the hill. We were so close. We pressed on. I was at the handlebars and all of a sudden I lost all power. I let it rest, hit full throttle and got a loud grinding noise with no movement. We had burnt the clutch out again.

We couldn't believe it. Idiots! Before we left Santiago, we had actually put on a new clutch. Luis and Jan from Gazeboshop had very kindly paid for a few spare parts to be sent out to us and they had really saved the day. We had changed it, so we had the new one running and we kept the dodgy one we had cobbled together in Ethiopia as a spare. The stress of the Lagunas Route must have given the clutch a battering and this last steep, sandy incline had been the straw that broke the camel's back. Fortunately, we were in pushing distance of Oscar's house, so he got his mate, Juanito, to come down and the four of us pushed it over the finish line. It was a 300-400-metre push up a very straight hill and we were absolutely pooped. Oscar took one look at us, opened his garage door and said, "Put that in there, it will be safe. Let's go and get you serviced first." He took us off to this fantastic burger joint with his partner, Maka, and we had a beer and a burger on him.

After dinner, we went back to Oscar's house and we instantly understood why he chose to live at the top of the hill. The view from his flat was incredible. He had huge windows across the front of the place and could see right across the city. We chilled out with a few beers and enjoyed hanging out in his lad's pad. He lived there alone and it had a proper bachelor pad feel. There was a big flat screen TV, a fully stocked beer fridge, and craploads of motorcycle memorabilia on the walls. Oscar was pretty well-off, but he'd earnt every penny himself through starting his own printing company. He was a work-hard, play-hard kind of guy and fun to be around.

The following morning, we woke up and got straight to work on the scooter. We took off the crankcase and sure enough a load of melted metal fell out. We had done it again. Fortunately, Oscar's mate, Juanito, was a bit of a handy man and happy to help us out. The bloke seemed to be a complete genius. He'd never seen a scooter like ours before but somehow knew exactly how it worked. We watched in amazement as he casually took apart our clutch and put it back together with such ease. The hardest part of the fix is to compress this almighty spring that sits inside the clutch. We had done it in Gondar through brute force and tenacity. We spent a few hours just pushing and pushing and, in the end, we managed to do it by lying on the floor and ramming it in with our legs. Juanito casually pulled the whole thing out, pushed it down against the floor and got one of us to pop the nut on, a thirty-second job.

He spent a few hours working on the bike and fixed it right up. We even went across town and picked up a new set of shocks for the sidecar; the originals broke on the Lagunas Route (not the Hagon ones, they were on the main bike and they really did take the load from the road exceptionally well). We chilled out in La

Paz for another day and took Oscar and Maka out for dinner to say thank you before pressing on.

The next morning, we headed off for Peru. It took us ages to crawl out of the crater that La Paz sits in. Steep inclines and lots of traffic are a lethal, clutch-burning cocktail, and we were really concerned that we might end up retreating back to Oscar's with another broken bike. Eventually, though, we clambered out of the top of the crater and started to make a decent pace along the plateau, heading for Peru. As we were still at nearly 4,000 metres above sea level we were struggling to push 45 mph and we realised we wouldn't quite make it out of Bolivia. Instead, we stopped for the night in Copacabana on the shores of Lake Titicaca. Much like its namesake, the Copacabana beach in Rio, Copacabana is awash with tourists. It's full of people trying to get a peek at the underwater Mayan ruins or explore the many islands, where ancient traditions are still acted out by indigenous communities on the highest lake in the world.

We had a beer and played a game of chess while watching the sun drop. It was quite a nice spot, actually, and an interesting evening at the board. We were still neck and neck some 300-400 games in. There's a lot of time to kill on a trip like this. After doing some social media work, we woke up the following morning, ready and prepped for a big day on the road. We were hoping to make it all the way to Cusco, some 530 km. That's quite a distance on a good day but at altitude and with a border crossing it was going to be a real push. We had tried to get away at the crack of dawn, but we had breakfast included in our hostel. It didn't start until 7:30 a.m. and wasn't served till 8 a.m., but we weren't going to pass on free food in our current financial situation. When it did arrive, it was marvelous. Toast, tea, coffee, jam, fresh juice, two eggs, and thick pancakes coated in chocolate and caramel spread.

While we were waiting, the guy put on the BBC World News and we were treated to thirty minutes of highlights from the royal wedding. We felt like adventurers of old times, receiving news of England via the BBC World coverage of the monarchy. Eventually, we pulled ourselves away from Harry and Meghan and set off for Cusco. The journey started with 10 km of winding up and down along Lake Titicaca to Peru. Unfortunately, the scooter couldn't handle the inclines combined with the altitude again. So, we spent the morning pushing it up steep hills and jumping on just in time to floor it down the other side, hoping the momentum would carry us up the next one.

Eventually, we arrived at the border for Peru, where I got done for a fiver from the local police guy. He checked my passport and while I was looking the other way, he pocketed my immigration card. He then pointed out that I didn't have my immigration card, which was certainly in there two seconds before. He took me around the corner and sold me another one for fifty bolivars. This delay also put us behind a full coachload of tourists, meaning we spent well over an hour at customs rather than five minutes. We finally got through and realised that the royal wedding and the royal jerk at the border had meant we would be driving at night.

We pressed on for the next nine hours, only stopping for fuel. That kind of driving time, with no breaks, sends you delirious. I remember clapping frantically at a passing train out of the sidecar. It did look marvelous; we were flying along the ridge of a magnificent valley and down below us a steam train went hurtling along through the fields below. It was there we decided our next project would be "As Seen From The Train," a far more comfortable way to circumnavigate the globe. We also had a ridiculous incident where we stopped to fill up just after dark at what I thought was a lay-by but turned out to be a dump site. It was littered with nappies. Reece said he was off for a wee and I said, "Why don't you just pop one of those on and we can keep going!" We were then crying laughing in a field of nappies, in the pitch black, halfway up a Peruvian mountain. It's those completely absurd, delirious moments that are the funniest to think back on. Never did I imagine that one day I would be thrashing it through the Peruvian mountains at night, trying so hard to get somewhere that I would say, "Reece, pop that nappy on so we can keep going."

Eventually, we did make it to Cusco, where we spent another hour or so trying to find our Airbnb before gorging on a dodgy take-away and passing out. We took the following day off to take stock once again. In reality, our bike was really struggling, and we were in real bother with our long-term finances. We had a couple of grand available on our own credit cards which we were happy to rinse but it was never going to be enough to get us home. Plus, the sidecar was still cracked pretty seriously, and our exhaust was still bent in half from the Lagunas Route, which we thought might be adding to the altitude problem.

We spent the morning trying to sort out our dire financial situation. First things first, we wrote off to all of our existing corporate sponsors and asked them if they'd be up for helping us get home. We framed it so that we could do a big press release closer to the final stretch and we could thank them for getting us over the finish line. That seemed like it was a pretty good idea but it would be weeks if not months before we had any serious response so we had done all we could. Then we went off to get the bike fixed and we managed to find a guy who was up for taking Kuishi off our hands for a day or two and giving it a proper service. He agreed to fix all the cracks in the rig and fix the exhaust too. We were pretty pleased about that, because it meant we had two days to kill in Cusco. We had no choice but to hop on the train and check out Machu Picchu.

For me Machu Picchu was another one of those places that lives up to the hype. We took the train along the river and into the town of Aguas Calientes, which is only accessible by foot or rail. It was a standard tourist town but set against the surrounding mountains, with no road in or out, it felt like a pretty special place. We just went up to the ruins as tourists for the day, but I can imagine hiking in along the Inca trail is incredible. The dramatic peaks that the Mayan ruins sit on are unreal and the views are completely breathtaking. It's really an amazing place and well worth a visit.

After Machu Picchu we spent another couple of days stranded in Cusco. There were strikes and the roads had all been dug up. We didn't mind that either, as it gave us some proper time to explore the town, which is also well worth a good look around. Walking up the steep, ancient cobbled streets and looking down on the city, all lit up at night, was a really cool experience. Eventually, we managed to get out of there, and having been off the road for four days we were keen to get going. We decided to try and rack up another 500 km to a town called Puquio. We got off bright and early and the break had done Kuishi the world of good. It turned out the bent exhaust had been chocking the engine and was the main reason for the loss in power. We could now make it uphill without pushing, only just, but we could keep a steady 10 mph and that made a huge difference. It was lucky too because the roads were ridiculously mountainous.

We were essentially trying to cross the spine of the Peruvian Andes and it wasn't easy. The road surface itself was great but it was non-stop snaking up and down mountains. We loved it at first. The mountain views were just stunning: big, jagged, snow-topped peaks all around us and seemingly untouched countryside just waiting for us to scoot past. There were very few towns and villages on the route but those that were there were a joy to pass through. People were just going about traditional Peruvian life. At one point we got caught up in a local celebration and followed a parade for a while. There were all sorts of entertainment and we got stuck behind a group of thirty or so girl`s doing some kind of traditional dance. It was pretty incredible.

By late afternoon, it became increasingly apparent that we weren't going to make it to Puquio, the next town, before dark, so it was either press on or camp up for the night. It had begun to get quite cold already and we knew that it would be well below freezing throughout the night. We didn't really have the kit for camping on a sub-zero mountainside, so we just cracked on into the night. By nightfall we were only around 100 km away from Puquio but the mountain road was such slow going that we knew it could be another three hours until we arrived.

Two hours later and we were still going. We were absolutely frozen to the core and just 20 km away from the town. We were pushing the bike to its limits and that meant flooring it on the uphill but also not slowing down for the downhill sections. We were taking icy bends far too fast and I remember one where I overcooked it and had to use both sides of the road to make it around. Had a car been coming the other way, we would have been toast. We came around a corner and saw a trucker stop on the side of the road. Despite only being 20 km away I decided I had to get inside, and I was right. I hadn't realised how cold I was getting, and it had reached dangerous levels. It took me half an hour inside with a cup of hot coffee just to stop shaking. I had never been that cold in my entire life, it genuinely felt like I had pushed it too far, I just couldn't get my body temperature back up.

After about forty-five minutes of chatting to the truckers and watching a South American version of Takeshi's Castle on the TV, we pressed on for Puquio where we arrived about 45 minutes later. We checked into a warm room, ate some fried chicken, and passed out. The following day, we managed to get out of the Andes and started making our way up the coast. The coastline in Peru is not particularly exciting at all so our plan was just to stick on the Pan American highway and charge towards Ecuador as quickly as possible.

The highway runs right alongside the Pacific, but most of the time there is just a big bank of sand and grit to your right and, for us, a grey sky with a moody-looking ocean to your left. It was okay but not somewhere I felt guilty about speeding past. The best part of each day was the lunch. The cheapest thing around was always a set, two-course lunch with a soup and a main. We had no idea what we were ordering so it always came as a surprise and it was usually really tasty. On the third day of our journey north though, something hadn't sat quite right with me and I had a serious case of the squits. That happens from time to time on a trip like this and it's not usually a big problem. On this occasion though, the only toilet available was the one in our bedroom at the guesthouse we were staying at, and for some reason that toilet didn't have a door. It must have been absolutely disgusting for Reece. The room stank and I was getting up every half an hour or so with food poisoning. Truly gross.

I was feeling pretty rough the following morning, and before we could set off for another day of riding towards Ecuador we needed to change the sidecar wheel. It was fouling against the new shocks we had bought in La Paz and we finally decided it was time to do something about it. We took it to a local garage and started working on it in the forecourt. Pretty much done, Reece was lying under the bike just doing some final checks and tightening it off when a guy behind us nearly killed him. He'd had some news he wasn't happy about, got in a strop, and I saw him jump in his car and slam the door. Then he bashed it into reverse and sped backwards way too fast, heading right for Reece's lower half. I watched it all unfold but I was like a rabbit in headlights and for some reason couldn't shout. Fortunately, my legs were still functioning, and I threw myself into the back of his car and bounced back off, at which point he slammed on his brakes, grinding to a halt about two inches from Reece's feet.

I flipped off the handle. I don't know why; I never really get angry at all but there was something about this guy's idiocy that really got on my wick. I ran around to the driver's side and gave him an absolute rollicking. He was completely shocked, he'd had no idea Reece was there and certainly didn't expect a nerdy English bloke to fling open his door and call him a blithering idiot. Just as in Sudan though, it was another case of me getting food poisoning and then saving Reece's life in the morning to make up for it. They say things come in threes, so from then on if I ever got ill I made sure Reece was wrapped up in cotton wool for the following day.

We got the tyre changed and pressed on north. After the best part of a week cheesing it along the Peruvian coast, we were excited to turn inland and head for Ecuador. We skipped through the border no problem and made it to the town of El Guabo. The drive was fantastic and we swapped the long barren coast in Peru for rolling hills full of luscious green forest in Ecuador. After a good night's kip we pressed on north again and the environment changed dramatically. We had gone from rainforest to banana plantations out of nowhere. They were incredible to see and seemed to extend to the horizon in every direction. We were pressing on happily and then all of a sudden a plane flew right over the top of us.

"Wow, Jesus, he was low! What the hell was that about?" I said to Reece over the intercom.

"I don't know mate but there he goes again," replied Reece. The plane banked to its right and started tracking towards us. As it approached, a load of mist dropped out behind it.

"Pesticide planes!" I shouted and, as I did, it swooped over the top of us. I was driving and my visor was open, so I got absolutely soaked in the stuff. It took me a minute or two to breathe and the chemicals felt nasty. It felt like somebody had just chucked a load of weed killer on me—because they had. Spraying crops in that way is used on big agriculture plantations all over the world. I think they even use it in some places in the UK. It's fine if used appropriately. Fly low, drop on a day when there's no wind, make sure you hit the target, etc. Here in El Guabo, they most certainly were not doing that and instead they were drenching the local population in the stuff. Two minutes later we passed a lady stood outside her home, in shorts and t-shirt, and she got drenched head to toe.

It was awful. For us, it was no problem, we were in full motorcycle gear and had a couple of seconds of discomfort. For the lady by the roadside, she has to bring up her family under the constant bombardment of planes releasing potentially carcinogenic, highly hazardous substances on her. I've studied this kind of stuff in the past at university, so I was aware of the fact it's fairly common throughout Central and South America. It can have devastating impacts on communities. There are horror stories where 90% of the kids in the town have lesions on their skin and parents are dying from kidney disease and skin cancer as a result of the overexposure to the pesticides. I thought it would probably be the case here, too. I knew the region couldn't be an ethical producer because the only proper way to use that technique is not to drop pesticides near the roads, on people or near water sources. However, when I jumped on Google it became apparent that this region of Ecuador is known for its Fair Trade banana plantations.

I was pretty shocked by that and felt a bit betrayed but, in reality, it is still worth spending the extra 40p per bunch on a Fair Trade sticker. At the end of the day nobody set up Fair Trade to con anyone, it's just a complex thing to manage. Remember when you were at school and the teacher used to say, "Behave today because the inspectors are coming in." Well, that surely happens on plantations too and it's far more complex with an issue as big as this. Big agriculture is incredibly powerful, and bribes and intimidation techniques are common. It's easy to jump to the conclusion that we shouldn't buy Fair Trade because they don't make sure that the product is as good as they say it is, but in reality we should actually buy more, to give them the resources they need to make sure it is Fair in the future. Not buying Fair Trade just leaves the lady on the side of the road entirely at the mercy of big business and, in reality, with no hope at all.

That night we pulled into Quito where we were going to be staying in absolute luxury. Reece's mum, Debbie, and stepdad, Marc, had flown out to see us. They had been to see Reece's little brother get married in Vegas (congratulations once again Liam and Jasmine), and then they tagged on a little trip to see us. They had rented out an unreal Airbnb for about a hundred quid a night. Normal money by normal adult standards but it gets you a lot in Quito. We had a two-bedroom, gorgeous flat, with access to a Jacuzzi and a steam room. Incredible stuff. They had brought us another clutch too, so we decided we would take a week off, do some repairs, and have a bit of a holiday with them. Before I knew it, we were off the expedition and I was on my holibobs with my mate and his parents.

It was all good fun, until I fell off a horse. Really nasty business. We had got a cable car up to the mountains around Quito and you can press right onto the top on horseback if you like. I loved the idea but, on the way back down, my saddle slipped off and I fell with it. I had landed really hard on my back, and I was in complete agony straight away. It seized up and I could barely move for the next few days. It was fun to have Deb and Marc there and it was great, too, because Reece was still crying most nights since Paris, so their comforting presence gave us some time away from the tears. They decided we should hire a car and go and explore Ecuador a bit. We went out to the fringes of the Amazon rainforest and had a lot of fun messing around in waterfalls and the like.

Before long though, it was time for them to fly off and the waterworks came back on. Not only because Reece was missing his mum again but because the next part of the ride would mean crossing into Colombia, through a region where there had been a recent rise in kidnappings by rebel groups. We were praying that we wouldn't be mistaken for a bright red pot of ransom money scooting through at a snail's pace!

"You're here for a blister?" At Land's End, Cornwall. The start of our 'UK tour,' which led to Reece winding up in A&E.

"Time to 'suck it and see.'" At the start line with the London to Paris Rally attendees all sticking their middle fingers up to modern slavery.

"That's better!" Reece feeling cheery with sausage and mash at a secondary school in Kranj, Slovenia.

"One and a bit!" Measuring the length of the bike using Reece's height in Athens.

"Pass the thing Farouk!" Midnight football with our new friends in Alexandria.

"Scooting the Sahara." One of the many long, searingly hot stetches of perfect tarmac cutting through Egypt.

"Watch out for the crocs!" Camped up by the Nile in Sudan. With only the sounds of farmers singing in the distance and a blanket of incredible stars to gaze at above, there is no better place to spend a night.

"Where's the tarmac gone fellas?" Confusion all round as we come to the end of a road in Ethiopia.

"It's done for mate!" The police beating back the crowd as we break down in the middle of Timkat Festival, Ethiopia.

"Live well" The Kuishi na Kuishi team in Tanzania. It was great to help build the place the sidecar is named after. I hope to one day go back and stay in one of their eco-lodges.

"We made it!" Reece and I with Chels and Brian—the Irish guy we'd met in Ethiopia—having made it to Cape Town.

"Bloody gorgeous, mate." Warming up in the naturally hot pools at the start of the Lagunas Route in Bolivia.

"Gasping for air that just wasn't there." Pushing the bike uphill at 5,000 meters above sea level in the Andes.

"I can't feel my arms." Riding pillion, with a broken sidecar, along the final stretch of corrugated track towards Uyuni, Bolivia.

"Want to swap guys?" Upstaged by the Mexican police in the Yucatan!

"Coffee boys?" Sunrise from my hammock at the Handle Bar and Grill on
Route 66 in Amarillo, Texas.

"We look cool in these hats, mate." Pretending to be cowboys at a longhorn cattle ranch in Dallas. (*Photo courtesy Jill Coultas*)

"It's like Mars!" Scooting the Garden of the Gods in Colorado.

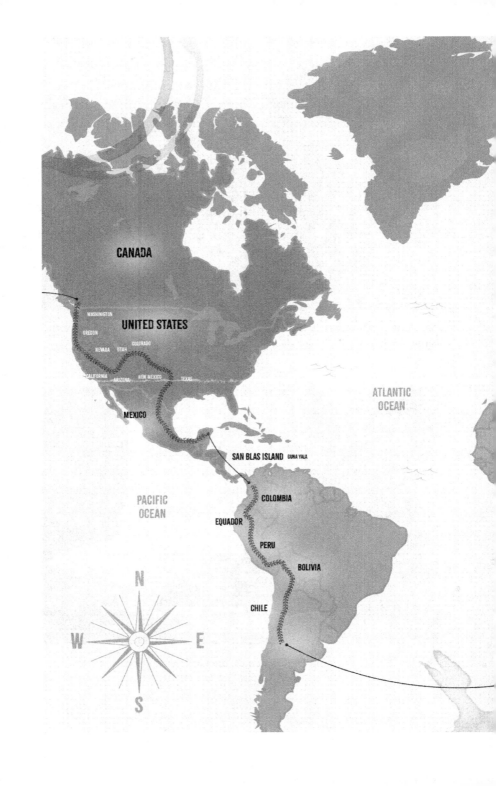

THE SIDECAR GUYS

RUSSIA

TRANS-SIBERIAN HIGHWAY TO ST PETERSBURG

ESTONIA

UNITED KINGDOM

LATVIA

LITHUANIA

NETHERLANDS

GERMANY POLAND

BELGIUM

FRANCE SWITZERLAND

SLOVENIA

ITALY BOSNIA AND

CROATIA HERZEGOVINA

ALBANIA MONTENEGRO

GREECE

VLADIVOSTOK

EGYPT

SUDAN

ETHIOPIA

KENYA

INDIAN OCEAN

MALAWI TANZANIA

ZAMBIA

ZIMBABWE

SOUTH AFRICA

5 CONTINENTS VISITED ✓

35 COUNTRIES VISITED ✓

34K MILES TRAVELLED ✓

455 DAYS TRAVELLING ✓

1361 HOURS ON THE ROAD ✓

Map by Oliver Bennet of More Visual

"Are we nearly there yet?" Fighting the trucks at sunset along the Trans-Siberian Highway.

"Thanks for warming us up!" Waving goodbye to Sanya and the lads in Krasnoyarsk, having survived our first night of proper Russian hospitality.

"That's better!" Warming up at a roadside services in Siberia.

"The Visor Dilemma." Frozen visor vs frozen face.

"Don't want to ruin my trousers!" Doing repairs in his underwear, our new Russian friend welds a fix-up for the road ahead.

"I'm not convinced we'll get up that, mate." Snowy hills in the Ural Mountains.

"I think I'll make yellow snow!" A Russian roadside toilet.

"More borscht, please." Warming up our toes and insulated boots in a roadside café in Siberia.

"You're starting to realise the real danger is Russian hospitality!" Bike post fun in Chelyabinsk.

"I am not crazy, I am an athlete" Bartosz and I trying to stop Gerard's bike falling back on top of him.

"You did it for Britain and you did it for Banbury!" Charlie Prescott welcomes us in at the Ace Café in London.

"Thanks for everything fellas!" With the team that built Kuishi na Kuishi at the Ace Café. Left to right: me, Malcolm Kew, Charlie Prescott, Richard Prescott, Reece.

"Congratulations boys, you made Banbury proud!" Arriving to a mayoral reception at the Banbury town hall.

"Catch you later, mate." Waving goodbye as Reece drops me off at the end of trip.

– 14 –

"I TURNED AROUND TO SEE CHELS STOOD AT THE END OF THE JETTY SOAKING WET, ANGRY, AND EFFECTIVELY DRIPPING IN RAW SEWAGE."

I looked around me and the entire room was on the edge of its seat. I looked back in the direction of Reece and he was shaking with nerves. I don't know if it was the heat or the anticipation, but I could feel beads of sweat dripping down my forehead. Could this genuinely be about to happen? Were we about to witness the unthinkable? Jitske was looking away, she couldn't bear to watch. Reece took a step closer, looked around the room one last time, knowing that whether he pulled this off or not, life would never be the same again. Then he zoned in on the task that awaited him. He slowly lifted his shaking hand towards the block, grabbed it with his index finger and thumb and gently pulled it out. The tower shook, but it didn't fall, and the room erupted with cheers! Reece turned with a stern scowl. His work was not yet finished. He turned back to the table and placed the block back on top of the tower. It held. We'd done it. Pints flew in the air. Cheers and high fives all around. We actually did it, we actually completed Jenga!

After Reece's parents left Quito we decided to stay on for a night or two and hang out with an old friend, Jitske, whom we had met back in New Zealand in 2011. Jitske said we could stay at her place if we liked and she'd show us around the non-touristy side of Quito. That's what had led to us playing giant Jenga with Jitske and her house mates in a micro-brewery. We were amazed when we entered the brewery. It was like being transported back to Bermondsey in London. Top-quality pints all served in a hipster-style setting with massive board games to play if you so desire. It was a lot of fun and cool to see a different side of the city.

We stayed at Jitske's place for a couple of nights, mainly because it was fun and there was a gorgeous little balcony to hang out on but also because we needed a base to work out plans for getting around the Darien. We had a lot of decisions to make. Originally, we decided we would try and get the bike onto a boat and sail through the incredible San Blas Islands to Panama. It seemed a no-brainer. What a completely awesome thing to have to do. We made some enquiries about it and sent off to various companies to see if they could squeeze Kuishi on. At the same time, we started looking into other options. We had been writing off to organisations that might be able to set us up with modern slavery charities to visit in Central America when one organisation, the Environmental Network for Central America (ENCA), pointed out to us that the political situation in Nicaragua was spiraling out of control. They suggested that we organise a Plan B just in case and look into shipping north of Nicaragua. We thought it would be unlikely that we'd end up skipping Central America but we did send out some emails and put some posts on the overlanding forums before setting off to Colombia.

Our first day from Quito to Otavio was a breeze, just a couple of hundred kilometres. We could have gone a lot further, but we wanted to be absolutely certain that we wouldn't end up driving at night through the area that had seen the spike in kidnappings. The following morning, we set off for the Colombia border. We arrived and found queues that seemed to snake back for miles. The language barrier meant we couldn't find out too much, but we got the distinct impression that people had been there for days. We later found out that it was due to the troubles in Venezuela at the time. At first, we thought we should join the queue but then we remembered we were white and, relatively speaking, rich, so we probably wouldn't need to. Sure enough, we walked straight past the line of fairly desperate looking families, who had been there for days and got put to the front of the queue.

We felt pretty guilty, but us waiting for a couple of days in a border queue not being able to interact with anyone on account of the fact we were ignorant (as well as white and rich) and didn't speak the language, would have been a fairly pointless way to cleanse said guilt. We grabbed some fried chicken, stamped in the bike using our carnet de passage and pressed on into the kidnap zone. Of course, as is nearly always the case, we were completely fine and had no trouble at all in the area. We made it all the way through to the first big town of Colombia, Pasto.

We pulled into Pasto and pulled out our laptops to see if we'd had any news on the Darien Gap situation. We had three emails. The first was from the Stahlratte, a popular sailing boat that takes motorcyclists through the San Blas to Panama. They said there was no way any sailing boat would be able to take us across as it would be too difficult to get the outfit onto the boat. Damn, that's that dream done for, then. The second email was from a tour company called San Blas Adventures. It said that there was no way we would be able to get the bike on their boat but because they loved the trip they would give us two free slots on a tour that would take us from Cartagena to Panama. Incredible. So, all we had to do was get the bike in a container to Panama and we were sorted. The third email was from Martin Mowforth, my old university lecturer and chair of ENCA. He told us that there were reports of Nicaragua heading towards a new civil war. All of the main roads had been dug up and blockades had been erected with some of the protesters being heavily armed.

It was quite the conundrum. We knew we'd be fine going through Nicaragua. The protestors weren't protesting against scooter and sidecarists, so they'd be unlikely to use their machine guns on us. The problem was, though, that the roads were impassable. Some bike forums were saying that you could still get through but with big sections of off-roading. Fresh off the back of the Lagunas Route, there was no way we were going to plan for that. We decided that we would need to ship around Nicaragua. After much research, we realised the only way to do that would be to ship all the way to Mexico. Pretty disappointing but better than getting stuck in a country on the brink of civil war. We found a couple of overlanders online who had already come to the same conclusion as us and we decided we would all share a container to the Yucatan region of Mexico. We would be sharing with a Canadian guy called Che, on a motorbike, and a French couple, Victor and Mane, who had a motor home. All was good, we would put the bike in the container, take the San Blas guys up on their offer and then hop on a flight from Panama City to meet the bike, sorted. The only catch was that the boat left in a week and we'd have to blast through Colombia to catch it.

We had learnt by now that if you get any opportunity to ship you should take it, plus 1,000 miles in a week was just about doable. We decided that we would get our heads down early and be off at the crack of dawn to rack up some miles. We were staying in a small guesthouse that was ideal: super cheap and super clean. We had a tiny room that had two single beds and just enough space to throw our bags down the middle. We chilled out on our phones, watched a bit of something on Netflix, and then it was time to hit the hay.

"Bang!" Something hit the floor across the room and woke me up. There was a deep rumbling kind of sound and the whole room seemed to be shaking. "Oh my God! It's a fricking earthquake!" I thought to myself. I flicked on the light next to my head but the quake had already knocked out the power. It was still going and seemingly getting stronger.

"Mate, wake up!" I shouted to Reece. "Wake up!!"

"What's happening?" Reece was instantly awake too. The room was still shaking. We could barely see anything at all. It was shaking so much it felt like it could cave in at any minute. A car alarm started going off in the street outside. It was all very dramatic and then, suddenly, the shaking stopped.

"It was a fricking earthquake, mate. That was mental. So strong! Put your torch on your phone on."

The room was pretty much how we had left it the night before. No obvious damage or anything. It was 4:35 a.m. and still dark outside.

"What do we do now?" Reece said.

"I'm not sure, mate, what if there's an aftershock and it's bigger? Maybe we should get out of the building?" I replied.

We took a look out of the window. Nothing going on. "Maybe this is normal here?" I said.

Lay in our beds, we deliberated for a minute or two when suddenly another massive shake.

"Shit!" shouted Reece.

We both instinctively lifted the covers over our heads, a genius move. We just waited, praying the roof wouldn't fall in. Fortunately, it didn't. Still no action outside. We lay there for another minute and decided, "Sod it, it hasn't collapsed yet, it will probably be fine," and went back to sleep. We woke up a couple of hours later to find out it was 4.9 on the Richter scale and the epicentre had been just 20 km away so it had felt huge. It was genuinely scary. I can't imagine what it must be like to be in a truly massive earthquake—I hope I never find out.

We had a spot of breakfast and had that kind of buzz you get after surviving a bit of a scare. We were alive and today would be a good day. We set off for the next town, Popayan. The Colombian countryside is just breathtaking and we spent all morning racking up the miles as we twisted and turned through the luscious green mountains. All was going swimmingly and then, "Bang!" Reece had hit a huge rock in the middle of the road. He had seen it and swerved but it struck the sidecar tyre. We had a split second where we thought it was okay and then, "Dum, dum, dum, dum, dum, dum, dum." The sidecar wheel had gone completely flat. We pulled off to the side of the road and found that there was a huge dent in the wheel. It was done for. We made a desperate attempt to fix it using Quick Steel, which is like PlayDoh but sets like, well, steel. It didn't work at all. We had only one option left and that was to start flagging down the public.

It was scorching hot, so we changed into shorts and t-shirts and slapped on the factor 50 before holding our thumbs out. After about fifteen minutes, somebody pulled in. Dressed head to toe in airy white clothes, Juan asked if he could help. Unfortunately, he didn't carry a spare 12" rim sidecar wheel so couldn't do anything more than drive to the next town and send the police back to find us. About forty-five minutes later a police pickup truck arrived and out popped a couple of guys in full camo uniform. They couldn't speak any English at all but it didn't take much effort to tell them we were in a complete pickle. We used Google Translate to ask if they knew the number of any recovery vehicles we could call, but, incredibly, they didn't. They scratched their heads for a minute and then turned to the same conclusion we did and started flagging down the passing public for help. The first vehicle they stopped was a big, flat-bed lorry. The driver was happy to take us on to the next town but, unfortunately, we couldn't lift the rig onto the back. Incredibly, the next vehicle to pass was a car transporter. The police flagged them down and the next thing we knew we were loaded up and heading for a repair shop further along the road.

About 20 km later we pulled into the town of Remolino and set about trying to get the bike fixed. We found a little workshop and a few guys who were happy to give it a go. It soon became apparent that there was no way we were going to drive on that day, so we popped up the road and checked into the only guesthouse in this tiny town. The guesthouse was just a couple of rooms above a restaurant and the plastic mattress covers indicated the usual clientele were more likely to book by the hour. Still, for what was most likely a roadside brothel, it was fairly clean. By nightfall the fellas had managed to fix up the wheel and it was holding air. We weren't convinced it was going to hold but maybe it would get us to the next major town, and we could try and find a replacement. We awoke the following morning, jumped in the rig, and set off back to where we had broken down. We managed to get 500 metres outside of town when we ground to a halt with a flat sidecar wheel. It was done for. We pushed the rig back to the lads on the rim and they just laughed. The only option we had was to go back to Pasto by bus and hope to find a replacement wheel there.

We left the sidecar and all of our kit with the guesthouse before checking out and heading off for a one-night stay in Pasto. The bus we took was a pickup truck fitted with seats in the back and a bit of tarpaulin over the top to shield you from the elements. We were the first ones in the truck and waited for about an hour while the driver slowly crammed as many people as humanly possible in alongside us. An uncomfortable but scenic two hours later and we were back in Pasto.

We had no idea where to start looking and agreed that it would be a miracle if we found anything that would work. We asked the bus driver to point us in the direction of a wheel shop and we just followed his directions to the first one we could find. It had wheels alright, hundreds of the things, stacked two stories high and all bigger than the entire sidecar. It was a truck wheel shop. We asked at reception if they knew anywhere that might have something a little smaller and two minutes later a very polite man called Carlos came out to offer his help. We got chatting to Carlos who was the owner of this shop and, although he couldn't help us directly, he went above and beyond to help find what we were looking for. The three of us jumped into his car and drove around Pasto for hours on end, trying various motorbike shops until, finally, one came up with the goods. It was a miracle! When we tried to give Carlos money for urgently chauffeuring us around to find what we were looking for, he politely declined and just said, "This is life. Today I help you, tomorrow you help me." What a guy!

The following morning, we returned to the fellas in Remolino and got the bike fixed up ready to crack on again. We were pretty eager to get going and not keen on staying in the "guesthouse" again, so we left the wheel with the lads and went to pack up our stuff. We returned an hour later, expecting to set off, but found that they had stopped working on the bike. At first, we were a bit annoyed but soon realised it was for good reason. It was the opening ceremony of the World Cup in Russia and Robbie Williams was on stage strutting his stuff. We grabbed a Fanta, pulled up one of those tiny plastic chairs and huddled around the TV with guys. After watching the hosts thrash Saudi Arabia 5-0, we fixed the bike up, returned to where we had the breakdown, and trucked on to Popayan.

We arrived in Popayan to a message from a British couple called Paul and Yvette. They had been riding around South America on their motorbikes but had fallen in love with Colombia so stopped to set up their own guesthouse in the mountains. They said we could stop for free for the night if we were passing through and it just so happened that they were bang en route. It was important that they were on the route because we now had to rack up 1,600 km in three days if we were going to make our boat.

Fortunately, the following day was a pretty routine drive and we were able to make the 600 km to Paul and Yvette's. We twisted and turned through the wonderful luscious forest that makes up the Colombian countryside and had a great day. As we travelled, we regularly passed heavily armed members of the police force or the army. They were lovely fellas and almost every single one put their thumbs up as we drove by. We thought they were just super friendly or could appreciate a good scooter and sidecar when they saw one, but we later found out it was a signal to say there was no FARC in the area. Paul and Yvette's place was called the Steel Horse and it was incredible. The setting is out of this world and the place itself is gorgeous. We hung out with a couple of other bikers, ate some amazing fajitas, and planned for the road ahead.

Paul took us to the local village for breakfast the following morning and we had a delicious pork and bean soup. Well rested and fueled up ready for the ride ahead, we set off hoping to rack up another 600 km or more. Unfortunately, the Colombian roads had other thoughts. There was maintenance going on and large stretches of road were down to a single lane of traffic resulting in queues for twenty minutes or more while hundreds of cars came from the other direction. We must have waited in that kind of queue ten or fifteen times and the progress was exceptionally slow. Having only made it 300 km, we would have to make over 700 km the following day if we were going to catch our boat. It was further than we had ever tried to go in a day and it wasn't as if we would be going down a straight desert highway, we would have to contend with twisting mountain passes and Colombian road works.

We set off the following morning at 4 a.m., an hour before first light. We scooted through the hills and past Medellin, the city made famous by Pablo Escobar. Apparently, they've cashed in on his story there and you can go and play paintballing in one of his old mansions. One of your group will be given the role of Pablo and the rest of you will hunt around the house pretending to be the police, trying to find him. A pretty messed-up concept when you consider how many lives were lost. In fact, the house is supposedly owned by one of Pablo's ex-servants and he gives a talk about how he shot at the police in gunfights at the house. With no time to check out Pablo's old stomping ground for ourselves, we cracked on towards Cartagena.

We arrived at the outskirts just after 8 p.m. We were completely shattered and verging on delusional. We were so out of it that Reece actually left his wallet on the roof of the sidecar and drove off, leaving it in our dust. We did eventually make it to our guesthouse though, where we met a very relieved Che. We were hugely relieved to have made it, too. It was a rushed finish to the end of the South American leg of the trip, but we were super excited to have reached another milestone and to be shipping on to another continent.

The following morning Chels arrived on a flight from Jamaica. It had been a few months since we had seen each other in South Africa so we were super excited to be able to spend some time together again. The bike would take the best part of three weeks to make it to the port in Veracruz so Chels had decided to book on and join us on the trip though the San Blas. As we had planned well in advance, we knew it would be simple to get the bike shipped and it would just take a day of me signing things at the port before we were free to enjoy Colombia. Obviously, as is always the case with shipping, it wasn't that easy. We arrived at the port to find that the boat we had been chasing had been cancelled and we would have to wait a few days to catch the next one. Pretty annoying considering how much we had rushed to get there, but we were all happy with a few days off and a chance to explore Cartagena.

It's an awesome little city. You can spend days exploring its quaint cobbled streets and admiring the colourful colonial architecture. Each building seems to have some kind of vibrant artwork plastered across it and there's an excited buzz about the place. Although, that buzz may have just been because the World Cup was just getting underway and the Colombians are huge football fans. While we were there, a 3-0 win over Poland sent the city into a full day of celebrations, with street parades and cheering everywhere.

When it finally came to the day in which we would check the bike in at the port, Che became really ill. We went by to pick him up from his hostel and he was a complete mess. He could barely stand up and wasn't at all safe to ride down to the port. In the interest of not missing another boat though, he flopped into the sidecar and I rode his motorbike down to the port. It was a long, hot day of organising paperwork and Che spent most of it curled up in a ball or chucking up in the toilets. He was as white as a ghost and shaking all day—I don't know how he did it.

With the scooter on the boat we could say we had finally finished this part of the journey. We had scooted 6,000 miles through five countries and had a great time doing it, but we couldn't help but feel a bit disappointed that we hadn't managed to learn anything about modern slavery on this continent. It had proved difficult to find organisations all over the world and even more so in South America. I guess the language barrier didn't help. Jo, Reece's sister-in-law had helped us translate emails and we reached out to as many organisations as we could find but just as was the case with many other parts of the world we couldn't find an organisation from which we could learn from and, crucially, which we could help rather than just waste their time. Not all anti-slavery organisations have 'awareness raising' and 'fundraising' at the top of their agenda.

It wasn't a lack of time or anything we'd had a month of waiting for the shipping to get stuff arranged. We just couldn't find any organisation for whom telling us about the issue would be a good use of their time. Still, we thought we could at least do some research about the issue and what it looked like in this part of the world. Colombia itself has a population of over 48 million people and over 300,000 of them are thought to be living in a life of slavery. But that's just Colombia. It's estimated that there are a massive 1.2 million people enslaved across the South American continent. The main forms of slavery within the continent are forced labour, usually targeted towards uneducated men; sexual exploitation, which mainly affects LGBT groups, women and children; and, at times, there have also been reported cases of forced begging.

Through our research we also came across a small town called San Basilio de Palenque. San Basilio is said to be the first town in the Americas free from slavery and it just so happened that it was little more than 50 km from Cartagena. As we hadn't managed to connect with any anti-slavery organisations, we thought it would be a good idea to check out a place of considerable historic importance in the fight against slavery. Naturally we thought the only way to get there would be by motorcycle and amazingly a local rental place called Motorcycle Hire Cartagena offered to lend us a couple of bikes for the day.

To our surprise, when we arrived at San Basilio, it felt like we had stepped back three months into Africa. Very few, if any, "Colombians" live there, and most people identify as African. We spoke to a few people, who were extremely welcoming, and asked them about slavery and San Basilio de Palenque. They took us to the statue of Benkos Bioho, who established the community of San Basilio when he escaped from a life of slavery in the sixteenth century.

We tried to chat to them about modern slavery in Colombia, too. We asked them if they thought slavery still existed and they of course said no. We tried to let them know that Benkos Bioho's work was not yet done and there were still 300,000 people enslaved in Colombia, but we would have needed a few months in the village to get that message across.

After Cartagena, we caught a bus to a town called Necocli, where we caught a local boat over to the very edge of the Darien Gap, to a tiny village called Sapzurro. The boat ride there was hilarious. It was a small motorboat that carried around twenty people, sat in rows, like a bus. The first two minutes were a bit bumpy and I looked at Reece and laughed knowing that he gets awful sea sickness and would likely be a mess in five minutes. Then out of nowhere the captain cranked it up a gear and we were suddenly tearing towards Sapzurro at double the speed. The water was pouring over the sides of the boat non-stop and we were getting completely drenched. There was no respite whatsoever. No chance to be seasick. It was a solid hour of being nailed in the face by wave after wave of sea water. Thoroughly cooled off and

191

soaking wet from head to toe, we arrived at the other side completely baffled by the whole experience.

We stayed in Sapzurro for a couple of days and trekked off into the forest to swim in some waterfalls. The village is like a time capsule. There are no roads and subsequently no cars. There is one stretch of tarmac in the village and it's a small air strip. When you fly in, there are no arrival halls, just a horse and cart waiting to whiz you into the village. The village itself is a tiny tourist town and made up of about ten or twenty hostels, guesthouses, bars, and restaurants. We celebrated Reece's birthday there with several empanadas and several pints. It was a pretty cool place to have a birthday, but I think Reece was probably missing home more than celebrating the moment. It was easier for me, as Chels was regularly flying in and making it feel like home, but the previous love of Reece's life was still dating that bearded bloke while Reece was circumnavigating the globe with his idiot mate. I think he probably questioned what the hell he was doing again. That's not to say he wasn't over Anuschka, I'm pretty sure that train had sailed long before. It can just feel a bit lonely on your birthday, when you're away for a long time. A bit like being away for Christmas, I guess.

Reece was suitably cheered up the following day, though, when we were introduced to the group we would be touring the San Blas with. To Reece, nothing says happy birthday like four nights exploring Caribbean islands with a boatload of girls on their gap year. We set off into the San Blas Islands the following morning. Known locally by the name of the Guna Yala, the San Blas Islands are inhabited by the indigenous Guna people. The Guna people are an autonomous group who still live by their own rules in their traditional way. They are an incredibly open and friendly group of people who welcome anyone to visit the islands, although the area is so protected that solo travel is more or less impossible, and you either have the option of racing through on a sailing boat or island-hopping with the Guna people on their local boats. San Blas Adventures do the latter, which is something we were very pleased about, as it gave us loads of time to hang out on the islands.

There's said to be an island for every day in the Guna Yala and the 365 tiny, picturesque pockets of sand and palm trees that make up the archipelago are absolute paradise. We spent four days lounging around in hammocks, snorkeling in the crystal clear water, and trying to keep up with the Guna guys on the volleyball court. Then at night we either stayed in a hammock on the beach or headed to a Guna village to stay in local lodgings. The island villages are incredible places that are made up of mainly wooden houses which the community builds for every newly married couple. The lodgings are of course very basic, but when else do you get to stay in a room where you can watch the fish through the cracks in the floorboards?

The highlight of the trip was without a doubt getting to know the Guna people en route. As I mentioned earlier, they continue to live very much in their traditional way. For example, there are no police on the islands but instead if you do something wrong you are fined by the village elders. Something wrong can include breaking any normal laws that we live by in the West but also traditional things like drinking the wrong alcohol at the three-day long parties they have every time a girl is born. If I was ever lucky enough to attend one of these parties I would happily accept the fine as the alcohol you must drink is a kind of moonshine that's made in big cauldrons in the days leading up to the event, the secret ingredient being the chef's saliva.

But even though the Guna keep hold of their traditions they are very open to the modern world. Guna people are allowed to do whatever makes them happy. For example, many young people go off to study at university in Panama City and either return with skills to help the community or go to live on the mainland. Equally, the community welcomes you to express who you are and there's no judgment or persecution of the LGBT+ community. Their small shacks and humble way of living may seem like a hard life for us, but at the same time our western world could certainly learn a thing or two on community living from the Guna.

The Gunas have a rich history as well. On the tour we heard tales of how the population decreased to just eight people before they left the mainland to live on the islands. And we visited the village where the Gunas revolted against Panamanian rule on the islands in 1925. All of this history and culture, set in complete paradise, made for an exceptionally interesting and enjoyable few days. Equally, the food was incredible. We dined on a mixture of octopus ceviche, sea snails, and lobsters, which we knew had come straight out of the sea because we found our Guna guide, Edgar, swimming back to shore with a couple of massive lobsters in his hands.

Aside from hanging out with the Guna people, the other main highlight of the trip was arguing with Chels. Sounds odd, but on the second day we were paddling across the islands in a local dugout canoe when I had a big old barney with Chels. It was nothing serious, just me not being very sensitive to the fact that I had driven off around the world, but we were more or less shouting at each other, out there in paradise. As we approached the island Chels decided she just couldn't look at me anymore and jumped ship in order to swim ashore. I pulled up in the boat and our guide, Edgar, told us that we shouldn't swim on this side of the islands as it's where the Guna empty their toilets. I turned around to see Chels stood at the end of the jetty soaking wet, angry, and effectively dripping in raw sewage. I saw the funny side straight away, but it took Chels a few drinks before she started laughing, too.

After our trip through the San Blas Islands, Reece flew off to Las Vegas to meet his dad. A bold move you might think, but we still had a week to kill and Reece's dad and step-mum, Cindie, had flown out to see us. Only problem was that we were a couple of months behind schedule. Fortunately, the flight direct to Mexico City that we had to take was the same price as the flights to Mexico City via Vegas. I was pretty pleased, too, as Chels and I decided to book an Airbnb on the beach in Panama and chill out for a few days. It was a brilliant few days of relaxing on the beach and a great way to say bye before I boarded a flight to Mexico City and Chels stayed to explore Panama.

– 15 –

"I CAME OUT TO FIND REECE SAT DOWN ON THE SOFA, PEN IN HAND, SIGNING A HUMAN LEG."

It was the 11th of July, 2017. The clock in the top left-hand corner of the screen showed five minutes played. England's right back, Kieran Trippier, stood with the ball, ready to take the biggest free kick of his life. He coolly placed the ball down, took a few steps back, ran up and smashed it into the top right-hand corner of the goal. The English bar that we were in erupted with cheers. Beer flew everywhere as we all sang, "It's coming home, it's coming, football's coming home," but of course, it didn't come home. Mandžukić, the Croatian centre forward, ended England's dreams with a 109th-minute winner. We were gutted but, in all honesty, we were quite pleased football wasn't going home because we weren't going to be there to greet it. The English bar we were in was, of course, in Mexico City and we were still some way off returning to the UK. We still had to ride to Alaska and then back across Asia and Europe.

We were killing time in Mexico City because our boat was predictably delayed. It was going to be another week at sea, and we knew by now that when a shipping agent tells you a week, they really mean at least two. The World Cup had been a welcome break from the frustrations of arguing with the customs agent, but not on the 11th of July as that was the day the dream ended.

Instead of celebrating a place in the final we were sobbing pathetically into a dodgy pint of Guinness with a load of other Brits abroad, all wondering whether to drown our sorrows in a £10 fish and chips that would blow a few days' food budget and wouldn't be the same anyway.

Fortunately, by the next morning, we had got over our loss and we were ready to crack on with the project once again. We had managed to arrange a visit with another charity fighting modern slavery and we hopped on the subway to meet with an organisation called El Pozo de Vida. Based in Mexico City, El Pozo de Vida is set up with the sole goal of eradicating modern slavery and human trafficking from Mexico.

It turned out El Pozo de Vida has a huge challenge on their hands. First and foremost, it's huge because they focus on Mexico City and that's just a huge place. Twenty million people live in the city, making it the biggest city in the Americas and the biggest Spanish-speaking city on the planet. It's a really brilliant place to explore. If you're a foodie, you'll instantly fall in love with it. Every corner is littered with street vendors all trying to whack out the best tacos and tortas in town. The city is bursting with culture and you could get lost for days as you dive in and out of the tiny streets, huge boulevards, and quirky undercover markets. But behind its flamboyant surface you'll find modern slavery, the same issue that plagues every other major town and city on the planet.

We met Nicole, an El Pozo de Vida employee, to talk about the issue. She told us that El Pozo de Vida estimates there to be 18,000 people living in slavery in Mexico City and that the Global Slavery Index estimates there to be 300,000 across the entire country. In Mexico City that means that roughly one in every 1,100 people is living in slavery. Worldwide, it's believed that 70 percent of modern slavery victims are women and girls and it's the women and girls of Mexico City whom Nicole and the team try to help the most. Nicole told us that in doing so they are often putting themselves on the front line.

Organised crime is what keeps the trafficking going and it turns out that the Cartel don't like it too much when you try to take away their profits. El Pozo de Vida's team has actually received death threats and even had a hand-delivered one turn up at their safe house for survivors. They carry on, working under these huge pressures despite receiving little support from the government or law enforcement. We sat with Nicole and discussed the issue for a few hours. She said that she would love to introduce us to some of the survivors and take us to see their work but because of the situation with organised crime groups they couldn't. It sounded like they were working under immensely difficult conditions. We decided not to take up any more of Nicole's time and told her that we would add El Pozo de Vida to our list of charities that we were raising funds for before we pressed on.

We left Mexico City the next day and jumped on a 36-hour bus to the port town of Progreso in Mexico's Yucatan region. Victor had found out that the boat was stopping south of Veracruz, where we were supposed to be shipping to, so he asked if we could just get our vehicles out there. Amazingly, they let us, and our boat was suddenly in the port! It was a long bus ride south but quicker than waiting another couple of weeks for the boat to crawl up the coast. Plus, the bus ride was absolute luxury compared to travelling by scooter and sidecar.

Another week later and we had survived the port process. It seemed like we were the first people to ever get a vehicle out of the port of Progreso, let alone a scooter and sidecar. We were useless in the whole process and had it not been for Che, Victor, and Manet, who could all speak fluent Spanish, we would probably still be there. After a day of servicing the rig and welding up some broken sidecar joints we were ready to crack on north again.

First stop on our road to Alaska was exploring the Yucatan. We decided to check out a couple of the region's towns and take in the amazing colonial architecture. They did not disappoint, and the towns of Merida and Campeche served as great places to grab a taco and rest our heads before pressing further on. Having camped in Merida we opted for an air-conditioned hostel bed in Campeche. Our night in the tent was one of the hottest nights we've ever had. It was just so humid and after twenty minutes we felt like we were lying in a puddle of sweat. What made it worse was the onslaught of mosquitos. They flooded the tent and completely peppered us all night. It was misery. Fortunately, our spirits were lifted the following day, when we were able to nurse our wounds in one of the Yucatan's cenotes.

If you've not heard of them before, a cenote is a giant sink hole filled with crystal-clear, cool water. Shaded from the sun, with their steep sides, and full of freshwater fish, they are a huge amount of fun to explore. I can't stress just how good it is to be riding along in full motorcycle kit, whip your gear off, and flop into one of these little pockets of paradise. There seems to be a bit of dispute about how they got there but most people we met said the holes were formed by a meteor strike; specifically, the meteor strike that wiped out the dinosaurs. We chose to believe that option, as it's far more interesting than underground rivers carving out holes in the semi-porous rock that makes up the Yucatan's karst environment.

After we had finished frolicking in the paradise that was left behind by the destruction of the dinosaurs, we carried on with our apocalyptic-themed road trip and took a trip to the Palenque ruins. The Mayan ruins at Palenque are considered by many to be the most impressive ruins in all of Mexico. They're over 2,000 years old and date back to 226 BC, when they were known as the ancient city of Lakamha. These particular ruins are famous for being the place where the 21st of December 2012 doomsday prediction was made. Apparently, on the 21st of December 2012, both the local town and the ruins were overrun with believers who had come to Palenque to witness the end of the world. However, the world didn't end. Which was good for most people, but Palenque was in a kind of weird post-apocalyptic chaos with hundreds, if not thousands, of stranded people who had travelled on one-way tickets and had no return passage, or accommodation booked for the 21st.

We pressed on north from Palenque and headed up the spine of Mexico towards the US. We were behind schedule after delays with the shipping and if we wanted to make it to Anchorage before the winter, we had to really put our foot down. We decided we'd rack up a few miles by sticking to the highways, paying the expensive tolls and having a big week or two up to the States. After a couple of days on the road we were making great progress and I put a Facebook post out that said just how well it was going compared to the start of our journey in South America, which had been littered with breakdowns. I could not have jinxed us more.

The next thing we knew, we were on the side of the road sucking petrol out of our tank again. We were making a terrible job of it. After about thirty minutes we had only managed to get around half out and I think a quarter of it was in our stomachs. We were drinking our fuel through a giant straw more successfully than we were siphoning it out. Fortunately, two guys named Gilberto and Francesco saw us struggling and couldn't bear to watch the gringos drink anymore fuel. They took it off us and siphoned it out first time. We cleaned up the filter and were back on the road half an hour later.

We racked up another 100 km or so and began climbing up through the mountains on the way to Puebla. By this time it was about 2 p.m. and despite our earlier problems we were making good progress. However, while we were crawling uphill at a snail's pace, another biker pulled alongside and waved for us to pull over. He had spotted that our front tyre was completely flat. The guy on the bike, Josue, stopped with us and offered to help us get a recovery truck. "No thanks," I said. "We've got a puncture repair kit. Ten minutes and we'll be back on the road." It turned out we couldn't plug the gap and three hours later we were still sat on the side of the highway. Amazingly, Josue was still there with us, as he wanted to make sure we were okay before he left. It was incredibly nice of him to stay and help. It's part of this unwritten code of conduct that seemingly all global bikers know about and adhere to: If another biker needs any kind of help you are required to do everything within your power to get it for them. Everyone does it willingly and I think it's probably the most selfless, universally adopted policy on the planet. We benefitted from it hundreds of times on our trip.

We had been riding along a main highway when Josue pulled us over. It was a hugely expensive toll road which we had previously been moaning about. One good thing about these monstrously expensive stretches of tarmac, though, is that they usually include free recovery. At a cost of around £7 every couple of hundred kilometres, they should include something. Josue got in touch with the recovery people around ten minutes after we couldn't fix it and they were dispatched to come and find us. Three hours later and they still hadn't arrived. The local police force had, though. They dropped in to make sure everything was okay. Josue was really nervous when they first arrived but then breathed a huge sigh of relief and wrote in his translator app, "These are good police," and "They are scared of your embassy." We were quite pleased about that and we all decided to carry on waiting together.

Another hour later and the recovery truck turned up. Josue asked them to take us to the nearest town where we could find a garage and a hotel. They declined and said they could only take us to the next exit of the toll road where we would be left to sort ourselves out, not such good value after all. By this time, it was pitch black and there was no way we were leaving the relative safety of the police guys and Josue to sit on the side of the road somewhere else. Instead we asked the police guys if we could just lift the bike onto their pickup and then they could take us to the next town. To our amazement they said yes. Exciting stuff, we hadn't been on a police truck since Ethiopia! Somewhat experienced in the matter, we got the rig on the back of the pickup and strapped it down ready to go in no time. Then we climbed on and clung onto it for dear life as the police flew down the motorway at what must have been 80 mph, at night, with us hanging on in the back.

We arrived at a hotel about twenty minutes later and were told there was no room at the inn. One of our new friends in blue walked in with us and asked again, and suddenly there was a twin room available and we stayed the night in relative luxury. The following day we fixed the tyre and did a few kilometres up to Puebla, where we decided to relax for the afternoon.

Next, we set off north, headed for Queretaro. We piled on another couple of hundred kilometres before we broke down once again. Another flat. This time it was the sidecar tyre. Again, we couldn't plug it. It was leaking from a patch that the guys back in Pasto had put on. We couldn't believe it. This time there was no Josue so, with no mobile phone, and nobody to call anyway, we put our thumbs out and again hoped for a saviour. The recovery guys came again. They blew up our tyre and it held long enough for us to get into a roadside café. We sat down, grabbed a Coke, ordered a massive torta and rang for a proper recovery truck through our Mexican road insurance. They asked us to wait for a while. After six hours of chess, they finally arrived. We stuck it on the back of their truck and made our way to the nearest town. We were annoyed about the wait but couldn't stay angry at the recovery guy for long as he had an absolutely brilliant selection of music for the drive north, mainly power ballads. I'm talking Meatloaf, Tina Turner, the full works. He seemed to know every word but couldn't speak a word of English.

The following morning, we patched the tyre up in a local repair shop before returning to our breakdown spot and cracking on further north again. After those nightmare few days the jinx was lifted and the riding became less troublesome. We were able to enjoy scooting through the beautiful Mexican countryside, appreciating the colonial towns, and gorging on cheap, fantastic street food as we passed through. Everyone worries about safety in Mexico but ultimately if you're not into drugs or prostitutes, you'll be fine. Don't get mixed up in stuff the cartels like to be involved in and you (probably) won't come across them. There are reports of dangers for sure and people definitely get caught in the crossfire from time to time but, generally speaking, don't be an idiot and you'll get to appreciate Mexico for the incredible place that it is, an awesome country full of awesome people.

We decided to cross the border into the States at Laredo, as we were heading in the general direction of Reece's cousin's house in Dallas. The biggest headache was getting our road insurance sorted, but once that was done, we were ready to enter the USA and start a road trip most people could only dream of, riding all the way from the Mexico border to Alaska. The border crossing was super simple and nobody was questioning us. It's probably one of the most stringent border crossings in the world, but at the end of the day we're a couple of white guys in a quirky vehicle, doing something crazy for a good cause. We could have cocaine coming out of our ears and nobody would have noticed. In fact, at one checkpoint, the border guard said, "Wow, yahoo, I'm not even gonna bother checking you guys, through you go!" As easy as that and we were into the States!

"Hello, just the petrol please," I said as I approached the till in our first petrol station, after we crossed the border. The comment was met with nervous giggling by the lady, in her mid-50s, who was manning the cashier.

"Where y'all from?" she responded in a thick Texas accent.

"England."

"Wow . . . hehehe . . . I figured!" said the lady, as she tried to control her nervous outbursts of laughter. She had gone bright red and was completely hysterical. I had never experienced anything like it. I had been in the USA for ten minutes and suddenly, I was Bishop, Matt Bishop, and my voice was now a lethal weapon. Colin from Love Actually had been right all along, American girls would dig my cute British accent. I had just been on the wrong continent. Well, of course, I was—and still am—a spoken-for man, so I hadn't been on the wrong continent at all. Reece, on the other hand, was still free, single, and ready to mingle. I came outside to inform him of the good news and found him already using his powers as an international man of mystery on an elderly chap in his mid-60s. They were deep in conversation about our rig. It was a conversation we would have more or less every time we stopped from here all the way to Canada. You can say what you like about people from the States, but if you're a couple of Brits on a quirky bike then they are an exceptionally friendly bunch. Reece's chat went on for about thirty minutes and after a family picture, we were free to head on into the fried chicken joint that was next door to the petrol station.

After a solid month of tacos, the cheapest thing we could eat in Mexico, we were keen to eat the cheapest thing we could find in the US. Usually, the cheapest thing isn't that healthy, but you can survive on it. Granted, tacos are greasy, the chips in Kenya got a bit much, and the chunks of meat in Sudan would eventually have sent us to an early grave, but nothing could prepare us for the cheapest things to eat and drink in the land of the Big Mac. In Texas a Pepsi is half the price of a bottle of water and a bucket of fried chicken that will fill you for the day will come in less than a ham sarnie each. That day we spent a solid hour sat in the air-conditioned Church's Chicken, gorging on fried stuff and trying to find the bottom of a bottomless cup of Pepsi. It was grotesque.

We stumbled out of Church's, had another chat about the rig, and got back in the seat to start our US road trip. By this time, it was getting pretty late and just because we could, we thought we'd pull into a motel like they do in the movies. It was expensive. Forty dollars for the night. Looking back that seems pretty cheap but we were going around the world and our budget was half that, tops. We stayed nonetheless; our chicken coma was catching up with us and we had little choice but to get out of the heat and into the relative comfort of another air-conditioned room. We were celebrating, too, as we had hit 20,000 miles for the trip. I don't know why that was something to celebrate but any excuse for a treat. I think that was probably the only night we paid for accommodation in the States. It's a wild camping paradise and there are plenty of friendly people to take you in.

The following day we chalked off 200 miles to Austin. It was incredibly hot, the kind of heat where being on the bike doesn't help, you just get the hair dryer effect. Fortunately, air-conditioned convenience markets were plentiful, and we frequented them regularly for fifty-cent pints of Pepsi and a quick cool-down. We got to Austin in no time, there's no slowing down at all in the States. If you're on the highway you're full throttle. Massive carriageways seemed to make the flow of traffic a few miles an hour faster than in Europe and we were pushing Kuishi's limits, just to keep up.

In Austin, we stayed with the all-American family. Jewels, Jason, and their three boys were a really friendly bunch. Jason was a military veteran turned local cop and Jewels a high school teacher. They lived in a Malcolm in the Middle-style suburban house and the whole set-up was about as American as you can possibly be. They were a great family and Jason had taken the day off work to welcome us. They offered us an ice-cold beer as soon as we walked in at about 3 p.m., so it was pretty clear we were going to hit it off.

We sat and talked all day and night about life in Texas, covering all range of topics that relate to something called "The Texas Way." If you're not aware, "The Texas Way" is a slogan that most

Texans use to finish most sentences. The Texas Way is a funny old "way." Some things I can jump right on board with, massive steaks for one, but others, I find harder to understand. In fact, I would go as far to say that Texas is as culturally different to the UK as say, Egypt or Sudan. It sits on the "Bible Belt," the name given to the USA's hyper-religious Deep South. Religion here is as in your face as the call to prayer blasted over the tannoy that we heard all the way back in Alexandria. As you drive along the highway, you see billboard after billboard with messages like "900-900—For the truth" or "Jesus is looking for you call 100-100." Religion is king and if you're not a Christian then you're really not doing stuff The Texas Way. According to our friends further up the road in Dallas, strong Christian beliefs are so engrained in society that there has been a battle raging to allow creationism to be taught as scientific theory in state schools. That's state schools, not some funky independent school. I found that just so shocking, I guess I was about as shocked as Farouk was in Alexandria, when I told him that I thought humans had essentially evolved from fish.

Armed with a better knowledge of The Texas Way, the following morning we left our new friends in Austin and cracked on north again to Dallas, where we met Reece's cousin, Jess. She lived on the outskirts of Dallas with her two boys, Austin and William. We stayed for a week and did the usual stuff like repair the bike. It was a brilliant break and probably the first time we felt like we were in a proper home since we left the UK. It was cool just to hang out and plan for the road ahead, but it also gave us an opportunity to find out about modern slavery in the States.

We arranged to meet with an organisation called New Friends, New Life who are set up to tackle human trafficking in Dallas. What we found was that the USA was not at all the land of the free and in fact modern slavery was a major issue. New Friends, New Life focuses on helping women and girls who are victims of sex trafficking. As we were still pretty close to Mexico, we figured we would hear all about how victims were being trafficked across the border but actually victims were mostly from the USA. The most common type of victim they were dealing with was young girls who had run away from home in rural Texas with a "boyfriend" and had ended up in Dallas. However, their "boyfriend" wasn't their boyfriend at all, and it was all part of the work of organised crime gangs who were manipulating young girls into leaving their homes and heading for a new life, with the new love of their life. When they arrive in Dallas, they're told by their boyfriends-turned-traffickers that they need to sleep with other guys to pay for their new life and they are manipulated into becoming sex workers.

New Friends, New Life estimates this to be a $99 million a year industry just in Dallas and they say that one of the main challenges they have with it is that the girls generally don't know they have been trafficked. Even after researching the issue in each country we had passed through, we were shocked to hear just how big a problem it was for the leaders of the free world. We added New Friends, New Life to the list of organisations we were raising money for before heading back to Jess' place for a truly Texan evening.

That night was rodeo night. Jess and the boys wanted us to see proper Texas and so we went to see probably the craziest thing I've ever seen. It's so extreme and not for the faint-hearted. It feels like you can actually hear bones shattering as cowboys get flung from the animals. I think getting on an angry bull or seeing how quickly you can tie up a sheep is a really odd way to spend your time, but you can't deny that it's entertaining. There's just something about putting a four-year-old on a sheep and seeing how long they can hold on that's fun to watch. Yep, it's probably a bit messed up, but it's part of The Texas Way.

We chilled out in Dallas for a few more days and did some cool stuff like visit a longhorn cattle ranch before we scooted off north once more. We were heading to Amarillo, another 350 miles or so. Texas is massive; Lands End to John O'Groats is a shorter distance than one side of Texas to the other. We hadn't quite factored that into our travel plans, and we had new tyres waiting for us in Colorado. We were thinking it's just the next state, whereas we should have been thinking, it's another 1,000 miles. On our drive from Dallas to Amarillo, the rear tyre was so thin that it attracted the attention of a local guy called Cal. He came over to have the usual chat about the rig and why we were taking it around the world, and then said "Boy, that rear tyre is so thin, here's a hundred bucks. Buy yourselves a new set in Amarillo!" We were blown away. This was another characteristic of The Texas Way—generosity!

We pressed on north again and were about 100 miles south of Amarillo filling up in a Walmart when a lady in a big SUV pulled up next to us, dropped the window down, peered out, and said, "Wow, would you look at that. Where y'all heading?" We told her we were heading to Amarillo. It turned out her name was Janet, she lived there and offered to take us to lunch the next day. We of course accepted and exchanged numbers.

We arrived in Amarillo a couple of hours later. We had been told about the Handle Bar and Grill from Jill Coultas, one of our new friends in Dallas. It was a biker's joint right on Route 66 and Keith, the owner, let bikers camp on the patio. We thought that sounded like a lot of fun so we headed straight there. We arrived as minor celebrities. It turned out it was bike night and Keith knew we were coming in so had been putting the word around that two British burks on a scooter and sidecar would be the entertainment for the evening. We arrived and instantly had a beer put in our hands by a guy called Jason.

Jason had come down especially to pick our brains. He was planning on heading around the world on a sidecar outfit, too, and wanted some advice. However, when he realised just how little we knew about anything to do with motorbikes or sidecars, he was the one dishing out the advice. The conversation quickly turned from sidecars to discussing what was good to see and do in Amarillo and he offered to show us around the following day. Jason went off home and we cracked on to the early hours of the morning.

At about 2 a.m., it had all died down and we strung our hammocks up across the decking. Keith closed the place up and as he was leaving, he said, "Boys, it's kind of a sketchy area out here. Want me to leave you with my pistol?" Maybe he was messing with us, but it really did seem like he was willing to leave us with his gun. It was crazy. We were probably eight pints deep, swinging in a hammock, and he was suggesting we poke the pistol out every now and again to make sure all was safe and well. We politely declined.

Eight a.m. and Keith was back with a steaming hot pot of coffee and two plates of bacon and eggs. We fell out of our hammocks, tucked in, and dropped Janet a line. We told her we had slept on the patio at the Handle Bar and Grill and she was horrified. She said we must come to her house for a shower and then she would take us out for a proper lunch. We thought that sounded like a good way to spend the day, so we drank Keith out of coffee and went off to Janet's. It was hot, we'd had a night on the booze, and then slept on a patio—we really did need a shower. I was very aware of that fact so when we arrived, I said a quick hi to her husband, Jackie, and dove straight in. Ten minutes later, I came out to find Reece sat down on the sofa, pen in hand, signing a human leg! I nearly fainted. My first reaction was, "Oh my God, what has he done?" Then Reece explained that Jackie's leg had to be amputated after his donkey stood on it, and he wanted us to be the first people to sign his new prosthesis. It was a very bizarre situation. I took the leg off Reece, he went in the shower, I popped on a "Best Wishes, Matt Bishop" and then handed it back to Jackie to screw in.

Janet took us down to the Big Texan for lunch, a place where you can buy a 72-oz. steak. We tucked into a 10-oz. one and we were stuffed. It was a lovely lunch and a great opportunity to learn a bit more about The Texas Way. Janet told us that she didn't have a gun on her right now, and she knew we didn't, but she would usually want someone to be packing at lunch. We were bewildered. Next, Janet dropped us off with Jason and he and his dad, Gary, took us out to Palo Duro Canyon. It's the second largest canyon in the States, after that other very grand one, and is an awesome place to visit. After the canyon, we were chilling with Jason when he said, "I bet y'all ain't never shot a gun before, have ya?" We admitted we had not and he said that we would have to stay another night and hit the range with him in the morning. Janet had offered us a place to stay so we thought, "Sure, why not?"

At Janet and Jackie's that evening, we explained that we were sticking around to shoot some guns. They were very pleased about it and quickly got their guns out to show us. Jackie admitted that he sometimes gets confused as to whether his gun is loaded or not and just last week, he had accidentally shot out their new flat screen TV. Janet, too, wasn't sure if there was a bullet in her revolver and asked Reece to go outside and fire it into the air, to make sure it was empty. Bizarrely, Reece said he would do it and with his legs quivering in fear, he pointed the gun to the sky, braced himself for impact and pulled the trigger six times, all the while wondering if what went up, really did come down. Jackie later explained that he keeps his pistol by his bedside and if a stranger came through his bedroom door at night he would just shoot. His bedroom was the only access to the toilet and at about midnight I was busting for a wee but decided it was best to wait until morning.

The following morning Jason took us out to the range, and we did have a proper go at shooting a gun. I jumped in the back of his truck and found myself sat next to a small armoury. Jason's an Iraq veteran and he loves guns. He explained that guns calm him. He was a gunner on the back of a truck in the military and he said that when he was shooting that gun, everything slowed down. He said that the rhythm of it had actually sent him to sleep once. I found that bizarre at the time but twenty minutes later when I shot my first gun, I found it certifiably insane. They are so, so loud. How you could fall asleep while operating one is just beyond me. We shot a pistol, a shotgun, and some sort of assault rifle. We were both terrible at it and although I probably won't do it again, I will admit it was a lot of fun.

After we had finished shooting, we scooted north again and headed through New Mexico into Colorado. Our Texas road trip was over and our time experiencing The Texas Way had come to an end. I'm still not sure what to think about The Texas Way. It's generous, it's friendly, and it's pretty tasty too, but at the same time some of its characteristics just didn't sit well with me. One thing, I'll tell you for sure though, is that The Texas Way is here to stay. Don't worry about rushing out there to experience it. You'll be able to buy a 72-oz. steak at a restaurant and a pistol over the counter at Walmart for some time yet.

– 16 –

"THERE'S A FRICKING MOUNTAIN LION EATING MY BREAD WHILE IT STROKES MY BACK."

We set off from Amarillo excited to be heading into a new state but nervous that we might not get there. Our rear tyre was now a racing slick and we still had 300 miles to go to Colorado Springs where we had ordered some spares to a local bike shop. Sure enough, before we had even got to Dalhart, the last town before the border, the mesh on the wheel started to show. There was no way this tyre would make it to Colorado Springs, so we decided to swap it for our already worn-out spare. The spare was so thin it felt like you could push your little finger through it, but there was no mesh showing so it was at least slightly better than the one we were running.

It was a Sunday so there were no repair shops open in Dalhart. That was a bit of a problem for us as we didn't carry tyre irons and had no way of actually replacing it ourselves. We spent some time lingering outside what seemed to be the only tyre-changing place in town when we noticed a few guys hanging out back, drinking energy drinks in a pick-up truck. We went over to introduce ourselves and asked if they could help. Turns out they worked at the joint and were happy to open up for a few minutes. We pulled into the shade behind the building and got straight to work. It was unbearably hot. The kind of heat that makes you go lightheaded when you move too much and has you dripping in sweat after five minutes. We set about the process of removing the exhaust and swinging arm, so we could slide the wheel off and swap the tyres. Easy stuff. We'd done it a few times by now. The fellas switched the tyre in two minutes flat and it looked like we would be racing off towards Colorado Springs in no time. We slotted the wheel back on, mounted the swinging arm and then tried to slot the shock back into place. It lined up perfectly but for some reason we couldn't tighten the nut that held it on. We spent the next hour and a half, dripping in sweat, cursing at this nut. I tried to remind myself about the guy from Zen and the Art of Motorcycle Maintenance but there was no way we were keeping our cool. It was so flipping hot and annoying. This one little bloody nut, ruining the day for everyone. I was going at it with such frustration that when I stood up to take a minute, I found myself seeing stars. We took five minutes to cool off and then just put a different nut and bolt in the hole, screwed it up nice and tight and drove off. Idiots!

Half an hour or so later and we crossed the state line into New Mexico. We passed through the town of Raton and pressed on north again and into the third state of the day, Colorado. The scenery had started to change, and we climbed out from the flat dusty shrub land in Texas and New Mexico to find glorious rolling green hills in Colorado. The roads were weaving through the most magnificent countryside and it was a fantastic way to spend an afternoon, but it soon became clear that we weren't going to make it to Colorado Springs before dark. As we drove along, we started to notice loads of warning signs for deer. With a tyre close to the edge and the imminent risk of riding into the side of an animal, we decided we should stop for the night. We pulled into the next place we came across, which was a rest area. Just a block of toilets and a car park. With a nice picnic bench and a great view, we decided it would be a good place to pitch up. We kicked back with a jam sandwich and a cup of tea, before getting down for the night next to the bike.

We placed our hammocks on the floor and hung their built-in mosquito nets up off the bike and a bag. Then we slid in our thick Alpkit inflatable sleeping mats before climbing in and doing up the mosquito net. On a dry night it's the ideal way to camp, super comfy, you can see the stars, there are no unwanted critters climbing in with you and it's completely free. I was out like a light in no time. Reece, on the other hand, was up most of the night. He's a worrier. Which was ideal for me, I always slept sounder knowing Reece probably wasn't sleeping at all.

The following morning, we trucked on towards Colorado Springs. We were full of relief as we pulled into a hotel car park with an inflated tyre. We had made it! The hotel was vastly too expensive for our budget, but they were playing the Arsenal match, so we decided to grab a coffee. To our delight the hotel breakfast was just finishing up and the lovely waitress offered us a free run at the massive pot of coffee they had left over. We contacted the bike shop, but it was looking like it would take a few days until the tyres would arrive. This left us in a bit of a pickle as we were now stuck in the city and it's not a cheap place. With nowhere to camp, we would be destined to rack up a bill at a horrible motel somewhere. Incredibly though, when we sat down to breakfast we received a message from Jasmine Gilkes, who is Reece's younger brother Liam's wife. She was still waiting on her visa to move to the UK and was stopping with her dad, David, and step-mum, Lynda. We had never met any of them, but they had always been super-supportive and had been following the trip from the start. They lived just an hour north in Denver and said they would come down and meet us for lunch at least.

We thought that was great. At the very worst we had something to do for a couple of hours and it would be great to meet them. The next thing we knew, we were in a BBQ joint tucking into an absolute whopper of a lunch. We hit it off with the Bacons straight away and were laughing at Liam's inability to put the ring on the correct finger at the altar, while the vicar, an Elvis Presley impersonator, asked if it was just the other way 'round with English people, you know, like the roads! They were a lovely bunch and David instantly offered to put us up in a hotel while we waited for the tyres, as Lynda said in the same breath, "Why don't you come and stay with us?" Both seemed to be far too generous for us to accept but in all honesty, we were broke and either would be a huge help. In the end, we decided we would head off with them and truck on to Denver. It seemed a lot more fun than sat doing work in a hotel somewhere. Lynda insisted that we shouldn't risk the tyre popping on the highway, so we went down to a local U-Haul place and David hired a trailer for us. We offered to pay, of course, but were shot down straight away. That kind of generosity set the theme for the next few days.

We hitched the bike on the back of David's awesome Jeep Wrangler and headed off for Denver. En route we detoured through the Garden of the Gods. It's a completely otherworldly landscape—imagine what Mars would be like if trees grew there and you'll be somewhere near. Big towers of red rock surrounded by awesome greenery. We arrived in Denver that evening and got settled into a place we'd call home for the next few days. We met another member of the family, their awesome dog. It was probably one of the best dogs you'll ever come across. So friendly and smarter than most humans. We marveled at their perfect home. Everything in the house was immaculately clean and well kept, except us and all of our things. We'd been sleeping in pub gardens and lay-bys and we were clearly rank. We jumped straight in the shower and put a wash on, but it would take days to get rid of the smell. Lynda and David politely said we didn't smell at all at the time, but a few weeks back, Liam let us know that Lynda had said, "It was lovely to have the boys but my word they did stink." Hilarious.

We had a couple of drinks at their house that night and just got to know each other. We were amazed. David Bacon was an ex-military guy who trained the toughest of the tough in hand-to-hand combat. He had excelled so much that he had been on the all-American mixed martial arts team and fought internationally for the States. He had reached such lofty heights that he had regularly gone for lunch with Chuck Norris and had even sparred with Steven Seagal who, by the way, we're assured, is as much of a tosser as he seems, and David landed one right on his hooter. Obviously, Reece and I were completely absorbed. We would have believed David had fought the Queen at Buckingham Palace if he had told us he had, but rest assured Lynda got the pictures out later and proved he was the real deal. I can't imagine what it must be like to have a guy who's punched Steven Seagal as your father-in-law but I'm pretty sure Liam will never break Jasmine's heart. If he ever does I'd advise that he turns himself into David and begs forgiveness straight away. He has a special set of skills, he will find you and he will . . . probably just be a bit disappointed, but I think I'd rather get a pasting than disappoint the Bacons.

We hung out there for a few days and borrowed David and Lynda's Jeep to head back south and pick up our tyres from Colorado Springs. Jasmine joined us for the day, and it was a lot of fun to be cruising through Colorado in a soft-top Jeep. We also met up with fellow sidecar enthusiast, Scott, who had set up a company called City on the Side. It was a sidecar touring company using new Ural outfits. He had worked a normal job for the best part of three decades. It was okay, but he wasn't passionate about it. He then lost a close family member and decided life was too short, so decided to follow his dream. He worked tirelessly at it and now his sidecar business is thriving. He loves his job and his enthusiasm for life was infectious. I'll definitely be back one day for a ride in of his rigs.

After a day of fixing the bike up and changing tires with David, we declared that the bike was in the best shape it had been since leaving the UK and we left behind the blissful comfort of Denver for the adventure of the open road. Next, we would need to check south to Colorado Springs, where we had been towed from, before turning west, headed for the Frisco Bay. We made it about ten miles south before realising the bike was overheating big time. Reece and I had changed the coolant the day before as we were blindly following the servicing schedule. It was a stupid idea; it didn't need doing and we had messed it up. We had broken the number one rule of mechanics: "If it ain't broke, don't fix it." We relaxed in a garage forecourt for a while and waited for Kuishi to cool down. Hoping it was freak, we pressed on again. Five miles south, it was overheating once more.

We called David, who told us it was most likely an air bubble in the radiator. He said it might come out if we left the cap off, ran it and kept topping up the radiator. We did exactly that and sure enough, after about five minutes Kuishi swallowed a load more coolant and we were looking good. We pressed on south again and although Kuishi's temperature was still creeping up, it was riding okay. With all of the faffing with the radiator, we didn't even make it the hundred miles south to Colorado Springs and just after dark, we pulled into the town of Monument looking for somewhere to stay. Unfortunately, the only places available were way out of our budget. It did, however, have a Walmart. We had heard on the grapevine that Walmart is pretty cool about people sleeping in their car park. A lot of people in motor homes do it so we reasoned that they wouldn't mind us either. After all, Kuishi had a motor and it had been our home for the best part of a year now.

The shop itself was closed by the time we arrived so we grabbed some food over the road at a dodgy fast-food joint. It was a cheap but huge burger, coupled with a whopping Pepsi. After dinner we pitched up camp. We found a couple of massive RVs camped along one side of the car park so we pulled in next to them. We parked up next to a lamp post and stuck our hammocks around the post and the sidecar. We were hanging just a couple of inches from the floor and the bike and lamp post seemed to be able to take the strain so in our minds it was another perfect spot. Again, it took me ten minutes and I was out like a light. I think Reece was watching the local teenagers mess around the car park all night. We woke up in the morning to find the guy in the RV next door waving us over. He had fixed us some breakfast. A couple of waffles and a cup of coffee each! Who'd have thought that a night in a Walmart would come with breakfast included?

You meet some interesting people, camping in a Walmart car park. The couple that made us breakfast were just on their holidays. Bikers at heart, but not up for the long miles anymore, they had just returned from the biggest bike rally in the States, at Sturgis, South Dakota. Camped up opposite was a guy sleeping in the back of a small van. He hadn't kitted it out for camping, it was just a van and a sleeping mat. He went by the name of Vagabond and had now given up everything for a life on the road. He said life with a stressful career had got too much and now he just cruises the country, from Walmart to Walmart.

We left Walmart refreshed and full. Next stop was Colorado Springs and another scoot around the Garden of the Gods before we tracked west. As we headed out of the city, we came across a huge number of riders on Harley-Davidsons. They were all headed to Cripple Creek, a nearby town, for the biggest Veterans' Bike Rally in the States. We decided we would have to check it out for ourselves and headed out there too. As we scooted towards Cripple Creek, we entered the Pikes Peak National Forest and the views were breathtaking. I sat in a t-shirt, in the sidecar, put my feet up on the outside of the rig and kicked back to enjoy the ride. Hundreds of Harleys passed us and very few riders wore a helmet. Just jeans, a leather vest, and a pair of shades. They looked like they were straight off the set of Wild Hogs.

We pulled into Cripple Creek to find the streets lined with bikes. Two cranes were fully extended and holding up the biggest flag I have ever seen in my life. The festival was in full swing. Native American dancers, dressed in traditional wear, danced in the street, while a country and western band played next to a BBQ pit around which the Wild Hogs drank beer and patriotically got pissed in salute to America's military men and women. It was all very USA and interesting to watch. We checked out a couple of the local joints, but the town was basically one giant casino and seeing as we weren't planning on stopping the night, we decided to press on to find somewhere to camp. The great thing about riding in the US is that you can camp pretty much anywhere. The best time to do it is when you're passing through national forests, though. It's almost always okay to camp and they're pretty much always gorgeous.

Pikes Peak National Forest is a coniferous forest and it's home to over a million acres of wilderness. Populated by black bears, mountain lions, and a whole host of other less-scary animals, the area is truly wild. We camped up on the fringes where you still get the odd holiday maker but, generally speaking, we were well and truly on our own. We hung up the hammocks and started getting ready for a good night's kip in the forest. We'd never really wild camped in woodland before, it had always been deserts or fields, so it was an exciting but kind of scary prospect. There's something about a dark forest at night that's just a bit creepy. As the sun sets you start to look harder through the gaps in the trees to try and make out what's beyond as far as you can see. Then, when vision is almost completely useless, you switch to listening mode and tune in to the finest details. A crash in the distance, what could it be? A bear, a lion, a person out to get us? Those thoughts went round and round in my head until I actively knocked them out and managed to convince myself that nothing was there. Well actually, I more came to the conclusion that something may be there, but if it was, and it got close enough for me to see or hear it, then I was dust anyway. We're both weedy and stupid. We're not streetwise or prepared, nor do we have any kind of knowledge on avoiding being killed by wild animals and murderers alike. If there was something there, we were dead, so we might as well enjoy our last evening.

As the last light finally disappeared, we both climbed into our hammocks, clambered into our sleeping bags and settled in for the night. It was a perfectly clear night and you could just about see stars glistening through the canopy above.

"Hey, mate, do you reckon we should put our rain covers on?" said Reece.

"Are you kidding mate? You say this now? Just as we get in!" I angrily replied. "Well, we'll have to now won't we, because you've full-on jinxed us!"

We began the process of shuffling back out of our bags and both flopped out onto the floor. It was a chilly night, so we worked fast to get our rain covers up as quickly as possible. We'd never used them before but the principle is pretty simple and it didn't take long to get sorted. Now pretty cold, we clambered back into our swinging cocoons. Though there were no longer any stars above, the rain cover wasn't entirely bad. It came down the sides a bit so you couldn't see anything and it kept us from peering out into the trees, wondering what's out there.

We lay there snug and comfy in the cold night for about fifteen minutes and then I started to hear a pitter-patter on the sheet above me. Sure enough, it was raining. Two minutes later and it was nailing it down. "Well done, mate, bloody well done!" I shouted to Reece.

"Thank you, mate, thank you!" Reece replied.

And we went off to sleep with the sound of the rain wonderfully masking any creepy distant sounds.

"Hoooooooooowwlllll!" I was suddenly awake. What the hell was that? A coyote? A wolf? Again another "Hoooooooooowllll!"

"Holy crap that is fricking creepy," I thought. Laying in my cocoon, I could see nothing all around me. "Reece, Reece, are you awake?" I loudly whispered. Nothing. Then out of nowhere, I heard something coming from the distance. It was a weird kind of sound, but it was getting closer and closer, quickly. It sounded like it was building and then a deep, bellowing, singular gust of wind rocked my hammock from side to side. Suddenly, I'm swinging in the air. Pumped full of adrenalin, I start laughing to myself. What the fuck is going on?

"Reece, Reece." Still nothing. No point in waking him up, we're not going to do anything anyway. I lay there, ears pricked up, clasping my torch. The next thing I knew it was morning. I must have heard nothing and eventually drifted off. I woke up with an absolutely freezing cold back and all 'round chilled to the core. The morning light was just creeping up through the forest. I flopped out to try and get warm. Reece was already up shaking and doing star jumps. Hammocks get cold through the night.

"Mate, did you hear that last night?" said Reece.

"The howling and the fricking wind?" I replied.

"Yes! Bloody nuts wasn't it?"

We agreed that it must have happened on more than one occasion because we'd both checked the other was asleep at the time and got nothing back. But we both agreed exactly on the details. Some kind of howling and then the most creepy, almighty gust of wind that knocked us from side to side. I've never experienced or heard of anything like that at all. Is wind ever a singular gust? Well it bloody was that night! It felt like a stampede of spirits knocking me from side to side.

After a morning coffee, we pressed on west again. Once more, we were buzzing with that kind of feeling you only get when you've survived a night you thought you might not. We pressed on further into the beautiful Colorado countryside. Our goal for the day was to make it onto the famous Kebler Pass, which takes you through the largest living organism on the planet. No, it's not a whale, it's an aspen grove. Apparently, it's the same plant, as it all feeds off one singular root system. On the surface, it's just a big forest but a really pretty one. The best time of year to go is supposedly autumn, when the area is a sea of glowing oranges and reds. We were there in summer when it was still pretty impressive. You access it via the town of Crested Butte, which feels like it's been plucked out of the Swiss Alps. It's a very cool place to visit.

It was a slow ride up to the pass with regular long breaks for Kuishi to cool down as we were still having big problems with overheating. It's the kind of area where you don't mind having a break, though. After a long day of riding again we pulled in on the Kebler Pass and strung our hammocks up in the aspens. We had found a clearing where others had camped before. It had a big wooden structure that I think is used by hunters to hang the deer they've shot, but I really had no idea. There was a fire pit, and some leftover beer cans. We hoped we weren't pinching anyone's spot and that they weren't going to come and string us up in the night. With every item of clothing on and our sleeping mats in the bottom of our hammocks, we got down for the night.

As we were high up in the mountains, temperatures plummeted that night but there was no howling, and no creepy gusts of wind, so all was well. We woke up in the morning about as cold as the night before which, as it was about 10°C colder, meant our new technique with the sleeping mats in the hammock had worked. The following morning, we pressed on along the Kebler Pass and then tracked north towards the I-70, headed west for Utah.

Hitting Utah is a very weird thing. The sign marks the start of a new state and an entirely new landscape. Within a mile the scenery turns from rolling hills and forests to flat, sandy desert. Temperatures soared instantly. We must have climbed twenty degrees in a couple of hours. Before we knew it, we were stripping layers and trundling along slowly as Kuishi overheated. It took us all day to drive through to the first major town of Moab.

On the ride into Moab, we scooted downhill along a wonderful stretch of tarmac that is cut into the red sandstone cliffs which frame the valley. We checked into a little campsite on the outskirts of the town and found a great spot to hang up our hammocks. It was fairly late by the time we got there so we decided we'd wait until morning to explore the nearby Arches National Park. Instead we popped to the shops and bought a couple of cheap tins of soup and a loaf of bread, and had a chilled evening in the campsite. It was the usual routine, we inhaled some food, did some social media work on the Wi-Fi, and jumped into our hammocks for a good night's kip. No need for the air mat underneath us, it must have still been 25°C at night. You barely needed a sleeping bag. I drifted off to sleep in no time.

I woke up some time later to find something stroking my back. "What the shitting hell is that?" I thought to myself. I was wide awake and hanging about two feet from the floor. Something was rubbing up and down my back. I could hear it scoffing away. It sounded like an over-enthusiastic dog scratching at scraps of litter. I suddenly realised I left the bread under my hammock. We were out of bear country, so I didn't think I needed to hide the food. I was wrong. Something had spotted a meal. It was pitch black and I could only hear and feel what it was as it frantically attacked the bread and battled with the plastic sleeve. It could be anything, a dog, a cat, a bigger cat, Christ—it could be a mountain lion. My imagination ran wild. There's a fricking mountain lion eating my bread while it strokes my back. What the hell should I do? I couldn't just get up, I might have startled it and got attacked.

"Reece," I whispered quietly. "Reece, Reece, Reece." Nothing. "Useless prick," I thought to myself. I lay there for another five long minutes. It was disgusting, scurrying up and down fighting the plastic. It tossed the bread a foot to the left of my hammock and suddenly an opening presented itself. If I jumped out then, I wouldn't be in its direct scratching, biting range and maybe I could scare it away. I went for it, jumped out to the right of the sleeping bag, shone my torch on it and shouted, "Arghhhh! Get back you bastard!" A raccoon stared up at me completely shocked before darting off in the dark never to be seen again. Gross! Reece didn't stir at all so I just binned the bread and got back off to sleep. Little git ate our breakfast!

The following morning, still feeling like a raccoon was rubbing up and down my back, I had a thorough shower before we scooted off towards Arches National Park. We were there for sunrise and it was absolutely out of this world cool. If you get there nice and early, you get some time when it's just you, an eerie silence, and some incredible rock formations: big towering piles of red rock, placed alongside almighty arches that frame the most incredible views over the surrounding valley. We stayed to appreciate them for a couple of hours.

Next we pressed south toward Arizona, headed in the general direction of the Grand Canyon. It was a day of slow riding, with nobody minding. We were appreciating the views. Next visit en route was the Valley of the Gods, much like the Garden of the Gods in Colorado but this place gets no rain and it really is Mars. I expect it's where they will one day film the Mars landing. Not as popular as the surrounding national parks, and you can almost expect to have the place to yourself. There's no tarmac either so a nice bit of trail riding, with sweeping bends, steep drops and tough climbs. It was a misty day but it didn't ruin the view, it made the experience even more atmospheric. With every turn a new weird rock formation would appear out of the haze and you'd have to quickly analyse the tracks ahead and plot your route to scoot around it. It was a remarkable place.

We rejoined the tarmac after a while and pressed on towards Arizona. Just as we hit the border that breathtaking iconic view appeared in our visors, Monument Valley. How cool, we had driven our vehicle all the way from old Blighty to the scene of a Wild West movie. We messed around taking pictures for a while before pressing on into Arizona. It was starting to get dark so we pulled into a designated rest area. We pitched our tent, overlooking an incredible canyon, which would be the UK's number one attraction but wasn't even deserving of a name in this crazy landscape. We originally put our hammocks up but as we stood and admired the view we could see storm clouds brewing. It looked nasty. It was. The rain was so loud that we couldn't hear Reece's laptop on full volume inside the tent. With nowhere to go and nothing to do in the cramped two-man tent, we had no choice but to listen to the rain and get an incredibly early night.

We awoke to a very soggy campsite. Before the storm had come, we had burnt some beans to the bottom of our pan. Incredibly, a friendly passing creature had licked it clean for us, how helpful! Next stop on the horizon was the biggest attraction of them all, the Grand Canyon. I was skeptical. How good could it really be? Could anything live up to that much hype? Only one way to find out. We had to get there first though, which turned out to be more troublesome than we first envisaged. We were cruising down the highway when the sky in front turned a deep, dark, hazy red. It was weird. It looked like the kind of scene you'd expect the devil to walk out of. We pulled into a petrol station to fill up while we ogled at what lay in front of us.

"Oh yeah, she's coming boys, you're going to wanna stay off the road in that thing," said a guy filling up on the next pump.

"What the hell is it?" I replied.

"Sandstorm, big fucker too, nearly knocked me off the road in my truck. Wait for it to pass."

That was all the warning we needed. We put the GoPro on the bike, grabbed a coffee and stood at the door waiting for it to hit. And my word, did it hit. We went outside for two ticks just to see what it was like. Horrible. That's what it was like. Felt like we were getting sandblasted, because we were. Twenty minutes later and it had passed.

An hour so of clear riding after and we arrived to a lot of tourists and a lot of mist at the Grand Canyon. We stayed for an hour or so just hoping it would lift but we couldn't stay all day, we had to get to Vegas that night. Then just as we were about to give up, the curtains lifted to unveil the most magnificent view. It more than lived up to the hype. The grandeur of it was truly staggering. Never has a name been more apt. I felt like I could have stared at it all day. There were so many layers to the view, it just went on and on. Finally, we managed to tear ourselves away from the views and scoot on towards Vegas. Again, though, the view from behind the handlebars was pretty intimidating. This time there were huge black storm clouds with forked lightning crashing into the hillside in front of us. We put our waterproofs on and drove into the storm. It was as bad as it looked, the kind of rain that hits you on the way up as well as the way down, falling with such ferocity that it felt like the drops would cut a hole in your coat. We were absolutely drenched. Ironically, though, it meant we could drive faster. The constant flow of water over Kuishi's radiator meant we weren't overheating for the first time since Denver and we were getting a risky 55 mph along the highway.

We eventually arrived that night to the place that calls itself the entertainment capital of the world, Las Vegas! After an intense day's riding we were feeling absolutely zonked. We checked into our beat-up motel, carried all of our sodden luggage upstairs, which we were pleased about as the ground floor rooms had all had their windows broken in, and flopped onto our beds. We were ready for a good night's kip, but that wasn't going to happen, after all, we were in Vegas.

– 17 –

"SUDDENLY, I WAS PARALYSED IN SHOCK. WHAT THE HELL WAS THAT?"

At about 4 a.m. we were still walking around Las Vegas wide-eyed and bushy tailed. We'd had no sleep since peeling ourselves off the bed at the motel six hours earlier. We'd had a couple of beers but we weren't drunk, we were high . . . on oxygen! Apparently the casino's air-conditioning units push out pure oxygen to keep you awake and to keep you gambling. It works, well, not the gambling bit for us. We put $5 on red, lost, and agreed not to do it again. We just walked around full of oxygen, ogling at all of the entertainment, and in awe of the sheer scale of the place. It's a truly barmy town. The lighting is so bright in the casinos that it feels like daytime and with the free drinks while you gamble and all that oxygen, you can see how people could stay for days never leaving the tables. The place is so fake that the streets are actually cooled down by the air-conditioning pouring out of the permanently open casino doors. It's probably the only city we drove through on the trip where something as weird as a bright red English scooter and sidecar coming through isn't weird at all.

I can imagine it's great for a stag weekend or a hen do, but for a couple of broke sidecarists there are better places to visit. We spent the next day sleeping off the crash from the oxygen high before pressing on again. We headed north out of Vegas before tracking west again towards the coast. We had planned to head for Yosemite National Park. It was a bit of a stretch but we were up bright and early and thought we could probably make it. Half an hour later and we weren't so sure. Kuishi was instantly overheating. It was an exceptionally hot day, probably pushing 30°C at 10 a.m. and we were skirting up the side of Death Valley so Kuishi's rising temperature was understandable. By lunch time it was probably more like 40°C and Kuishi was really struggling. We were cruising at a max speed of 20 mph in the hard shoulder. Fortunately, in the middle of the desert we randomly came across a service station. It was perfectly timed and we were desperate for a massive Pepsi and some air-con. With no wind chill and in full motorbike gear we were cooking, Sudan-style.

It turned out that the service station was called the Area 51 Alien Center. We were as close as you can get to Area 51 and somebody had decided to cash in on the elusive history of the place. It was an odd joint—a big, bright-green, wooden building with a massive alien head on the outside. Inside was nothing more than an alien-themed restaurant and a gift shop. I can't imagine how underwhelmed you would be if you travelled here to actually visit the "Alien Center." Of course nobody really does visit it, they get passers-by like us, who are more than happy with the Pepsi and air-con and then there are those who want a souvenir after visiting the place next door. Nope not the military base, the brothel. Yes, really. In the middle of the desert, next to the bright-green Alien Centre, there's a bright-pink building called the Alien Cathouse. I asked the cashier if it was really a brothel and he said, "Sure is, you can have a free tour if you like!"

"Um, no thanks, mate, I'm good with the Pepsi and the hot dog," I replied.

I gave it a google after and it turns out it's crazy popular. Apparently it dubs itself as the number one spot to fulfill your fantasy of being abducted by aliens. If you do happen to fantasise over being abducted by aliens, though, I wouldn't suggest you give it a go. Maybe just have an honest chat about it with your partner because frankly this place should dub itself as another seedy, rundown, roadside brothel, as that's certainly what it is. After spending as long as we possibly could inside with the truly out-of-this-world air-con, we got back on Kuishi and cracked on north once more. Ten minutes later we were again reduced to crawling along the hard shoulder in the highway. With trucks hurtling past and the sun beating down, it was a hot, stressful experience.

After a couple of hours we arrived at an unexpected junction. It turned out to be a small side road that cut off the corner and allowed us to take a shortcut east. Gary the Garmin didn't know we couldn't keep pace with the trucks so he hadn't pointed it out before. I took the turn and started heading off into the desert. After a few miles we started to climb into the hills and with the climb came some greenery. After about another ten miles, and with us still maxing out at 20 mph, I decided to lose all the gear. No helmet, no jacket, just a slight breeze and a pair of shades. It was bliss. Even though it's not legal to ride without a helmet in Nevada, it just felt absurd to be wearing all the gear at 20 mph with no other cars around on such a hot day.

Around four hours later we rejoined the highway and turned left to head towards California. We were now in rolling hills and we were well and truly on the way to our destination for the evening, Yosemite National Park. The conditions were incredible. The hot desert air had disappeared and we were into a cool, California summer's evening. The sun set as we crossed the state line into Cali and as it did we were treated with the usual cocktail of gorgeous views and nervous apprehension. Before we knew it, the glowing sky had disappeared and we were riding along in the pitch black with no idea where to stay. We had been heading to a wild camping spot we had identified on iOverlander. It was just a spot on a map and there were no facilities there, but we knew it was legal and had been a safe place to sleep for others, so it seemed like a good choice. Now though, thanks to our overheating bike, it was still fifty miles away and wasn't an option. Fifty miles at night in this area would be a really bad idea.

We were back in wildlife country. There would certainly be a lot of deer and the usual scary beasts too, including bears. It's not the kind of place you want to just pitch up and camp in an area you don't know, after dark. We had blown it. We decided that we would press on slowly to the small town of Benton, where we would just check into any motel or campsite and admit defeat.

Arriving in Benton, we pulled into the first thing we found, a fuel stop. Great stuff, we were starving, we hadn't eaten since the alien centre, so we grabbed a couple of sarnies and asked the cashier where the nearest place to stay was. "Oh there's nowhere around here. The next place you'll find will be up by Mono Lake."

Mono Lake was fricking miles away, probably another twenty miles after the original place we decided we would camp. It was now completely pitch black so we were no longer racing the clock. We took a few minutes to fuel up and assess the situation before agreeing all we could do was crack on slowly. If we got to somewhere that looked like a reasonable place to camp then we'd pull over, and if not we'd just press on to our original spot. We pulled out of Benton at about 25 mph and didn't go any faster. We wanted to give ourselves the best chance possible to not hit anything wild that stumbled into the road. There were no other cars on the road either, it was just us and the moon. It was out in full force and actually gave us the opportunity to see into the fields around us. We probably passed hundreds of suitable wild camping spots but none really felt like the spot.

After a few miles of riding through farmland we started to scoot up into the hills. The narrow, climbing road twisted and turned around the distinctive massive rock features that this part of the world is famed for. They weren't quite El Capitan but they were big enough to block any view around the corner and the environment had gone from a vast flat landscape where the moonlight allowed us to see what was coming, to a path overshadowed by huge rocks which could be hiding anything. We were starting to get a bit creeped out. We hadn't seen a car or any kind of settlement since we left Benton, it was just us and the outdoors and it felt like we riding through the set of The Hills Have Eyes.

Still holding strong at 20-25 mph, I was at the handlebars when something suddenly popped out of our secretive surroundings. It burst into sight in an instant and my headlights were full with its incredible wingspan. I swerved and so did it. I went left and it went up. We avoided the collision, which was great, as with no screen on the scooter it would have been a fairly big whack of owl to take to the face, had the wise old thing not climbed so quickly.

We were already pumped full of adrenaline but now my heart was beating out of my chest. There really were critters hiding in the shadows.

We had no choice but to press on again. We were still crawling up the valley and holding our breath every time we turned around one of the massive rocks. Always half expecting another owl, a deer, or perhaps, with the full moon, it would be something more supernatural. It's safe to say we were freaked. A while longer and we pulled out at the top of the hill. The landscape opened up a bit and there were small fields to our left and right but backed by big areas of forest.

"Here it is mate," said Reece through the headset. "Slow down, it's just coming up on the left." We pulled up next to a left turn. "Yep, down there."

"Are you kidding?! It can't be down there," I replied.

"Yeah it's about a mile or two down there mate. It'll be alright!"

I couldn't believe it. The "road" to my left was a sandy gravel track. We were now staring down the barrel of going deeper into the wilds, down a road, towards a forest, that might well grind us to a halt and render us as complete sitting ducks.

"You do know bears live in forests don't you, mate?" I jokingly said as I blindly followed Reece's instruction. The road was sandy but rideable. We were trail riding but it was soft stuff and as long as I kept going, we would probably be fine. We scooted closer and closer towards the towering, pitch-black forest. The landscape changed from The Hills Have Eyes to The Blair Witch Project in an instant as we scooted under the almighty pine-tree canopy above us. The moon was no longer around to guide our path and the only light came from our headlight. We could see absolutely nothing to our left or right. It was genuinely pretty scary. We scooted on for about five minutes and then I saw a reasonable sized clearing. It looked like a designated camping spot so I turned off and pulled in. We jumped out with the engine still running and our helmets still on to have a look around. "Yeah this will do it, hey, mate?" I said to Reece through the headset.

"As good as place as any," he replied. I switched off the bike and the wall of light in front of us disappeared with the headlights. The sidecar lights have their own switch and they still provided a bit of a glow onto the white sand below. We took our helmets off and had a bit of a nervous laugh at how ridiculous the situation was. We'd done stuff like this before though, and we knew that we just needed to adjust to the environment and make this weird, spooky place the new normal. We placed our helmets on the scooter roof and just took a couple of minutes to take it all in. The silence was incredible. It took a while to get the grumble of the scooter and the horns of the truckers out of my head but then I did and it was complete silence.

A couple of minutes later and I was starting to get to know the place. There was the odd crack of a branch falling and rustle as the wind gently passed through, but all was very normal for a night in the woods.

"Matt, come and look at this." Reece was stood peering at the floor in front of the sidecar.

"Oh get out of it," I said, as I instantly knew what he was going to point out, a footprint. It wasn't all that clear in the light but there was a pretty sizeable paw print on the floor in front of the sidecar.

"What the hell do we do?" Reece said.

"Put the tent up and go to bed, mate," I replied.

"But the print, it looks like a be . . . ."

"Shut up Reece," I interrupted. "We're freaking ourselves out, that's all. The likelihood of it being a bear's footprint is far lower than the likelihood that we are seeing things in the dark. Plus, if it is a bear, I'm sure it's run off after our bright red, really loud spaceship has just burst in out of the dark. Let's just put the tent up and all will be fine."

Reece reluctantly agreed and we set about unstrapping the bags. I took the tent bag off the scooter seat and Reece started unbuckling the luggage rack on the rig.

Suddenly, I was paralysed in shock. What the hell was that? I had stopped what I was doing and was staring blankly in the direction of what I had heard, listening with all my might. There it was again but this time much louder and more distinctive. A deep grumbling, groaning kind of sound. I turned my head to look at Reece. He was now transfixed too. As white as a ghost. We looked back at the darkness and heard an even louder grumble and then "thud, thud, thud, thud, thud, thud, thud." Humongous footsteps getting closer and another deep, angry sounding moan.

"Fuckkkkkk!" We both said to each other as we crammed our helmets on our heads, started the bike up and got on to drive.

"We're fucking stuck!" I exclaimed as I jumped off to give a running push out of the sand. I got it going and I floored it as fast as I could, bags still open on the back. I had no concern for our stuff, just an overwhelming desire to get away from whatever was moaning from the woods. I floored it as fast as I could down the track, whizzing under the dark arms of the trees above, looking into the trees to our left for any sign of something in pursuit.

"That was a fricking bear wasn't it, mate?" Reece shouted through the headset.

"Yeah! I think it was!" I replied. And then suddenly again out of nowhere my headlights were filled with feathers. The enchanted forest had chucked another owl at us to make sure we really did piss off! It swooped up again and narrowly missed us. We emerged out of the trees and into the relative comfort of the moonlight once more. With nothing in pursuit, we pulled in at the tarmac.

"Christ, we have got to swap helmets," said Reece. In the rush we had put on each other's and Reece's head is about eight sizes bigger than mine. I've no idea how he managed to get it on. We swapped, buckled up the bags, and sped off down the tarmac. Still pumped full of adrenaline, we were going as fast as the bike would let us. We agreed that there was no way we were wild camping after that, we would just keep driving until we found another human and if that meant driving until dawn then so be it.

Around thirty minutes later we pulled up in the small town of Lee Vining. To our relief we found a campsite with an honesty box, so we were able to just drive in and pitch up. We were very happy to be behind a fence.

The following morning we awoke to another gorgeous day in California. We had survived the night before and were excited to truck on into Yosemite National Park. Plus we were planning to stay indoors that night so we didn't have a worry in the world. The scenery in Yosemite was pretty remarkable and we had a great ride through. After riding for a short while we pulled in by a lake and decided to take some shots of the sidecar riding through the park. Reece climbed up a bank to get a decent high, wide shot and I sped off down the road to get out of view. I then quickly whizzed the bike around like I had done a million times before but somehow got it horribly wrong. The chair lifted up and I drove in a straight line into the ditch on the side of the road. It was our first ever crash. Fortunately, there was no damage and a passer-by helped me pull it out of the ditch. Reece was pretty pissed off when I came back down the road a solid twenty minutes later, though.

We spent the morning exploring the park and took in the sights. One of the most staggering things to see that day were the bare, scorched hillsides that had been decimated by forest fires just a couple of weeks earlier. Some of the park had been saved but huge chunks of it were just charred remains of what was there before. We eventually left the park and made a final push for the coast. At around 6 p.m. we took the Oakland Bay Bridge into San Francisco and arrived to our destination for the evening, Marc's house.

We had met Marc back in South Africa when Flight Centre had sorted us with that freebie in Kruger. He had said, "If you're ever in San Francisco, you have to stay at mine. I'll make it the best stop in the world." I don't think he thought we were serious when we said, "Well, give us six months, Marc, and we'll take you up on it." Yet, here we were, on his doorstep, stinking as usual and looking gross. We were welcomed into his downtown flat and handed a drop of top-quality red wine. We more or less didn't put down said glass of top-quality red wine for the next three days.

Marc and his girlfriend, now fiancée (congratulations guys), Sarah, showed us what life was like as a twenty-something in a good job in San Francisco, and it is good. We spent our time hanging out in cool bars, watching movies on his projector screen, and checking out all of the incredible scenery. We did the usual stuff like Alcatraz, Fremont Street, and Fisherman's Wharf, but also lived life as San Franciscans for a few days and just enjoyed the local area. We even went and did our clothes in a launderette; it was all very "city life in the States."

After hanging around like a bad smell (literally) for too many nights, we finally clawed ourselves away from Marc and Sarah's awesome life and back to ours as a couple of idiot sidecarists on the road. Marc lived about five miles from the Golden Gate Bridge and that was our route out of town so we headed straight for it. We didn't get away until the afternoon, having spent far too long trying to find any excuse not to leave, so we pulled up to the bridge at around 4 p.m. If you've not been, then go. It's as awesome as you'd imagine it to be. We were somewhat distracted, though, because despite doing a bit of maintenance at Marc's place the bike was a complete mess. Here's a list of problems that we posted on Facebook from the Golden Gate Bridge car park:

Exhaust sounds like it's fallen off (sounds even louder when the back brake is pulled on).

Back brake fails now and again.

Struggles to start in the morning.

Overheats after ten minutes at high speed or after a big climb.

Transmission sounds like a dog's dinner.

Back wheel wobbles a bit.

Centre stand has half fallen off.

So it was a complete mess. We spent some time trying to tinker with it in the car park but were getting nowhere. We had planned to press on a bit and camp up in the redwoods, but after our last forest experience, we decided it wasn't worth the risk and I suggested we just sleep by the bike, overlooking the bridge. It seemed stupid at first, seeing as we were about three miles from Marc's gaff, but actually it made a lot of sense. We had made progress and we'd get to watch the sun set and rise over the incredible Golden Gate Bridge. Also it meant there would be no rushing and we even had a chance to pop down to Sausalito, a little tourist town and home to many of the city's mega-rich stars. We had first been here back in 2010 and it was the first stop on our "gap yah." I remember sitting on the seafront eating fish and chips and feeling an overwhelming excitement and appreciation for how lucky I was to be out of the factories and living the dream. We decided to do the same again that night and, sat watching over the bay, I felt like I had been taken back in time. It's a truly incredible spot and is the place where Otis Redding wrote "Sitting on the Dock of the Bay," so you can imagine how peaceful it is.

We returned back to the car park by the bridge in time for sunset and watched as the glowing red sky surrounded the towering red structure that sat in front of us. It was an incredible sight and after a night under the stars in our usual hammock and sleeping mat set-up, we saw it all over again, this time with a cup of hot coffee, ready for a new day on the road. We woke up to a message from a guy called Roger Vise. We didn't know him but he was a sidecar enthusiast who had been following our trip and lived just a hundred miles up the road in a place called Lower Lake. He said he had loads of experience of working on rigs like ours and said we'd be welcome to stay at his place while we fixed it up together. What an offer! We of course took him up on it, and after a glorious, misty sunrise by the bridge we pressed on to Roger's.

We arrived at Roger's house in Lower Lake to find a very welcoming man in his 60s stood waving and smiling in a super-bright, tie-dyed shirt. He looked like he'd come straight from a Jimi Hendrix set at Woodstock or a Vietnam protest or something. We knew we'd get along straight away. Roger showed us around the place first. He lived on his own and as a result the garage and the house had become one. The dining room table had another motorcycle project on it, and everywhere you looked in the house —and I mean everywhere you looked— there was some kind of motorcycle project, textbook on how to fix stuff, or tools to do the work with. He lived and breathed fixing stuff and was keen to dig straight into having a look at the bike.

As we started to strip the bike down and unpack, it became apparent that Roger is one of those guys who has an ability to find a story in absolutely everything. If you were taking the nut off the scooter wheel he'd say, "Now these nuts are pretty good, reminds me of the nuts we used to have on the old scooters down at Burning Man festival . . . ." And then he'd go on to recount some awesome story of riding to Burning Man festival in a vehicle shaped like a shoe. Which is a true story, by the way, he really did that. So for those of you who know about Burning Man festival you'll know quite a bit about what Roger's like already, as you have to be a certain kind of person to go. If you've never heard of it, then think Glastonbury but even more eccentric people and quirky ideas, and instead of a muddy field, you're in a scorching hot desert. One of Roger's passions was to take quirky things he had made to the festival. Ironically and sadly, bushfires had swept through the area the year before and he had lost most of his contraptions when his barn caught fire. He also lost about $100,000 worth of rare vehicles that he had acquired through a lifetime of work. He was only able to show us the remains and a couple of vehicles he'd been able to save.

We spent all afternoon stripping the bike down and working out the problems. Turned out we had snapped a bolt that held the engine in place and as a result the engine was only held on by one fixing. If that was to go, it would fall out beneath us and the bike would be a complete write-off. That was top of the "to-fix list," then. Further to that, we had to fix a hole in the exhaust pipe, bleed the brakes and coolant to put those right, fix the centre stand, service the shocks, and repair and replace a couple of other sidecar fixings. We stripped it all down that afternoon, ready for a full day of repairs the following morning. In the evening we decided to hit the local town for a bit of fun with Roger.

We went out for a ride in his old Citroen 2CV. It was a convertible, and they have no back seats, so we were crammed in, all sat on each other's laps along the front. It was a very cool car, maybe even more of a head-turner than Kuishi. We cruised down to the lakefront and went to one of Roger's favourite bars for a couple of beers and some wings. There was live music, country and western style, and Roger was in his element. No sooner had we sat down, Roger had approached a lady and asked her for a dance. Two seconds later and they were strutting their stuff on the dance floor. Proper dancing too, the kind of stuff you see in old movies. Next, we pressed on to a local pool hall and Roger started to strut his stuff on the table. We had a couple of games with the locals before sitting down to chat about hot topics in the USA. Roger was a fairly opinionated guy and all of it was clearly well-substantiated with a crapload of thought and reading. He talked us through why Trump's the worst thing ever and why growing weed should be and is becoming legal right across the States.

We rolled back into Roger's house at about one in the morning having had a corker of a night. Just as we were going to bed Roger said, "Sorry if I wake you in the morning boys, I'll be in the tub at first light."

"Well, we'll join you then Roger!" I replied.

Cut to about 5 a.m. I look up through exceptionally blurry, still half-cut eyes, to see Roger in his swimmers, holding a towel, hooting like an owl to wake me up. "Comin' tub boy?" he said, after he saw me stir.

"Uhhh, no thanks actually Roger, I'll give it a go later!"

We got up a couple of hours later and paid a visit to America's favourite restaurant, McDonald's. It was a Saturday and Roger spends every Saturday morning chewing the fat with his pals at Maccy D's. There were four or five regulars there when we arrived, and one riding an old Ural outfit, so we really had found our people in Lower Lake, California. We all tucked into a glorious double Sausage and Egg McMuffin meal and talked all about sidecars and travelling for an hour or so. Hangovers cured, we headed back to Roger's, where we met his son Avery, who had come by to hang out and help us fix up the scooter. As you can imagine, Avery was as well versed with mechanics as his dad and was actually the top engineer for a classic car collector down the road.

Breaking for an absolute corker of a burrito at lunch, we had a cracking day fixing up the sidecar and sharing stories. We also had to break to do a Facebook Live session with Freedom United. They had connected us with HAART in Kenya but we had actually been working with them since the early days of planning for the trip and they were a huge reason for it happening. When we first approached them we were desperately trying to find anyone who would be associated with us. We had been for meetings with the charity Anti-Slavery International in London, but then they had a change of heart and decided we would probably die as our plans were far too dangerous. We couldn't believe it when Freedom United, called the Walk Free Foundation at the time, said they would be up for getting behind our plans. We loved the idea of the organisation and thought it was completely in line with our goals. Their plan is to unify and inform the fight against modern slavery, and they try to work as an umbrella network for charities and non-profits that fight modern slavery around the world. They have about six million Facebook fans and we went out to them live in Roger's back yard. It wasn't really a resounding success as most of the Freedom United fans didn't show up, but it was a nice way to catch up with Reece's entire family, who were prepped with questions to ask in the Q&A.

It was a family-oriented day for Reece because that night we popped up the road to stay at his grandad's house. He lived in a cabin in the woods with his wife, Jek, literally just up the road. Reece hadn't seen him since his early teens and barely knew him at all. Sadly, we found, Mel, Reece's grandad, in his last months. He passed away in 2019. He was more or less trapped by his bed when we went to stay, but I think he was genuinely thrilled to have Reece come by and visit. He told us some interesting stories about his extraordinary life. Most notably, tales of working on a listening post during the Cold War. His lovely wife, Jek, made us an absolutely glorious dinner, too. We stuffed ourselves silly and then enjoyed a few beers with them, something Mel probably shouldn't have done, but it put a smile on his face, and that's all that really mattered at that point. They lived in an absolutely idyllic spot— you had to walk over a really bouncy bridge to get to the cabin. Behind them was mountainous woodland and in front a river trickling by. I imagine if Mel could have chosen anywhere in the world to spend some of his last days, it would have been there.

The following morning we waved goodbye to Mel and Jek and met with Roger for one final morning of repairing the bike. Kuishi was looking absolutely brilliant. It had been fixed up wonderfully, so much so that it was handling as well as it did when we left Richard Prescott's barn.

Before we left I asked Roger how much we owed him for all of his and Avery's work, he replied with a big smile and, "I don't want any money boys but what I do want is a t-shirt from a sidecar club in some weird part of the world." Incredible, three days of helping us and he wanted nothing but a t-shirt in return. We thanked Roger and then headed north towards Canada. I said to Reece as we did, "You know what, mate, I think this thing will get home without another problem now. It's in the best condition ever."

– 18 –

"WE ADMITTED DEFEAT, ADMITTED CERTAIN DEATH, AND STOPPED TO STARE AT THE HEADLIGHTS GETTING CLOSER."

"Just ridiculous," I muttered under my breath, as Reece filmed me pushing the bike through a giant drive-through redwood tree. We had made it about a hundred miles up the road from Roger's house and we had broken down again. This time it really was absolutely ridiculous. All had been going smoothly, we had made it into the area famed for having some of the biggest trees in the world, and they are staggeringly gigantic. We couldn't really appreciate them though, because we were focusing on our staggeringly stupid scooter and sidecar. As we scooted in the shade of the redwoods, we came across a sign for a drive-through tree so after agreeing that it's not every day you get to drive through the middle of a tree, we pulled in. Unfortunately, it was a national holiday so the tourists were out in full force. We queued for a while and as we slowly edged closer down the single lane of traffic to drive through this big tree, I noticed the back brake didn't quite feel right. I jumped off the bike and went to take a look. Sure enough, there was a problem, a fairly major one too. Melted metal was everywhere.

"Oh my word, mate, it's buggered," I said to Reece.

"You are kidding?" Reece exclaimed.

He got out to have a look, too, and we saw that there was no nut on the rear wheel and it had moved sideways, crashing into some bolts and melting them into the disk. It was a wonder we were still on the road at all. Not wanting to risk worsening the situation, we agreed we should turn the bike off and push it through the tree. The minibus full of Japanese tourists in front found it to be a very strange way to go through the tree and looked truly puzzled by us.

We assessed the situation after and realised that we were in for another long repair. We had no spare nut and had completely lost the existing one. Plus we somehow had to get the melted metal off the disk in order to get our brake working. We pulled up Google Maps on my phone and saw that we were less than a mile from a campsite. With no choice, we jumped on the scooter and drove down to the campsite at about 5 mph.

It was actually a brilliant spot and we were able to sling our hammocks up between a couple of the smaller trees. To give you an idea of the size of some of the trees in the area, if we had joined our hammocks and straps together, we wouldn't have got around one trunk. Our next door neighbours were getting settled in for the night and needed a hand carrying firewood, so I mucked in and earnt us a couple of ice cold beers in return. We were broken down but it could have been a lot worse.

After visiting the little campsite shop and finding out that they didn't stock Honda SH300i wheel nuts, we decided to just settle in for the evening and plan how to get to a town in the morning. By the time we had finished setting up camp it was dark anyway and we decided to just have a cheap night on our camping stove. I popped in two boil-in-the-bag vegetable curries and we sat down to a game of chess while they cooked. Around five minutes later, the owner of a local shop came by with a nut. It looked like the right size! We quickly put the bike on the centre stand, whipped off the exhaust and placed the nut on the spindle. It did fit but unfortunately it was the wrong size thread. I thought it might just be a bit of a dodgy end so I decided to push the bike off the centre stand and give the nut a good turn with no movement in the wheel. As I pushed the bike, we were suddenly plunged into darkness. I had pushed it onto my phone light. It was completely smashed into pieces, having had the whole weight of the bike roll onto it.

It was one of those days—a broken bike and now a broken phone. "Let's just have some dinner and hit the hammocks," I said to Reece.

"Balls! Dinner!" Reece replied.

We returned to a pool of melted plastic on a dry stove, we had completely forgotten about it. Admitting defeat, we bought a hot dog from the campsite's food stand and turned in for the night. What a day.

I awoke the following morning having had a fantastic night's kip in the hammock. They're truly cracking if it's warm enough or you have the right set-up. I started the morning off by banging a cup of coffee on and just enjoying being in the outdoors. One good thing about breaking your phone is that you no longer have a phone. No need to take pictures, no need to reply to messages, no need to send emails, no need to post on social media. An opportunity to just sit and appreciate the place. I loved the parts of the trip in which I could do that.

About halfway through my cup of coffee, a park ranger came over and said, "I hear you boys are a bit stuck."

I explained we just needed a nut but had no way of getting to the next town, which was about fifteen miles away.

"No problem, I'll give you a ride. Jump in."

Amazing! The next thing we knew we were driving off to the local town to find a spare part. I, of course, started quizzing her about her job as a park ranger. It turned out they have the same authority as the police in California and they actually spend most of their time genuinely fighting crime. The biggest part of their job is shutting down weed farms. Apparently, the hills are full of people growing the stuff, as there are no jobs in the area and it's the only way to make cash. So, I certainly learned something that day. I thought park rangers just sort of mooched about, checking on the bears, but nope, they're practically the DEA.

We found a nut no problem in the next town and by lunch time we had packed up camp, fitted the wheel and were ready to hit the road. We drove about ten miles up the road and then suddenly the exhaust started to sound like it was falling off again! Kuishi really was playing up. We agreed to pick up some more parts in town and crack on five miles to another lovely campsite in the woods. We spent the afternoon fixing the bike up as best we could. I tried to get the melted metal off the disk by putting the back wheel in the air, holding a file to the disk and hitting the accelerator. It didn't work. We turned to sanding it off properly, which took all evening but meant we could use our brakes in the morning. The exhaust pipe was full of holes but we managed to get some high-temperature exhaust tape to wrap it up with and that held fairly well, too. A good evening in the workshop, all in all.

The following day was relatively trouble-free and we were able to make our way north out of California and into Oregon. The drive was incredible, just fantastic scenery the whole way with much of it through the giant redwood forests. Arriving in Oregon, we came across signs for bushfires everywhere and thought it might mean we would have a tough time finding somewhere to camp. Fortunately, that wasn't the case and we pulled up to a little camping area right next to a river. I went for a dip in it, too. It was completely clear but had a fast current so was quite the work-out. Again, we found a perfect spot for the hammocks and as I lay in mine I could watch the local deer population grazing in the grass on the river banks. It was a pretty cool spot.

A second day in a row with no mechanical problems meant we were cruising at high speeds towards Canada. We pressed on north through Oregon and stopped in the town of Bend to visit Reece's grandma's grave. It took us a while to find, but that didn't matter at all because we were only going as far as his cousin's house in Vancouver, Washington. Staying at Reece's cousin's house was amazing. They had a lovely home in the suburbs, with gorgeous beds and showers, and everything was super clean. It was just brilliant. They were incredibly friendly and welcoming, exceptionally generous, and made us the most delicious dinners.

It was also a really interesting experience. We spent a couple of evenings chatting around the patio table with Michael and Sophie. We covered all range of topics and I fundamentally disagreed with almost everything that Michael said. Amongst other things, Michael thought logging was a good thing and the NHS is bad for people in the UK and healthcare globally. Now they are two fairly strong viewpoints. I think he's one of very few people I have ever met who have had that view, or is he? It struck me that I actually come across people with these different viewpoints regularly in life but I choose to ignore it. I scroll quickly past on my Facebook feed, tutting and calling them misinformed or idiots as I go. Here, though, I couldn't scroll past Michael and I certainly couldn't tut or call him an idiot, he had just cooked me a fantastic steak and welcomed me into his house.

We dove into the chat and I think we both learnt a little. Michael said that he agrees with logging because he thinks it protects the forest. He thinks if it's done right it creates barriers to forest fires and ultimately saves more trees than it takes, at the same time as creating jobs. Well, I only had to give him five minutes and he had given me a bloody good argument, I mean if that was in any way true then it actually sounded pretty sensible. He just said pro-logging and I jumped to Republican right wing, Trump fanatic, wanting to tear down the Amazon rainforest to make a McDonald's coffee cup.

His reasoning for the NHS comment? Don't pay as much for your healthcare and there's less money in the healthcare system. Less money in the healthcare system and there's less money for research. Less money for research and there's less money for developing cures and treatments, meaning a worse healthcare system overall. Now, I don't necessarily agree with that but crucially it has good intentions behind it. He's not there saying, "Well if you don't got no money, you clearly don't work hard enough and you shouldn't get no treatment," which is what I instantly put him down as when he insulted my precious NHS.

I'm still not pro-logging and do really like the NHS, but I think the conversation woke me up to the importance of debate and listening to one another. We just don't do it anymore, our social media algorithms find us a bunch of people we like and a bunch we hate and then we just go about liking and hating on people. I actually had to drive 15,000 miles by scooter and sidecar and stay in someone's house in order to truly learn that I should stop and listen to people I don't agree with. If we could work out how to make listening to other people's views without judgment the norm, I think we'd get a long way in society. Also, Michael had just had a neck operation and sounded like Batman so that too could have been why I listened to him. I mean nobody ignores Batman.

We left the Batcave and cracked on north again towards Canada. Next stop was Seattle. Again, we had been invited to stay at somebody's house. This time it was another adventure sidecarist called Alan Ayres. After a fairly trouble-free day we arrived at Alan's house but still with a couple of problems to fix, namely a very loose exhaust and a broken sidecar joint. No problem for Alan, who got straight to it. He pulled his welder out, fixed up the joint and found a good bolt to fit our exhaust mounting to. Fixed as easy as that and we were free to enjoy our evening. Alan showed us where we would be staying for the night, which was our very own caravan next to the house. Absolutely perfect. We were able to keep all of our stinking stuff out of his home. As we left the caravan, Alan pointed out something in the garden, a full-size cut-out of Bigfoot with flashing red lights as eyes.

"Yeah, I believe in Bigfoot, boys, so my wife got me that for my birthday."

"Haha, love it, good one Alan," I said as I closed the caravan door.

"No really lads, I'm a believer. Don't worry though, I've been a believer for the last thirty years and I know it exists, I've no need to try and convince anyone else anymore."

We popped inside, sat down for a minute, had a bit of small talk and then I had to approach the elephant in the room.

"So, Alan, this Bigfoot thing, you pulling our leg or what?"

Alan then proceeded to spend the entire evening teaching us about Bigfoot and with my newfound appreciation for listening I was soaking it up like a sponge. Alan believes that Bigfoot exists all over the world. Whether it's referred to as Sasquatch, Yeti, or any other local term, they all describe the same thing: a hyper-intelligent, gigantic, ape-like creature with big feet. Alan goes to the Bigfoot conventions and has been reading up on this stuff his entire life. He is absolutely sure that all major governments are aware of Bigfoot but there is a global cover-up to prevent a need to rewrite the textbooks. He believes that if Bigfoot was proven to exist we would be lower down the pecking order and it would jeopardise human domination of the planet. He says that the cover-up is evidenced by veterans who have talked about how they were sent to Canada to help bury dead Bigfoots after their habitat was ravaged by forest fire.

Alan had brought in some pizza for us all and we spent the evening gorging on it and watching videos or hearing stories about Bigfoot. He showed us some famous footage of Bigfoot, which is commonly acknowledged as a hoax, but Alan argues they have done tests and not even pro athletes can mimic the walking style of the creature in the film. He then played us some audio that a team of researchers captured from the inside of a shelter they had made in a tree, in a forest in North America. It sounded like apes talking to each other and banging on the doors. There are, of course, no apes in North America. It led us on to a discussion of what Bigfoot sounds like and we took it in turns trying to nail it down. According to the recordings, it's a really high pitched, "Ooooooooooooooooo-up."

Alan says that some days he will get his sidecar and drive off into the forest near him just to look for Bigfoot. He'll get to an area where there's nobody around for a hundred miles and he'll stand in a clearing going, "Ooooooooooo-up." A risky business, he says, considering how dangerous they can be. There are reports of humans being kidnapped, probed and experimented with before being killed or released. Alan told us about one time he woke up at a campsite and finally thought it was the day he'd see one. Finally, what he was so sure of would be confirmed forever. The bushes in front of him were rustling, a huge area. "It must be Bigfoot," he had thought, and then out walked a cow. We told him our story about the unknown beast we had encountered east of Yosemite and he agreed that there was a very high chance we'd had an encounter with Bigfoot. It was an interesting night to say the least.

We drove off the following morning excited for the road ahead. We'd be heading to Canada and Alaska, camping as we went in the complete wilderness. Alan wished us luck and told us to take care, as we were heading into Bigfoot's most natural habitat, huge chunks of land with no humans and only trees. I've got to admit, I was a bit nervous after all the evidence he'd presented.

As we had been making our way through North America we had been trying to work out which way to go next. We had always planned to go from Anchorage, Alaska, to Chukotka, Russia, but that was now completely out of the question. We'd tried every single shipping and air freight company and we had two plausible routes: ship from Vancouver, Canada, to either Singapore or Vladivostok, Russia. We had decided to take the Singapore option and try to bring the bike back across the Himalayas and then through Iran as, with it now being September, we would be driving through Russia mid-winter, a more or less impossible task. Unfortunately, though, Iran-UK relations had taken a big hit and they had decided that any person on a UK passport wouldn't be allowed to take their own vehicle through the country, not even with a guide. That completely cut off the route home. We would either have to take a huge financial hit on China (at least US$10,000) or double-ship again from India. Russia it was then. That meant getting through North America as quickly as possible and getting to Russia before winter really kicked in. We put it to our Facebook fans and asked for people to vote. Should we go to Alaska and risk being even colder in Siberia, or should we just go to Vladivostok straight away and hopefully make it home?

The votes were counted and incredibly the final count was 52% to 48% in favour of Alaska. We made some jokes about the similarities with the Brexit result and said we would follow the will of the people, but we would opt for a soft Alaska and go to Hyder, the most southerly town, accessible by road. First, though, we would be heading to Vancouver to meet friends and family. Chels had flown there to meet with our friends Ally and Toby. Ally is from Vancouver and she offered for us all to stay with her at her parents' place. The drive there should have been incredibly straightforward. Nothing ever is by scooter and sidecar, though, and as we crossed Seattle's busiest bridge our exhaust completely fell off. Somehow, all of the bolts we'd put in at Alan's had come out. We were absolutely bricking it. We couldn't go back down the bridge as it was one way, and we had no idea if the exhaust had come off and crashed into someone behind, either. It could have been deadly. We dove into a garage as we pulled off the bridge and came across a highway maintenance guy. We explained what had happened and he went to try and find it for us.

Meanwhile we got a cup of coffee and chatted to some local people who told us we were over the road from Bill Gates' house. Good to know. Maybe he would shout us a new exhaust! The maintenance guy came back about thirty minutes later. He couldn't find it. It had disappeared entirely. This was a big problem, the scooter sounded so, so loud without a muffler and we didn't know if it was even legal to ride without one in Canada or the US. We were pretty concerned that we wouldn't get through the border to Vancouver. This was of even more concern because Chels had just sent us a picture of Graham, Ally's dad, preparing the most gorgeous joint of ham for dinner. We had to make it. We went to a couple of repair shops but had no luck. Finally, we decided to just buy some ear plugs and go for it.

The sound was unbearably loud but the bike drove fine. It wasn't long before we were queueing at the border point, trying to turn the bike off at any opportunity and praying nobody would notice. We got through the US side nice and easy, but getting into Canada we were asked to pull in so the bike could be inspected. We thought we were done for, but twenty minutes later, after a few stories from the road, we were allowed into Canada.

We arrived at Ally's house sounding like a Harley-Davidson and looking a complete state as usual. Chels was the first to greet us and it was fab to see her again. It had been a few months since we had parted ways in Panama. In the meantime she had been working at a women's co-operative in Guatemala and had lots of cool stories to tell. We met Graham and Judy, Ally's mum, as well as her sister Norma and Norma's boyfriend, Sam. The place was full of life and we had a brilliant evening laughing about our run-ins with Bigfoot and other stuff. The food was out of this world and we were stuffed. Over the next few days we chilled out and explored the city at the same time as getting the bike fixed up. We found a guy called the Muffler Man and he agreed to fit a car exhaust for us. It worked, too, and we looked pretty cool. It did melt the plastic away from the side of the scooter but nobody cared because we could hear again.

After a few days at Ally's we went to the other side of Vancouver to an Airbnb as my parents had flown in to see us. They had arranged to come to Canada from the start of the trip and had managed to line up the dates perfectly. It was awesome to see them but they had the same problem that Reece's parents had, in that coming on holiday to see us most likely meant using your time off work to traipse around mechanic shops looking for parts. On this occasion it was an oxygen sensor. We did get some sightseeing done and we all went for dinner with Ally's family as a last goodbye to them before setting off north towards Alaska. My parents hired a car and, along with Chels, they joined us along the Sea to Sky Highway towards Whistler. It's an incredible stretch of road with truly amazing views of the rugged coastline and fantastic mountains.

We stayed in Whistler for a couple of nights and just explored the surrounding area. We spent some time shopping for kit, too, and acquired some massive sleeping bags that would apparently be good down to −30°C for Russia. Then my parents and Chels turned south and we pushed on north for Hyder. Nobody was sad at all, though, no teary goodbyes, we were all just pissed off that Reece and I would be on a flight back about a week later. Well, Chels wasn't pissed off and neither were my parents but it was quite funny that they had come to visit us in the week we received the news that we would have to return to the UK. It turned out that Russia wouldn't let us in unless we gave our fingerprints in the Russian Embassy in London.

We tried everything to avoid going home to get it. We wrote to embassies in the US and Canada, we pleaded with the Russian Embassy in the UK and we even genuinely looked into getting Canadian citizenship. All we got back from every option was a no, though. Unfortunately, going home for the visa was genuinely the only option. Practically speaking it made no difference whatsoever. We had a month to kill while the shipping took place anyway, but for us it was huge. We both had this dream of driving out of the UK and then returning by driving in from the other way, having gone around the entire planet. Sadly, that really wasn't an option if we also wanted to be the first people to circumnavigate the globe on a scooter and sidecar as we had to keep driving for it to stand as one trip.

We were actually planning to be on a flight back about three weeks later. That would give us enough time to get up to Hyder for our soft Alaska, back down to Vancouver to ship the bike and then back to Banbury in time for my brother's wedding in early October. It's funny how things work out like that. I genuinely didn't let Lee's wedding into the decision-making process. Even though I really, really wanted to be there, I wasn't going to let anything get in the way of riding around in one complete circle. Incredibly, the timing fitted bang on and I would be back in the UK right when they were planning to tie the knot. Fortunately, Flight Centre were as brilliant as ever and completely understood our Russia problem, so shouted us the flights to come home. We booked them in, had an absolutely humongous breakfast courtesy of my parents (I think mum was trying to keep us full for the following three weeks), and then set off north from Whistler, heading for Hyder.

In case you didn't know, Canada is fricking massive and although it doesn't look far from Whistler to the southernmost point of Alaska, it's still a good 1,300 km. We started to experience problems with the bike on our first day heading north. The exhaust was sounding very loud again and we thought we could lose it at any point. We tried to tighten it up and kept pressing on.

The good thing about Canada is that, apart from Bigfoot, there's nothing there. You can camp anywhere. We pulled in on the first night to a car park that overlooked a wonderful canyon. It was small and filled with thick forest. We were the only people around for miles and looking out into that wilderness we couldn't help but think Alan had a point. It's massive out there; big things must live in it. They do, to be fair. They're called bears. The place is riddled with them. We still didn't have any bear spray or a foghorn either so, as always, we were completely reliant on luck.

However, we had at least arrived to this campsite in the daytime so could have a bit of a walk around to get comfortable with our surroundings. There was a hedgeline that marked one side, a road running parallel to the cliff and an opening to a path that runs alongside the canyon on the other side. There was only one way to explore, then. We went about twenty yards down the path and came to a grave site. Brilliant, just what you want when you're camping out in the wilds on your own, an unmarked grave. We decided exploring was a bad idea and returned to the tent with a cup of tea. After the sun went down, we went off to bed and got into our exceptionally toasty new sleeping bags. They were brilliant and we were off to sleep in no time.

Suddenly, I woke up to the sound of a train approaching. I thought I was going crazy at first. We had walked the area when we arrived and there was no train track, but then we were lit up from its headlight and it felt like it was coming right for us. It was getting louder and louder. Reece sat bolt upright out of nowhere and shouted, "Get off the line!" He wasn't joking around, he was deadly serious. I think he must have been dreaming about it. Or was I dreaming the whole thing? What the hell was happening? It was getting closer and closer. We both started frantically shuffling to get out of our sleeping bags but it was no use, it was coming right for us. We had really done it this time, there was no getting away, our luck had run out, we were going to get flattened by a train because of our own stupidity. We admitted defeat, admitted certain death, and stopped to stare at the headlights getting closer. And then it sounded its horn and veered off to the left. We opened the front of the tent and saw it hurtling past alongside the road. The track was hiding between two big hedges. We honestly thought we were dust. As soon as it passed I was in absolute stitches. Reece really had shot up and shouted, "Get off the line!"

We popped outside the tent for a minute to get some air after the ordeal, when we saw that we had company. Why on earth was there another car here? We walked straight over and introduced ourselves, we had learnt all the way back in Albania that it's far better just to say hi than it is to sit and worry about who they might be. It turned out he was a worker at a local timber mill and he just slept here when he was working late. We were pretty pleased to have him around and got our heads down for a trouble-free night.

The following morning we woke up and pressed on north towards Prince George. We made it there no problem and pulled into a Tim Hortons to grab some dinner before going out into the wilderness for another wild camp. We pulled into camp about ten miles outside of the town on the 37, which runs for about 500 miles all the way to Hyder. We had a soft Alaska well and truly in our sights. Our camping spot for the night was pretty cool again. A small lake by the roadside. Nobody around at all and completely quiet. I went off for a wild poo in the woods, which was always a fun thing to do. I have to say I never took Gemma's advice and held onto a tree, I was always pretty good at balancing. From my very rural lavatory I could see the emerald lake and nothing but pine trees. Having attended to my business I came back to a very quiet Reece. He pointed down by the lake and we could see a coyote. We'd never seen one before and it was pretty cool to sit and watch it for a while.

A guy came along to walk his dog later that evening, but apart from that we were all good: no trains, no bears, no problems at all. We woke up early the following morning thinking that with a good day's ride we might even make it all the way to Hyder, but after about ten miles, disaster struck. I was driving along when I lost all power in the scooter. We pulled over to have a look and there was mangled stuff coming out of the transmission again. This time it wasn't metal though, it was a rubbery, stringy fabric. The drive belt had gone. Fortunately, the person in the truck behind saw us lose power and pulled in next to us. His name was Nate and he was driving north for work so had a truck full of tools.

Nate helped us get the crankcase off and together we managed to fit our old belt, which we had been carrying as a spare. The only problem was that the old belt had been damaged in a previous clutch explosion and had three or four teeth missing. It was on its last legs and we were worried. If we pressed on for the remote town of Hyder, population 97, and got stuck there, we could easily end up there for the entire winter. The snows would be coming soon and the town would be cut off. Ordering parts in could take weeks.

If we got stuck there for weeks or the entire winter then we could end up facing Siberia in deepest, darkest winter or losing the Guinness World Record altogether. We came to the conclusion that we should go against the will of the people and ignore the

Facebook vote. We know people voted for Alaska and we had every intention on delivering on it, so went for a soft Alaska, but when it became apparent that even a soft Alaska could take our future out of our hands and potentially leave us much worse off, we decided we had to cancel it all together. It was a tough decision but one that ultimately turned out better for everyone. We turned back around and headed towards Vancouver, ready to ship the bike for the final and most challenging part of the trip: Russia!

"GUYS PLEASE WAIT FOR SUMMER, THERE IS NOTHING THERE, YOU WILL NOT MAKE IT, YOU WILL DIE."

We were surrounded by quintessentially breathtaking Canadian scenery as we stood in a lay-by holding our exhaust in our arms. It had fallen off again, but what a spot for it to go. Steep banks, lined with fir trees, emerged from the fast-flowing river below. The golden hills dotted with green trees soared off into the clouds above, and on the horizon we could see a train approaching. We stood and watched as it snaked its way along the riverside. It seemed to take forever to get into shot, but as we silently sat there watching it get closer and closer, we realised what was coming. We looked at each other and, without saying a word, both stood up and started waving at it as it came hurtling by on the track below.

We were in disbelief. Here in front of us was the Rocky Mountaineer! The best way to see Canada by far. Well that's what we would tell you on the phones at Flight Centre anyway. Of course, in reality the best way to see Canada is on a scooter and sidecar. Seeing this golden train with its curved glass carriages come past was a truly bizarre feeling. I think we both remembered selling the Rocky Mountaineer and dreaming of one day taking that trip for ourselves and now here we were holding the exhaust of a bike we'd driven from the UK, waving at the passengers below as they steamrolled past and into their holidays. We were genuinely stunned as this symbol of our lives before the trip just rolled straight into our adventure and took us back to behind a screen on Oxford Street.

After a few seconds it had passed through and we were back on our adventure. There was no way we were getting our new, dodgy exhaust back on. We admitted defeat and chucked it in the sidecar before agreeing that we would go back to Vancouver and have some choice words with the Muffler Man. The ride through this beautiful part of the world was easy on the eyes but hard on the ears as our scooter was back to roaring like a Harley again. After a long day's ride, we were nearly halfway back to Vancouver and, with sunset not far off, we decided to find somewhere to camp. I pulled up iOverlander and saw a decent, suggested wild camping spot by a lake, just off the main road. Perfect.

As always, we turned down the rough gravel track and started riding out into the wilderness, hoping for a good spot and a quiet night's sleep. After two or three miles, though, there was still no lake. We had clearly gone the wrong way but we pressed on regardless, looking for a nice spot out of the way. Again, anywhere would have done but for some reason we just couldn't pick a spot. About thirty minutes in, we decided we'd driven too far and that we would turn back and camp up on the side of this gravel road somewhere closer to the tarmac, ready for a big drive to Vancouver the following morning. Fifteen minutes later, just as we were about to pull into camp somewhere, a baby black bear jumped out of the bushes in front of us. It stood for a split second and then bounded off down the track before diving into the hedge on the other side. It was incredible to see. We were so excited to get to see a real-life baby bear in the wild, but at the same time we couldn't help but think, "Where's mother bear?" After our last fiasco, we decided we didn't want to hang around to find out and wimpishly drove back out to the main road. By this time it was dark and we were miles away from anything in the middle of the Canadian wilderness. Fortunately, we spotted a lay-by with a lorry pulled over in it for the night and we decided to pull in there and camp up for the night. At least that way, if the bears came back we would be able to jump in the cab.

We pressed on south again the following day but the weather turned on us and torrential rain was causing havoc on the roads. Someone up ahead had spun out at high speed and caused themselves some real bother. We found ourselves lined up in a queue that snaked back for miles. We waited on the bike at first but, with the rain coming in sideways, we decided to stand in the relative shelter of the truck in front. We were there so long that we actually ended up whipping our stove out and cracking on a cup of coffee. Eventually, the air ambulance came overhead, which a local person told me was a good thing because hopefully it meant we weren't waiting for the coroner to arrive. Firstly, because the coroner coming would mean someone had died but, secondly, because there are no other roads and with this one closed we could be queuing for hours, if not all night.

Fortunately, after a couple of hours, the air ambulance took off, the road opened, and we drove on. It was too far and the conditions too treacherous to make it through to Vancouver, so for the last time in North America we pulled into a roadside motel and got our heads down for the night. Then, the following day we hobbled over the finish line into Vancouver, again arriving to Graham and Judy's, and again with our ears ringing and our exhaust not where it should be.

This time, with Chels gone back to the UK and with Ally and Toby back in London, too, the Sheane house was a lot quieter, but it hadn't lost that incredibly warm welcome. We stayed with Graham and Judy for at least another week while we prepared to ship the bike on to Vladivostok. In that time we were treated like royalty. Graham has a bit of a passion for cooking and he made some incredible food while we were there. Wonderful roast dinners and sensational stews were a regular thing, but one night he pulled out all the stops with roasted halibut in a tomato sauce. It was served with rice and broccoli cheese. Just plain old broccoli would have done the job but Graham had turned it into this glorious cheesy mess. We asked him why and he said, "We didn't spend thousands of years climbing to the top of the food chain to eat broccoli. How many lions or sharks do you see eating broccoli?" I've got to admit I liked his thought process and I enjoyed the outcome even more.

We spent some serious time and money shopping for discounted outdoor clothes in Vancouver. We were trying to get ready for Siberia and the cold weather kit was much more available there than it is in the UK. We picked up the same boots and socks that the oil rig workers take off for the winter season so we figured we'd be pretty set with the footwear. Then we ended up spending £400 each on a £1,000 coat from Fjallraven. It was the real deal, a proper, goose-down, Arctic parka and was supposed to be good down to −40°C.

The shipping process should have been easy but as always there was another curveball. We had arranged to get the bike crated with the same company that was shipping it. We thought that would mean there would be no problem getting off on time. We drove the bike down to the port and left it with them, ready to head off to Russia. Two days before it was set to sail off, we just checked in with the agent to make sure it was all good to go, and she replied with a very calm, "Oh no, sorry guys, you've been bumped to the next boat in two weeks because we don't have time to crate it for you." Ridiculous. Completely ridiculous. Two weeks meant another two weeks into a Russian winter, plus we couldn't leave Canada until the bike was physically on a boat. We agreed we would take matters into our own hands and then move said matters into Graham's hands with one cool, calculated question: "Graham, how do you build a box?"

We decided to crate it ourselves and get it on the bloody boat! Graham was keen to help us, not because he was going to enjoy it but because, if he didn't, he knew we would be lingering for a couple of weeks and that would cost him a fortune. Through no fault of our own, we were a huge expense to the Sheanes, as Judy is the most insistently generous person on the planet. We could not buy a single thing when we were there. One day we had got to the end of our tether and we decided we would cook them a shepherd's pie. We all popped down to the shops to buy the ingredients and Graham had to physically pull Judy away from the till in order for us to get our card into the machine. We spent about $70 CAD. In the morning we saw that Judy had donated £100 to charities we support on our page. She had got her own back!

Graham built an absolute corker of a crate and we had the shipping company send a truck to his house to pick up the bike. We had done it, and with about three hours to spare we made the boat. We said our goodbyes to the Sheanes the following morning and jumped on a flight back to the UK. Touching down into a perfectly grey, drizzly London Heathrow, we were met by Reece's mum who had come to pick us up. We got in the back of her car and found ourselves breathing in as we went down the motorway because the lanes felt so narrow. Only once we got on the M25 did we realise just how big everything had been in North America.

It was a weird kind of feeling being back in the UK like that. On my first night, I got fish and chips and sat on the sofa to watch TV with Chels. I couldn't help but think about how I had actually dreamt of doing that while in a daze with food poisoning in the Sahara six or so months before. A few days later and it was my birthday. Twenty-seven at last. When I had turned twenty-six, I certainly didn't think I would be spending my twenty-seventh at home. We had a bit of a BBQ to celebrate. The following day, we were celebrating again because our Russian visas were done. We walked into the embassy in London, put our fingers on a scanner and walked out. As simple as that. We had flown home for a two-minute job. By the time we had got our fingerprints done our boat still hadn't left the port in Vancouver and with all of the necessary delays it would be at least a month until we could get it out of the port in Vladivostok.

We had two choices: go to Russia and spend a fortune waiting for the bike, or lie low at our parents' houses for a few weeks and then fly when the bike had arrived. We chose the latter but it wasn't wasted time, we were able to prepare properly for the long ride home. We still needed to get a crapload more kit to be ready for the conditions. Over the course of three weeks we had the most successful sponsorship campaign of our lives. We just relentlessly rang business, back to full Colonel Sanders mode, but this time we had 25,000 miles under our belts to back us up. We managed to get on board two outdoor kit companies, Snugpak and Alpkit. Snugpak provided us with insulated jackets and trousers and Alpkit chipped in with a long-term loan on a tent that could withstand Siberian winds, as well as some brilliant ground mats and a new stove, the Brewkit.

Oxford Products got on board next and they gave us some thermal base layers, a couple of scooter skirts to take the wind off us, some heated grips and some of their Aqua soft luggage bags, to keep all of our kit safe and dry. Michelin tyres gave us the most appropriate tyres they could find too, a winter city commuter tyre called the City Grip, great for a wet London but not designed for ice roads. We happily accepted though, as there really is nothing better out there.

Then finally we landed the big one, support from Honda. We finally got through to the right people at Honda and I think they were pretty amazed that we had stuck the whole thing out. They seemed genuinely passionate about the cause, too, and really wanted to get behind something that was fighting modern slavery with one of their vehicles. They gave us about a grand's worth of new parts: a fantastic new exhaust, clutch, brakes—the works. Better still they gave us a properly fitted screen that would take an enormous amount of wind chill off the rider. All of this support was a huge boost and just what we needed ahead of the biggest challenge of our lives.

We enjoyed our time in the UK and it was awesome to see Lee and Charlotte tie the knot (an occasion made even better by watching my usually sensible dad throw up out the passenger seat of my mum's car having had one too many celebratory pints), but we were itching to get back on the road. We still had a job to do and on the 3rd of November we flew off from Heathrow, heading for Vladivostok. It was a pretty sad goodbye, because even though we knew we'd only be gone a couple of months, everybody knew it was by far the most dangerous part of the trip. I felt a bit teary saying goodbye to Chels, but we'd had an unexpected prolonged chunk of time together which had been great. Plus, I was pleased too, as this was the last time we'd be doing a teary goodbye at the airport. Over the next twenty-four hours, we crossed seven time zones and arrived with our watches set to the same time they would be if we had landed in Melbourne. That's how far away Vladivostok is and how utterly ginormous Russia is.

There was snow falling onto the runway as we arrived into what many call Russia's capital in the east. The snow set the scene perfectly and we were excited to get out and explore. Unfortunately, Aeroflot had other ideas and we spent the next few hours trying to track down our tyres. It seemed they had been left in Moscow. The guys at the luggage desk said they'd send them to our hotel when they eventually turned up but we didn't have much hope for that, admitting that they were most likely lost forever.

Our hotel was an absolute monster of a building. A huge, Soviet-style, concrete block that sat on the coast looking out into the North Pacific, which Kuishi was still plodding across. After more than twenty-four hours of travel, we were completely pooped, but it was morning time so we had to stay awake. We took a stroll out into the city and got our first taste of the challenge we had bitten off. The temperature was around 3°C but we were freezing. Wearing our arctic parkas, it was bearable but with the wind whipping across it was still not the kind of conditions you want to be out in. Local people were pottering by in jumpers and it soon became clear that we were going to need to toughen up. We had a bit of a mooch around the town, nearly fell asleep into a bowl of soup, and then admitted defeat and went back to the hotel to sleep. It was a big mistake. I don't think we fully recovered from the jet lag for the next three or four days. No big issue, though, as the bike was still floating around in the middle of the ocean.

As always, there were delays with the boat and Kuishi didn't get to the port for a solid week after our arrival. That gave us a bit of time to explore Vladivostok. We spent our days pottering around the city, checking out some of the sights and learning a bit about its interesting history. With the city being a stone's throw from China, Japan, and North Korea, it's historically been a contested area but now, firmly in the hands of Russia, it is growing to become what its name directly translates to, the "Ruler of the East."

The city had been doing particularly well in recent years. Everywhere you looked in Vladivostok there was building work taking place. Tower blocks were popping up, old buildings being brought back to life and even many local people's homes were getting that much needed makeover. Surprising when you consider that the automotive industry which the city was built on had almost collapsed as a result of raised import tariffs from Moscow. How could the city possibly be doing so well with its main income stream in pieces? Yep, you guessed it, modern slavery. Turns out having North Korea for a neighbour isn't bad for business and Russia had made a pretty lucrative deal with Pyongyang, in which North Korean workers were being sent over to prop up the economy with super cheap labour. It worked perfectly for North Korea as they got a vitally important cash injection to keep the regime alive and Russian property developers and home owners got a perfect, dedicated workforce for bargain basement prices.

How it works is, teams of North Koreans are sent to Vladivostok to undertake any kind of building work. Accompanying them will be a government minder, who would be more appropriately called a state-funded slave driver. The teams then work from dawn to dusk without stopping to catch their breath. Nobody moans. Everyone just gets on with the work. Workers stay for months at a time, working all day and only stopping to sleep in squalid conditions, ready for another day's work. The reviews are great and the Russian people say the Koreans are incredible workers, they don't even stop for cigarette breaks. Then once the job is done, the Russian employer pays the government minder a low but legal fee and the government minder keeps the lion's share for the regime, with the worker returning home with a very, very small amount of cash in their back pocket. Apparently though, this is one of those incidences of modern slavery where the person in slavery is keen to take part. If your options are stay at home starving within the world's most repressive regime or travel to a faraway city to earn a tiny amount of money, I think anyone would take the money. Especially when you consider that turning down the opportunity could land you in trouble with the feds and a one-way ticket to a forced labour camp, where conditions are worse and wages are zero.

That lack of genuine options still means the situation is modern slavery, despite the fact that the individual is willing to take part. It happens in the UK, too, most commonly, I believe, with Albanian citizens travelling to work in your local car wash. Keep an eye out for it and next time you go to the hand car wash consider the fact that if it feels too cheap, it probably is. What I found most crazy about the modern slavery situation in Vladivostok is that it was a cultural norm. So much so, that if you give it a google now and follow the links for long enough, you'll find what I found, a genuine booking page for your own team of North Korean slaves. You might be able to afford that new kitchen after all!

We looked into trying to meet up with a local charity and find an organisation that could tell us more about it. We found a few but they didn't want to hear from us. "Awareness raising" was certainly not what they were after. It became apparent that we were likely to make the situation worse for any individuals involved and we were at genuine risk of getting in trouble with the FSB, which is what they call the KGB these days. We decided it would be best for us to just get the scooter sorted, enjoy the last few days of city life and then set sail for London.

Eventually, the bike did arrive into port and unlike Egypt it was incredibly simple. We had a local fixer called Yuri. He was a very serious kind of guy and a man of few words. The process was clinical and precise: you pay when Yuri says to pay, you sign what Yuri says you sign, and you and your sidecar get to go home today. Incredibly, once the job was done Yuri was a different man. He cracked a smile and we even had a few fun conversations via Google Translate.

It cost us US$475 to get the bike out of the port which is exactly what Yuri had said all along. There's no nonsense in Russia. You just pay the price and what you've asked for gets done. I quite liked it. I was also over the moon because it was the last time I would ever have to ship a scooter and sidecar. It was by far the worst part of the trip and it was done forever. Now, all that stood in our way of becoming the first people to ever circumnavigate the globe on a scooter with a sidecar was a 10,000-mile stretch of land followed by a quick trip on the Eurotunnel. First, though we had to get our maintenance sorted and fortunately Yuri fixed us up with a local repair shop to work in.

The place was called Rider2Rgot, and Roman and Leru, who ran it, were incredibly friendly and helpful. It was one of those bike shops that acts as a magnet to travellers riding across the country and we bumped into a French guy who had just come from the west. He told us that the road was already looking pretty bad and he'd bailed in Chita and put the bike in a truck and jumped on the train. He had been on a proper adventure bike and he'd had to bail. Here we were on our little scooter and sidecar, just gearing up to get started.

We spent a full eight-hour day working with the mechanics at Rider2Rgot and managed to make all the changes we needed, including fitting the new exhaust, putting on some stronger sidecar joints, replacing the new drive belt, changing all of our tyres (which did miraculously turn up) and carrying out some general maintenance checks. The following day we worked on the bike from the hotel car park and added a new screen, the Oxford heated grips, and some grip protectors. We messed up the grips and the throttle ended up sticking when you let go. It was a bit annoying but we just agreed to think of it as glass half full. We now had cruise control, we just had to remember to turn it off.

When we thought we were finished we took it out for a little test ride and to our surprise it felt like the bike was wagging its tail. Sure enough, we pulled in and the whole back end of the rig was rocking back and forth. We couldn't believe it. We'd been in Vladivostok for ten days and were finally ready to go but the bike had other ideas. We posted online and everyone following us on Facebook agreed it was most likely the engine hanger that had gone, a big problem which could eventually cause the whole thing to fall apart but most likely would just mean we'd rip through drive belts at a rate of knots. The sideways strain wasn't what they were designed for and it was likely why we weren't able to deliver that soft Alaska. We pulled it apart and found that there was a kind of fairing tube thing that had worn away. We'd have to get another ordered in from the UK and we'd be stuck in Vladivostok for at least another week, just waiting for winter to get worse.

Before we admitted defeat we took the part down to the guys at Rider2Rgot and asked them if they had any. Unsurprisingly, it was a no. But this was Russia, people fix things here and there's a solution for everything. The next thing we knew, Roman was on the phone to a local factory and they agreed to produce us a new part, made out of a hard rubber. Twenty-four hours later and we were ready to ride.

Getting ready to ride in all of our gear was hilarious and took some getting used to. Michelin was getting a good sponsorship deal because we looked like we were dressing up as the Michelin man. With all of our gear on it was more or less impossible to check our blind spot and the sticky accelerator made our journey out of the city centre a bit more exciting than it should have been. On the outskirts of town we met up with a local teenager we had found on a Russian version of Gumtree. He sold us his drone on the cheap, we stripped down a few layers so we could see and then we started our journey headed for London.

That first day was so dull. The landscape was about as bleak as you could possibly imagine one to be. Very flat, very grey, and only broken up by the odd concrete tower block or dirty plume of smoke coming from some kind of factory. We were cruising along, racking up the miles and heading north in order to get around China. We managed 180 km on the first day and stopped to check into a little trucker stop by the road. The following day was more of the same, long stretches of grey nothingness. At times it felt like the dull grey road had merged with the dull grey sky to create the most bland landscape imaginable. It was boring but we were making fantastic progress and by the time we stopped for the second night we were only 220 km away from the next big city, Khabarovsk.

From Khabarovsk we would stretch out into the true wilderness. We were told we were heading into hundreds and hundreds of kilometres of completely nothing. A place where temperatures would drop to at least 20 below. There would be thick snow and ice on the roads, and we would be unlikely to get through. We were told that there would be nobody around to save us when we eventually got stuck and we could genuinely perish out in some of the toughest conditions on the planet. We were receiving messages from bikers in Moscow pleading with us not to go, one said, "Guys please wait for summer, there is nothing there, you will not make it, you will die."

We figured they were just making a bit of a fuss and calmly replied saying, "Don't worry, we'll be careful, honest." We were taking it one day at a time and right now that was easy, we had another day of dull tarmac before we would be in Khabarovsk where we would look to get kitted out for the wilderness. There we would grab a shovel, get some spikes or snow chains, and some emergency supplies to help us make it through the snow. For now, though, we would just have a good night's kip and then rack up an easy 220 km.

The following morning, I woke up having had said good night's kip, drew back the curtains in the guesthouse room and looked out to see everything was a bright, glistening white, and the sidecar was buried under a foot of snow. Maybe those 220 km wouldn't be so easy after all.

– 20 –

"THE ADRENALINE HAD WORN OFF AND WE WERE NOW JUST TWO BLOKES SAT IN A SIDECAR, COLD, SCARED TO DEATH, AND STILL STARING AT THE BIGGEST CHALLENGE OF OUR LIVES."

We woke up to a complete winter wonderland. The boring grey landscape had been transformed into this wonderful, frozen, picture postcard of a place. Everything was bright white and glistening, including the roads.

We were super excited. This was going to be a real adventure. We were filled with nervous anticipation. What on earth was it going to be like? Having never driven our scooter and sidecar in the snow, we had absolutely no idea if it would move or how it would handle. It was time to see if the Michelin City Grip tyres, which were designed for rainy tarmac, would be able to cut the mustard on snowy ice.

Amazingly, the sidecar pulled off and we could drive fairly easily through the thick snow in the car park. We packed up our four 50L roll bags full of kit and headed up towards a small incline onto the Trans-Siberian Highway. Fully packed, with both of us in the rig and with very little momentum, Kuishi didn't even make it up the smallest of climbs onto the road. I had to get out and walk up to the highway while Reece went back down and floored it out of the car park in order to get up the icy strip. I met him there, sweating buckets, having walked 100 metres in my arctic gear. I jumped in the rig and we started trundling down the highway towards Khabarovsk.

"Hey, mate, give your brakes a test," I said to Reece over our headsets.

With nothing in his mirror, he pulled them on, and we carried on gliding down the road like a giant curling puck, eventually stopping as we hit a snowy patch.

"They've been better, mate," Reece replied over the headset. We agreed to go exceptionally slowly wherever possible, but at the same time we knew we had to keep some kind of momentum going in order to make it up any kind of hill.

We spent the next few hours creeping along at around 20 mph. We were slipping and sliding around but the roads were mainly just icy, as they had been cleared during the morning. Then, the snow came again. Out of nowhere we were in a white-out. We could barely see the handlebars on the bike, let alone where we were going. The road quickly returned to a thick blanket of snow and the only place we could drive was where the lorries had cut out a path for us. That meant that the drive wheel was in the icy rut left by the trucks and the sidecar was bouncing along in the fresh powder in the middle of the road. We pressed on regardless.

With the snow still dumping down, I found myself sat in the sidecar bouncing up and down in the middle of the road, when I was startled by a big noise to my left. Right beside me, a lorry's wheel had emerged from the blizzard. The truck was so close that I could easily have reached out and touched the tyre. As the truck started to overtake, it began picking up snow and dumping it onto me. I had my visor open at first and got a proper face full, it was a hell of a hit. I just sat there for a second or two as it buried me and then it had gone.

I let out a nervous laugh and said, "Holy shit, mate, did you see how close that thing was?"

"I know, this is insane," Reece replied. It really was. We had no control and we were bumbling along in the snow, dicing with death as lorries steamrolled past us on their way to Moscow. That first day was fun though. It was cold, it was scary, but it was exhilarating. The adrenaline was pumping and despite the conditions, we were actually moving in the right direction.

We arrived into Khabarovsk that night completely drained and in need of a good lie down. We found a suitably cheap motel and flopped onto our beds. Thirty minutes later our silent, lying-down time was rudely interrupted by a knock at the door. I opened up to a smiling Russian guy holding a bottle of vodka and some tomato juice. Behind him was a waitress holding two bowls of piping hot soup. "Eat. Drink vodka?" said the Russian guy, smiling from ear to ear. Starving hungry and keen for a stiff drink, we gleefully welcomed him in. He gestured for us to start eating. Five minutes later and there was another knock at the door. The waitress was back but this time with two steak dinners. We were blown away. We had been living off soup or noodles since we arrived in Russia and our eyes lit up. The guy handed us the steaks and gestured for us to tuck in again.

We spent the next few hours hanging out with this guy. He spoke no English and we spoke no Russian, but with every passing shot of vodka we understood his toasts even more. Through the aid of Google Translate and our exceptional charades skills, we had full conversations with him. All manner of subjects were covered, from Russia's involvement in Syria, to Brexit and even to the age-old Cristiano Ronaldo or Lionel Messi debate.

It turned out he was in the army and didn't want to be put on our social media or have his name mentioned anywhere. He just wanted to welcome us to his country and have a good laugh. In the end we all drank a bit too much vodka and, because he wasn't eating anything, he drank way too much and got a bit carried away. In fact, he threw a boot across the room, knocked a beer over and then spat on the floor in the hotel lobby while we tried to get him to bed. It was our first experience of Russian hospitality and it was brilliant. Full-blooded generosity with more than a dash of eccentricity!

The following morning, we woke up feeling pretty hungover and we were staring down the barrel of the most isolated part of the journey. This was where it got real. We would have to continue north to skirt around the top of China before we could start heading south again towards Chita, the next big town, some 2,000 km away. We knew there would be many villages and roadside motels between Khabarovsk and Chita but a look on Google Maps would tell us that there really could be stretches of hundreds of kilometres of completely nothing. With the warnings of our Russian followers still coming in on social media, we set off into Khabarovsk to look for supplies. An hour later, we'd had a coffee and a croissant but no luck with the snow chains. "Oh well, it'll be alright," we said to each other and, armed with our hangovers, we set off into the unknown.

We spent the next couple of days crawling up the side of China. The road conditions varied hugely; there would be stretches of really well maintained, smooth tarmac and others of thick snow, coupled with deep potholes and sheet ice. We made it 180 km on the first day to the town of Birobidzhan. We managed to find a quiet roadside trucker stop where we gladly pulled in for the night. The following day was more of the same but with every mile further north, the conditions seemed to get worse. It got colder but, just as bad as that, it seemed to get brighter. The sun well and truly had its hat on, and the landscape was dazzlingly bright.

At lunch time on the second day, we pulled into a small village to find a bowl of soup and some warmth. There was nothing in the town apart from this small bar with no windows. We went in and it was nearing pitch black. I could just see a lady behind the bar and a couple of guys sat drinking shots of vodka to my left. "Christ, we've dropped into some kind of Russian mafia hangout here," I thought to myself.

We approached the bar and said, "Kafe? Sopa?"

"Da, specibo," said the lady as she pointed to a seat.

We sat down, took off our gear and moaned to each other for a minute, muttering under our breath stuff like, "Mate, do you think we're okay in here? Seems fricking dodgy."

"I know, mate, why's it so bloody dark?"

I popped to the toilets and it was even pitch black in there. Where on earth were we? What kind of place has such a dimly lit toilet? I returned to the table through the darkness and we both took out our phones and had a flick through the morning's pictures. Then I looked up from my screen and suddenly I could see things I couldn't see before. I nudged Reece, he did the same and then we started laughing. It wasn't dark at all. Our eyes had just been destroyed by a morning's ride in the bright snow. Turns out the two gangsters sat opposite were just grabbing some lunch, too. They even offered to take us for a weekend's trip at the local ski resort. We politely declined, we said it was because we had to keep going but really it was because Reece can't ski and he'd taken a tumble a couple of years before when giving it a go in Latvia, which had knocked his confidence.

It was funny but it was pretty serious, we were at risk of going completely snow blind. We had no choice though. All we had to protect our eyes were our sun visors in our helmets and we couldn't use them because they froze up too quickly. In fact, we had stumbled across an issue which we later coined "The Visor Dilemma." Temperatures had dropped to around −25°C, which made any moisture instantly freeze up, causing a sheet of ice to form on our visors. It would freeze up on the main visor with or without the pin lock system in place and it would freeze up on the little sunglasses visor too. It was bad, it meant we couldn't see at all. So, the only option was to lift the visor up and take on the conditions with no protection. This led to fairly considerable short-term snow blindness but also completely frozen eyes. It would be really painful for the first few minutes and then the pain would pass and we'd just be left with a frozen face. We've got some hilarious pictures of big icicles hanging off our eyelashes. It was dangerous and stupid. We later found out that it can cause you to go permanently blind.

We pressed on regardless and managed to rack up a whopping 320 km to a small village where we found two guesthouses. Both were full. We had blown it. It was now actually dark, and we were looking at getting out our back-up camping kit when a guy pulled up in a car and said in English, "Problem, guys?"

"Nowhere to stay unfortunately. Do you know of anywhere?"

"Sure, follow me!"

We followed this guy through the dark, out of the village and back onto the highway. Blimey, where were we heading? About 5 km later we pulled into a trucker stop right on the highway that wasn't on Google Maps. The guy in the truck was called Dennis and once he had got us checked into a nice twin room, with a place indoors for the bike, too, he disappeared into the night. We hung out in the café, drinking beers, playing chess, and smiling at the locals. It was a hugely enjoyable evening when you compare it to shaking uncontrollably, trying to keep warm for eight hours in a sleeping bag, which is what we were destined for had Dennis not stepped in.

We set off the following morning into a fantastic sunrise. We had got up bright and early and wanted to get as many miles under our belt as possible before the midday sun. Today though, we had another element to deal with: wind. At those temperatures, when the wind really starts blowing, it's just awful. Each gust feels like it cuts right through you and any skin you leave exposed, even for a millisecond, feels like it's getting ripped off and carried away. Surprisingly, the coldest place to be in these conditions is in the sidecar. You'd think that the screen and roof would protect you a bit but because you literally sit and do nothing, you just freeze up. At least on the bike, you're fighting the sidecar to stay on the road and you're keeping warm that way.

By around midday, I had been sat in the sidecar for an hour and I was properly cold. We just needed to get inside to reset. I asked Reece to pull in at anything we could find. Travelling at around 40 mph, this can be a long time. Fifty kilometres passed and nothing. Sixty kilometres, nothing. Seventy kilometres, nothing. I was at breaking point. The pain in my toes and fingers was too much and I felt cold to the bone. I asked Reece to pull over on the side of the road so we could run around a bit at least. It didn't help. The wind just cut through us. I was a mess. I had let myself get too cold and all the running around I was doing wasn't saving me. Reece risked it all and whipped off his glove to look at Google Maps. He found that there was a restaurant just fifteen miles up the road. We got back in and headed straight there.

About forty-five minutes later we pulled into a trucker stop and headed for a cabin. It was an old truck converted into a little coffee shop, so it was super small. We must have looked ridiculous when we arrived. Both of us were so cold that we just flung open the door in full gear, helmets and all. The warm air from inside flooded out as we entered, and we appeared as a silhouette in the mist. I think the friendly Russian lady behind the till must have half been expecting us to say, "Tonight Matthew, I'm going to be . . . ."

After about ten minutes of faffing, we had got settled in and we were tucking into a bowl of soup and slurping coffee when a really friendly guy came in and started chatting to us in Russian. This had happened very regularly before, but this time it was different, he just kept going and kept smiling. Meanwhile, we were both trying to work out if we still had all ten toes and although he seemed like a nice guy, we really didn't have too much patience for a full game of charades. He persisted nonetheless and then eventually took out his phone and began to show everyone videos of us driving, as well as our SPOT tracker page. It turned out he had been tracking us since Vladivostok and as we were passing through his neck of the woods, he thought he would come and see if we needed any help. His name was Claus, or as he liked to put it, Santa Claus, and he stayed to drink some coffee with us for half an hour or so before heading back off into the distance.

Claus' presence had put us in good favour with the owner of the coffee shack and she came over with two absolutely massive meat and cheese pasties and another pot of coffee on the house. Having stuffed ourselves silly and recovered feeling in our toes, we got back on the rig and pressed on again. We were aiming for another 100 km to a town called Uglegorsk where we had seen that there were a few hotels. Knowing that we could safely get our heads down for the night, we pulled in about 10 km short to do some shots in the sunset. We threw the drone up and got some cracking aerial shots of the surrounding frozen forest.

It turns out we hadn't done quite as much planning as we had thought though, because we arrived to Uglegorsk and found a fifty-foot concrete wall surrounding it. It was a closed city. We had scooted into some kind of super-secure Russian rocket ship military base. You couldn't write it. It was now pretty much dark and the only hotels in town were on the other side of a massive wall. Honestly, it was like a scene in a Bond movie or something. Russian henchmen everywhere, guarding the entries to this top-secret base. We tried to flirt our way in and even drove up around the back to get to one of the hotels but we were told we needed a proper permit to stay. Worse still, the security guys were telling us that not only did we have to leave the area but that there was nowhere close by. We were flummoxed. I mean, what are the chances of accidentally planning to stay at Putin's secret space base?

We were looking at cracking the tent out in the car park when a guard told us there was a trucker motel in 10 km that wasn't on Google Maps. We drove off into the dark and sure enough fifteen minutes later, we stumbled across salvation. It was a huge relief. Looking back, we were incredibly lucky. Had we thrown the drone up closer to the base we'd probably still be sat in a Russian prison for espionage. As it happens, we did manage to get a couple of good shots of the intercontinental missiles there, and the CIA chucked us a few grand for the footage. In our dreams. In reality, I forgot to press "record" at all so didn't even get any nice shots of the trees.

The following morning, we woke up to colder conditions once again. Temperatures had dropped to below −30°C overnight and we hadn't been able to get the bike indoors. We got packed up and ready for the road as usual, plodded out to the bike with a few bags of kit, pulled off the bike cover and found a freezing cold Kuishi na Kuishi. I tried to start it up as normal but no luck. The cold had finally got to it. We figured it could just be a frozen battery, so I pulled it out and we went back in for a cup of coffee by the radiator. As we were sat there a Russian guy called Edward came over and started chatting. He was super interested in our journey and had just come the other way to us. He said conditions would be much of the same on the road ahead, thick snow in parts, clear roads in others. He asked us to stop and stay with him for the winter in Vladivostok but we politely declined. Then we told him about our plans to turn left at Chita and head down through Mongolia. He nearly fainted.

"Please don't do it. You will never, ever make it. There is very, very thick snow in the mountains. If you stick only to the Trans-Siberian highway you might just make it to Moscow but if you go to Mongolia, you will certainly fail and maybe die." It was a pretty serious and stern warning from someone who seemed to know what he was talking about. We agreed that it was probably best to take his advice and crack on west.

We ordered some breakfast while we waited and, to our surprise, we were treated with three fried eggs and two slices of the most rank sausage known to man. Yum. Incredibly, we had been right about the battery. Kuishi started straight away and we were ready to scoot on again.

As we inched our way up the side of China, the temperatures were getting colder and the roads scarier. The adrenaline had worn off and we were now just two blokes sat in a sidecar, cold, scared to death, and still staring at the biggest challenge of our lives. We were still a few days from Chita and it was likely to get worse before it got better. To make matters even worse our headsets had gone, so the guy in the sidecar would just sit there, watch the ice form on his visor and hope that the rider didn't slip into a passing truck on the treacherous roads. We were genuinely beaten down by the conditions and we were only a few days in. Here's my diary entry from that evening:

20th November 2018 – Day 6 on the road.

Fucking freezing. Went from Uglegorsk to a place just outside of Sivaki. Kicked off at −30°C or something. Frozen to the core. Every minute we're not on the bike, we're dreading riding it. It's shit. Just genuinely such a stupid, bad thing to do. It's fucking freezing beyond belief and nothing interesting to see. Worst thing I've ever done!

The following day was more of the same. We had managed to get the bike indoors, so it started fine in the morning, but the conditions were just terrible, still. So cold and so scary. Our attitudes were at an all-time low. We said at the time that usually when you do something terribly stupid and genuinely awful, you look back and say, "I won't do that again." Here, we were saying, "Hey, let's do it from dawn till dusk every day, for at least another month." It was ridiculous.

After a morning's ride, we were freezing cold and beaten down again. We rolled into the town of Magadachi and agreed we had to make a change. There's no way we would make it if we kept up this attitude and progress. We decided to book into a guesthouse and take an afternoon off to try and make some adaptations in order to make our ride more comfortable. We knew that there were two things that would make a huge difference: 1. Solve the visor dilemma; 2. Stop the wind whipping through the sidecar.

We'd had loads of people commenting online saying, "Guys, just buy some heated visors or at least a snorkeling set." Great tips but sadly we were a week out of the last place we'd be able to buy either of those things. This was the wilds of Russia's Far East and there were no snowmobile shops selling heated visors or scuba diving centres with snorkeling kits. Nope, we would have to get creative. There were about ten shops in the town, mainly selling groceries or clothes, but there was one hardware store. It was our only hope at finding some kind of fix. We went into the place and started looking around when we had a tap on our shoulder by a pretty stern looking local policeman. "Passport," he said, sharply. I questioned as to why he wanted my passport, but I got a stern look back so handed it over. He looked me up and down, nodded and then turned to Reece, "Passport!"

"It's at the hotel. Sorry, mate," Reece replied.

"Passport!" he came back with.

"Listen, it's at the hotel, besides why do you need it? Is this shop its own territory?" Reece replied.

"Hotel!" he pointed at the door where his colleague was waiting and marched us off back to our guesthouse. He led the way; he knew where we were staying. We got to the hotel and they followed us up two floors and into our room.

Obviously, he had put our noses out of place. Here were two average blokes just trying to get around the world on a scooter and sidecar and he thought he could waltz in there and boss us about. Reece picked up his passport and handed it over to him with a sarcastic, "Here you are flower, feast your eyes on this."

He looked through it and then said, "Bags!"

To which I replied, "Camping gear, dirty boxer shorts that kind of thing mate, want to have a look?"

"Bag!"

I put it on the bed and he saw our tent, which seemed to satisfy his need for knowledge.

"Anything else you need officer, fancy a flick through my diary while you're here, you nosey parker?" I said. They smiled and left us in peace. It was truly bizarre and a small insight into what it's like to be harassed by Putin's henchmen.

We returned to the shop to find the ladies behind the till giggling uncontrollably. Then, one of them shoved a phone into my hand.

"Hello?" I said.

"Hello, welcome to Magadachi. My mum owns shop. You very welcome. Please buy things you wish."

"Well thank you kindly. How nice of you," I replied.

We had a short chat about the young lady's English homework before I finally got around to looking through what the shop had available. Amazingly, we found the answer. A big roll of foil-covered insulation fabric and some washing machine tube. After an afternoon of duct taping and playing around with the kit we had turned the sidecar into a spaceship and created a breathing pipe for each of our helmets.

We called the insulation the sidecar curtains because they went straight down both sides of the rig. In theory it meant that no wind would get across, but it also meant you couldn't see the other guy. So, with our headsets broken we would have zero communication with each other for the ride home. We woke up the following morning and for the first time in days we were excited to get on the road. Hopefully the adaptations would make all the difference. Reece was on shift and he drove us out of the town. After five minutes he shouted through the curtains, "Waste of bloody time mate. I've got a frozen visor and a cut lip!"

Blast, the makeshift snorkel hadn't worked. I, however, was having much more luck inside the sidecar. It was −28°C outside and honestly, it felt −18°C. Absolutely glorious. Truly a huge difference. The outside curtain soon shook loose and started waving around in the road but the inside one was wedged in by the spare tyres and holding strong. It was brilliant, you could hunker down and feel snug as a bug in a rug, nestled up against the curtain. Better still, with the wind no longer whipping through, you could lift your visor up without getting frozen eyes. Sightseeing was back on the menu. It wasn't all bad news for the rider either, as we had managed to fix another problem we'd had, which was exposed wrists. Every now and then the wind would catch the right angle and get your wrists, but we sorted it by wrapping them in bandages. The locals must have thought we were a couple of suicidal scooter and sidecarists flying through their town. Probably why they were so nice to us.

The going was still slow, though, and as we neared the most northerly point of the journey the roads got worse and worse. Despite the nicer conditions in the sidecar we only made it 100 km from Magadachi to a roadside café next to a town called "Never." Never is situated at the turn-off for Yakutsk, which is the last big town before you pick up the Road of Bones and head east for Magadan. Apt, really, because never had I been more relieved that we were unable to ship to Magadan. It would have been colder still and genuinely, completely remote. Or so we are told. I bet there are coffee shacks along there, too!

Never was also the most northerly point of our trip and logic states that it should have been the coldest, too. We looked at a weather map and found that our logic was right, Chita was a barmy −15°C-a solid 15°C warmer than Never-practically shorts and T-shirt weather. We got a good night's kip at Never and then trucked on southwest for the town of Mogocha. In Mogocha, we accidentally gate-crashed a girl's night out. I think it might have been someone's 50th.

We were just having a pizza in the only restaurant in town, when it turned into a night club and the girls asked us for a dance. Unfortunately for them, we were both spoken-for men. Yep, that's right, Reece too. While he'd been back in the UK, he had received a message on Instagram from a secret admirer and they'd hit things off. I had warned him that it was most likely some catfish trying to con him or some obscure way of selling PPI insurance, but sure enough it had been a real-life girl named Hannah, who actually wanted to date him. How anyone could see that thing on Instagram and want to date him I will never know, especially with the goatee he was sporting at the time. However, it really is a ridiculous world and there are even people out there who like the look of Reece. Sadly for the women of Mogocha, Reece was off the menu and nobody would be getting a birthday dance with Gilko.

Before we left Mogocha, we had a message from Alex "The Devil" on our Facebook. It turned out he usually would have put us up with the local bike post in Mogocha but he had been away on work. However, we would be welcome to stay at the bike post with his friends in Chita when we finally arrived. That was still at least two days' riding away, though. Incredibly, temperatures rose considerably overnight and we woke up to a toasty −18°C which climbed to −12°C throughout the day. I wrote in my diary that it was the first genuinely good day since leaving Vladivostok. The conditions were incredible. Driveable roads, good weather, and great views. We were treated by a passing trucker to a cup of coffee, too. We had pulled in on the side of the road for a bit of a warm-up, and he pulled in behind us and popped the stove on. We couldn't speak to each other at all, so we just enjoyed the cuppa and went our separate ways.

The day was capped off with the most incredible sunset that went on for hours, literally. The sun takes forever to drop in that part of the world at that time of year and the sky is full of the most incredible burning, pink glow when it does. That sky, coupled with the frozen forest and glistening white trees, made for an unbelievable setting. We made it 320 km all the way to Chernyshevsk and we were in touching distance of Chita, the end of the most challenging part of our route. From there we would bail on Mongolia and take a relatively temperate journey home along the Trans-Siberian highway. It should have been good roads and great conditions all the way to London. Little did we know that Chita would be more like the start line of our challenge and our journey there had just been a taster of what Mother Russia was planning to throw at us.

– 21 –

"NO PROBLEM, WE TAKE IT TO AFRICA!"

"Mate, I'm not sure you should. Oh, no, you've gone for it." I squirmed as I watched Reece enthusiastically tuck into a slice of raw bacon, offered to him by the guys at the Chita bike post.

"How is it?" I said. Reece grinned and grimaced simultaneously as he tried to warn me of the fact it really was just completely raw bacon, without offending our hosts. The plate pivoted and was pushed in my direction.

"Mmm, yum, let's give it a go," I said as I reluctantly picked up a smaller sliver and started chomping away. As the cold, salty meat slid around my mouth I confirmed to myself that it was indeed just a raw slice of off-the-shelf bacon.

Next, another delicacy was cracked onto the table. Salted fish. Two of them lay there starring back up at me and then Vladimir reached down and snapped one of them in half with a sharp crack on the table. It split open and the guys dove in. Raw salted fish was less strange to me than raw salted bacon, so I grabbed a bit too. It was actually super tasty and, coupled with the ice cold beer I had in the other hand, it was a great set-up for the evening.

The final few hundred kilometres through to Chita had been relatively trouble-free. On our arrival we sent a WhatsApp message to a random number that Alex "The Devil" had given to us and arranged to stay at the bike post. The post was in the middle of nowhere and having arrived into Chita just after dark, we found ourselves following a car carrying four blokes down an icy dirt track into the night. As we drove there, we started to wonder if we had pushed our faith in strangers too far. Not many people would say it's wise to follow a random group of guys, whom you'd been introduced to by "The Devil," down a pitch-black road to an undisclosed location. We pressed on regardless. After what felt like some fairly intense trail riding, we arrived at a massive security gate, with a very serious-looking dog barking on the other side. We were ushered through, and with it being −15°C, we all went straight inside.

Inside was far more welcoming. We had been right to blindly follow The Devil's friends into the abyss. We found ourselves in a warm, glowing log cabin. It was a fully functioning bar and, in the summer, it would be a thriving biker hangout. Now, there were just two guys here. They lived there for free, permanently. It was kind of like a free hostel for lost people who like bikes. It turned out there are bike posts right throughout Russia. It's common for bikers from different districts to drop in at neighbouring posts and stay the night. You can use them to more or less cross the country without paying for a single night's kip, if you like. It's a network of bikers supporting each other on their journeys. There's never any money exchanged for a night at a post, it's just a safe place for bikers to rest their heads and carry out any maintenance required on their bike. Incredibly, this was a rare occasion where our scooter didn't need any work, so we were able to enjoy a night chatting to the guys.

It was a strange setting at this time of year. The bar was stocked with beer but redundant until spring. The stewards of the place, Vladimir and Sergiusz, seemed excited to have us. A welcome break from the monotony of watching over a bike post in the off season. These fellas had nowhere else to go, though. They were clearly struggling with life. Vladimir could speak pretty good English and he told us all about his life. He had been a fairly successful front man for a heavy metal band in Russia (it was true, he showed us the pictures). Now, his band had split up and he had no way of making a living. Up the road in Chita itself, he had a wife and young son. His wife wouldn't let him into their lives until he straightened himself out, which he said he was determined to do. He even had an interview for a job the following morning.

We carried on chatting, drinking beers, and eating weird stuff for hours. At around midnight, I suggested we all hit the hay. We had a big day of riding lined up for the morning, and Vladimir had his interview. Vladimir didn't fancy it, though, and wanted to stay up for longer. Reece said he would have another beer with him, and they cracked one open. An hour later, Reece came into the little dorm room I was in and told me that Vladimir was still drinking. Vladimir had been talking about how sad he was not to be with his wife and son all night. Reece had suggested he get to bed, smash that interview, and get his life back on track. Unfortunately, Vladimir had other ideas. I heard him flop onto his bed sometime around 4 a.m.

I woke up the following morning and walked around the place. It was a different kind of hangout in the cold light of day. A filthy bar. I had to step over a huge dog poo on my way to the bathroom where I crossed paths with Reece, who was just coming out.

"Mate, this place is rank. Let's get out of here," I said.

"I know! I think I've just seen a rat scurry off in the bathroom, too," replied Reece.

We got packed up fairly quickly and hit the road. It was quick for us but there's always a lot of packing and sorting to do. By the time we left, it was way past the time Vladimir should have been in town, sat down for his interview. He was still knocking about the house with a hangover. It was a really depressing scene. This lost guy with a hangover, cleaning up dog poo, in a closed bar, when in another world he would have been at his interview getting himself back on track.

We set off soon after and pressed on west again. Reece was riding and he shouted through to me in the sidecar to say that the conditions were terrible. I could feel it too. Huge gusts of wind that felt like they could pick us up and fling us straight off the carriageway or, worse, into the path of an oncoming truck. We pulled into a little roadside café to get some breakfast and discuss what we should do.

It was a tiny café—a typical roadside set-up: plastic tables and chairs lined up with a TV playing the news at one end, and the counter at the other. We ordered the usual, an undisclosed number of eggs and slices of overly processed sausage, loads of bread, and two coffees. It was a perfect café as there was a radiator by a window, from which we could see the sidecar. That and a hot coffee is all two scooter and sidecarists are ever looking for in a Russian roadside café. There were two or three other guys in the café, presumably the owners of the trucks outside. One of them stood up and walked over to sit at the table next to us. He smiled and just looked at us for a minute. It was a bit odd but not an irregular occurrence in Russia, or much of the world for that matter. We're not something you see every day on the Trans-Siberian Highway, so some people like to take a closer look. This fella went further, though, and actually angled his seat towards us. He then spent the next fifteen minutes loudly slurping his coffee while observing us. After he'd polished it off, he gave us a smile and pottered out to his truck. Truly bizarre. And honestly, quite annoying. It's funny looking back, but when you've been battered by life-threatening winds or frozen by the cold, the last thing you want is somebody slurping in your personal space, while you try to decide how to stay alive.

It was two eggs and two slices of sausage that day. Reasonable ratios. After much deliberation, we decided the wise thing to do would be to return to Chita and wait for the wind to die down. It was a decision we didn't take lightly because we were keen to rack up the miles while the weather was reasonable. Temperatures had soared overnight to $-5°C$ and looked like they might make it to zero by the end of the day, but there was a cold snap coming. A really serious cold snap that could see the mercury plummet to forty below, colder than we had ever imagined it would get and we were really quite worried about how we'd cope; $-20°$ had been bad, $-30°$ had been horrific, what on earth would $-40°$ be like? Still, we couldn't press on in these winds, it was just too dangerous and we decided to return to Chita. We skipped the bike post this time and checked into a cheap motel in town. As fun as it was, we didn't fancy another drunk night with the guys, plus we could have killed for a shower and a decent bed.

Having an afternoon off in Chita gave us time to sort out some bits and pieces. I had lost my immigration card and needed to get another, so I popped down to the local police station where I could grab one. After around twenty minutes, Reece joined me in the waiting area. Then, we were escorted through a series of doors and offices to a waiting room. An English-speaking police officer came out and interviewed us. He asked us all sorts of questions about the trip and it all seemed very serious. He returned to his office and left us in the waiting room. Half an hour passed, and we were still waiting for this little card. No progress. We were beginning to get a little nervous; why were we being kept in this waiting room so long? An hour later, we were still sat there and getting seriously worried, when a load of notifications came through on my phone. We suddenly had another five or six followers and they were liking everything. It was the bloody police officers that did our interview! I defied instruction and walked down the corridor to see them all at their desks ploughing through our Facebook page. We couldn't believe it. There's us thinking we're in some kind of trouble and they're just having a blast watching us ride into Cape Town.

We put our foot down and finally managed to convince them to hand over the immigration card. Next, we went down to a local burger joint we'd seen on Trip Advisor. We were really keen for some different kind of food. Since we'd left Vladivostok, we'd been on the borscht diet. Borscht is a kind of beet soup. The beetroot makes it a distinctive pink colour, but it has a load of other root vegetables and occasional lumps of meat floating in the broth, too. It usually has a scoop of crème fraiche in it, which we thought was an egg for a while, and it's the perfect winter warmer for lunch on the road. At nighttime the menu is almost always mashed potato, cabbage, and some kind of processed meat. A burger bucked the trend and it was a taste explosion. We needed it, too, because despite shovelling down as much borscht as we could, we had both lost the best part of a stone in the space of a couple of weeks. The cold and the energy required to keep the bike on the road keep you needing more and more calories.

We had a chilled evening in Chita before pressing on the following morning. It was a windy day again, but driveable, and we managed to rack up 320 km in the milder conditions. The ride took us all the way to the town of Khilok. Despite it only being -5°C it had been a really tough one. Exceptionally windy and a lot of trucks tumbling past us on the icy roads. We were well and truly ready to get off the outfit and into somewhere warm. We found a guesthouse on Google Maps and started heading towards it. As we did, we were stopped at a red light on a level crossing. The sun was setting, and we were completely knackered. The train approached and it slowly pulled past us. Fifteen minutes later we were still sat waiting for the thing to go but with no end in sight. A car pulled up next to us and a guy got out to say hello. He was smiling and wanted to shake hands. We were feeling run down and just so keen to get off the bike, so we had a less than enthusiastic chat with the guy. His name was Andre and when we told him where we were heading, he was disappointed to tell us it was closed down. He said that there were one or two other guesthouses in town, but they would most likely be full already.

Andre said he'd take us around and see what we could find. There was no room at the first inn but fortunately the second place had one twin room left. It was a dive, but we'd certainly stayed in worse, and we were just buzzed that we could get off the bike. Andre, his family, and his friend all helped us with our things into our room and we had a little chat for a while through Google Translate. Eventually Andre got up our SPOT Tracker page on his phone and it turned out he was one of Santa Claus' crew who were tracking us across the country. He must have seen us pull into his town and that's how he'd found us at the railway line. We couldn't believe it. He showed us some videos of us driving along, too. He was part of a WhatsApp group of bikers who were following along. Bizarre but very cool, and he had saved us from a night out in the cold.

We had a funny night in the guesthouse because it was full of drunks. One guy had so much vodka that he passed out on the floor right outside our door. We left them to it. We had parked the sidecar at Andre's friend's garage and in the morning Andre came by to take us down there. We arrived at the bike to find a puddle of petrol underneath. We had been getting really bad miles to the gallon on the ride the day before and we had found our answer as to why—a fuel leak. It turned out to be the fuel pump seal, so we needed a new one. Fortunately, Andre and the guys were keen to help and before we knew it, we were in his garage with around five or six guys peering at the tank. As ever, the first thing we had to do was siphon the fuel out. It somehow fell to me to do it and I really wanted to nail it with all of the fellas watching. I sucked it and incredibly I got it going first time. I looked like I knew what I was doing to the fellas, and better still I wasn't having any 95 Octane for breakfast.

The seal got fixed pretty quickly but as Reece was screwing the pump back on, he sheared a bolt. Fortunately, the lads had a plan and they drilled out the old bolt before reattaching a new one. We had filled the tank back up to check if the seal was working and incredibly Andre continued to work on the fuel tank with a fag in his mouth. The burning embers were hovering right above the tank and it made us pretty nervous. The guys didn't seem worried at all, though, and we later found out that it's not at all like the movies. Apparently, with it being so cold there you could actually put a cigarette out in a tank of petrol. We didn't bother to test that claim for ourselves, though.

We drove out of Khilok that morning with a fixed bike and having had a great night's kip. It was a slow day's ride as temperatures started to drop again and the road conditions worsened once more. Worse still, Reece spotted another puddle under the bike at lunch. We agreed that we had to get it fixed and we ended up pulling into another roadside motel for the night. After some considerable faff we managed to fix it back together and pressed on again in the morning.

The mercury continued to fall and we were back to cruising in the minus-twenties, which is never nice. We pulled in for lunch around 50 km from Ulan-Ude, where borscht was off the menu and the only things available were big Mongolian dumplings. Stuffed with minced meat and spices, these stodgy balls of flavour were a fantastic, very welcome break from the cold, and from the borscht for that matter. Again, we came outside to find another puddle under the scooter. We pulled in early in Ulan-Ude, where we tried to fix it again. It can be infuriating when you get a recurring problem like that but, fortunately, we woke up the following morning with no petrol under the bike.

We also woke up to −25°C, and we agreed there was no way that we would be using our Mongolian visas. The extreme cold, dangerous roads, and dodgy bike were plenty to worry about. The last thing we needed was altitude, exposed mountains, and six feet of snow to contend with. At the same time, if we're honest, we just wanted to get home. It was great meeting the Russian people, but we were still genuinely scared for our lives. The conditions were horrific on the road, and we were spending every morning wondering if we'd make it to lunch, and every afternoon wondering if we'd make it to dinner. It sounds dramatic, but the trucks were driving so close to us and, with the snowy roads and our slippy tires, it would only be a matter of time before we met our icy end. With the sidecar curtain and no communications, it genuinely felt like every time the bike slipped, we could be about to slip off the road or into a truck. No longer were we concerned with understanding the local culture or the place we were riding through, we were concerned for our lives and we were doing all we could to get home as quickly as possible.

We pressed on towards the shores of Lake Baikal and found busy roads full of trucks. The tarmac was showing and the roads were mainly cleared, with interspersed sections of ice and deep potholes. There was a wicked wind that day, too. It wasn't constant, but freak gusts would blast across the lake now and again and slam into us. I said to Reece at lunch that I thought it was the most dangerous stretch of road I had ever driven on. The intermittent clear tarmac leads you into a false sense of security, only to make sure you hit a hazard at high speed. This, coupled with the suicidal lorry drivers, tanked up on vodka, and the freak gusts of wind, made for a truly deadly cocktail. Reece took the reins at lunch and around forty minutes into the ride we came across someone who hadn't been so lucky with the roads. An arctic lorry was spread across both sides of the carriageway and half of it was hanging precariously over the side of a steep bank like the final scene of The Italian Job.

The traffic was snaking back for a few hundred metres when we arrived and must have been miles by the time it was cleared. I walked along to take a closer look and on my way I passed a tombstone, presumably from the last lorry driver who wasn't as lucky as this guy. This whole thing had us even more worried; not only were we struggling to keep on the road but so were the lorries. Only blind luck was protecting us from ending up under the wheels of one of these monstrous vehicles. Fortunately, this driver was completely fine and an hour or so later a recovery truck managed to tow the lorry off to the side of the road.

We snaked through the icy hills that line the banks of Lake Baikal until it was nearly nightfall. We were heading to a random person's house in a tiny village on the shores of the lake. We had received a message on Facebook from a biker in Moscow who offered for us to stay at their holiday home. We followed Google Maps to the location, but there was no sign of any kind of holiday home or guesthouse. We were just stood in a tiny village in the pitch-black at −20°C, wondering what the hell to do. Incredibly, a few minutes later a lady pottered along with her two tiny dogs and asked us to follow her. She didn't speak any English, but she opened the gates to her house and offered for us to come in. It looked like we had found the right place, or more, it had found us. Using the translate app, we eventually managed to determine that we were in the right house and Eleanor, the lady with the dogs, would be looking after us for the night.

It was just brilliant. We went from debating whether to get the tent out in the cold, to sat by a roaring open fire with a cup of tea in about thirty minutes flat. We chatted to Eleanor for a while and she showed us some pictures of her family enjoying the house and the lake over the years. She cooked us a fantastic dinner of chicken and rice, and we talked about all manner of things. Mainly, though, we talked about Lake Baikal. It turned out it's the deepest lake in the world, reaching a depth of more than 1,600 metres and containing almost a quarter of the world's fresh surface-water. We went for a walk along its shores with Eleanor in the morning, and I was amazed to see small waves washing up ice onto the beach. The whole lake actually freezes over throughout the winter, and some people ride sidecars across it. Standing at the shore that day was probably the one fleeting moment of the trip when I wished we had done Russia in deepest darkest winter. I would have loved to throw Kuishi around on the ice!

We left Eleanor and headed on towards the city of Irkutsk. Despite the plummeting temperatures we were doing okay and made it as far as Angarsk. We were keen to get as far west as possible before the cold snap, so we just checked into a roadside motel. It was a normal kind of night in a Russian roadside motel: mash, cabbage, meat, beer, and people staring at you while you try to focus on your chess. I popped outside the following morning to a chilly −28°C and found a shivering Kuishi na Kuishi. We'd been unable to get it indoors the night before and had paid the price: it wouldn't start. It wasn't the battery, as we'd pre-emptively brought that in the night before. This was something worse. We had absolutely no idea what it could be. It wasn't turning over at all, but the ignition was turning on. We thought it could be the immobiliser, as that had caused problems once before, but it seemed unlikely. We were completely stumped and with everyone in the UK in bed, Reece rang Honda Australia to see if they could shed any light on what it might be. It took him ages to convince them it wasn't a prank call before they finally said something along the lines of, "Struth lads, could be anything, can't help ya."

We ordered some breakfast and while we were working through three fried eggs and a single slice of sausage, we began discussing the very real possibility that this could be a completely done-for scooter and sidecar. We could be waiting in Angarsk for new parts for potentially weeks. Our only thought was that both of our batteries had gone flat and they just needed some juice, so we spent the morning shopping for a battery charger in Angarsk. As we sat in the café of the guesthouse charging one of the batteries, a guy came over and started chatting away in English. We explained the problem and he said he'd get a mechanic to come and take a look for us if the charger didn't do the trick. It was showing on the metre that the battery was full, so we popped it back in. Still nothing. We agreed that we were done for. We'd be waiting there for ages. The helpful stranger said it was time to let the mechanic have a go.

Twenty minutes later the mechanic arrived. He took one look and said, "No problem, we take it to Africa!" He pulled out a blue plastic sheet and pinned it down over the sidecar. Then he put a jet heater underneath and left it running for ten minutes.

"Okay! Try!" he said enthusiastically. Sure enough, it started first time. Amazing! It was now too late to set off so we arranged to put the rig in the mechanic's heated garage and then settled in for another night of mash, cabbage, meat, beer, and people staring at us while we tried to focus on our chess.

There were no problems the following morning and we were on the road bright and early trying to make up some miles. It was freezing cold, though, and at −31°C we were really feeling it. The roads were properly snowy as well. It was the kind of day where the trucks cake you in snow every time they pass, and we were hating it. We pulled in for some lunch and got back on the borscht. Warmed up and ready for an afternoon's ride, Reece jumped on the bike and turned the dial to start it. Nothing. We looked around us and the penny dropped. Everyone else's vehicles had been left running. We stood back for a second when we saw a puddle of oil under the bike. Reece checked the dipstick. We had zero oil left. It was completely dry. We had broken a seal when trying to start the bike and now it was all over the floor.

Incredibly, we had done so at the front door of a garage. We gave it a knock and Vladimir and Daniel, a father and son combo of mechanics, came out and started laughing at us. They flung open their big truck-sized doors and welcomed us into their warm garage. The fellas spent the next two or three hours searching for an oil leak. They were pulling parts of the engine apart, but they couldn't find it, and then they pulled out the starter motor to find a completely kaput O-ring seal. Straight away we jumped to moaning at each other about how that would be a couple of weeks at this trucker stop while we waited for parts, but the guys had other plans. They'd just make another. They used a gasket maker kit and by nightfall the bike was ready for the road again. We checked into a little motel above the café and again woke up to an extremely cold morning, somewhere around −30°C. There had been even more snow overnight and Daniel and Vladimir suggested to us that we should make some snow chains. They said they could do it in a couple of hours if we wanted. We decided it was a good idea and as promised we drove off a couple of hours later with some brilliant new snow chains. We also had a thick sheepskin coat to put over us in the sidecar. Vladimir wouldn't let us leave without it, and actually it really did help.

The snow chains were amazing, and we were sailing along a really snowy road at maybe 30 mph—so much faster than without them. I shouted to Reece through the curtain, "Mate, this is incredible! We'll be home in no ti—" when I felt a big jolt and heard a crunching sound from under the rig. I screeched to a halt and pulled in to see two sets of broken chains and a severely smashed-up bike. We were in the middle of nowhere, in thick snow, at −30°, with a really messed-up looking scooter, and we were thinking we could be in a real spot of bother.

– 22 –

"WE THINK YOU ARE FINALLY STARTING TO REALISE; IT IS NOT RUSSIAN WEATHER THAT IS YOUR BIGGEST DANGER, BUT RUSSIAN HOSPITALITY!"

Fortunately, the snow chain incident looked worse than it was and we were able to get it all sorted out on the side of the road. They had only really caused cosmetic damage and had ripped off a lot of plastic, including a big chunk of our front mudguard. We managed to use a bungee strap around the handlebars to keep the mudguard in place though, and after about twenty minutes of fixing it up we were ready to get back on the road. It's a good job, too, because after twenty minutes on the side of the road, we were starting to get seriously cold. We'd been riding for an hour already and the temperature was so low that we were both struggling to feel our toes. There was a dull pain in my feet and we really needed to get inside somewhere fast.

A few kilometres up the road, we came across a garage and got in to warm up. It didn't have a café or anything, it was just a very small room which you could walk into to get out of the elements while you paid at the counter. The room was no larger than four feet wide and six feet long and we decided we would take it over for thirty minutes. We bought a couple of litres of fuel and two double-sized Mars Bars at the till. Then we stripped down all of our gear, taking over at least half the room, before cracking open our flask of coffee and warming up by the radiator. It was inappropriate but it was survival and we had no complaints from the staff, either—they understood just how cold it was.

I needed to go for a wee before hitting the road, so I popped outside to use the standard roadside Siberian toilet, a long drop. We were really surprised when we saw our first long drop in Russia. I had thought, with Russia being one of the world's most powerful nations and all, that they may have flushing toilets, but no, they most certainly do not. Siberia is a very different place to Moscow and the country changes hugely as you travel from east to west. There are small pockets of wealth in some towns and cities, but on the whole Russia is completely broke. Nobody has much money and certainly not enough to buy toilets with. I read up on it a little bit and it turns out that Russia is one of the most unequal places on earth. It's a place where one percent of the country's population owns forty-six percent of the money in its banks. It's the land of the oligarch, and generally speaking, in Siberia anyway, you're either completely minted or you're doing your business in a hole at the end of the garden, at $-40°C$.

The long drops are pretty disgusting places, but unlike in most of the world they don't smell. Why? It's too cold. The poo instantly freezes up, which makes for an incredible phenomenon that I like to call the shite stalagmite. Each of these toilets has these almighty termite mounds growing up out of the ground. With every poo another layer is added. It looks a bit like the doner kebab meat you find down your local chippy. Pretty rank, but worse still is when the doner kebab stick starts to poke its head out of the hole and you have to be careful not to sit right on it! Now and again we did answer nature's call in these places, but generally speaking the guesthouses did have toilets. I would very rarely use them for a quick wee, and ordinarily opted to make yellow snow. As did most of the truckers, although many of the truckers weren't making yellow snow, it was a range of colours from deep red to florescent orange, an indication, perhaps, of what their homemade vodka was doing to their bodies.

Having warmed ourselves up a bit, we got back in the sidecar and rattled on down the Trans-Siberian. It was horrendously cold, and we were pulling in at every single coffee shop available just to get some feeling back in our toes. At lunch we picked up some Wi-Fi signal and had a message from a guy called Sanya who asked if we'd like to stay at his house. We, of course, took him up on the offer and after a long ride through another exceptionally long sunset we arrived at Sanya's house. It was a simple but lovely home. He had been building it himself throughout the summer and had just managed to get it ready to move into for winter. Sanya spoke a small amount of English and he was extremely welcoming. He had arranged a bit of a get-together for our arrival and his neighbour, Sergi, along with a group of other friends, came around to hang out.

We put Kuishi in Sanya's heated garage for the night and then went inside to find an incredible spread. There was pickled and smoked fish with potato salad and this weird but tasty fish-based coleslaw. Sergi burst through the door a few minutes after our arrival holding a big bottle of vodka and wearing an enthusiastic smile. Sanya asked us if we would like to have the full Russian experience. Not knowing what he meant we, of course, said yes. Sergi kicked off the experience by pouring out the first vodka. We ate a little food, then Sergi made a really long toast in Russian and then we drank the vodka. This happened on repeat for at least an hour. Occasionally, Sanya made a toast and so did we but Sergi certainly had the most to say. We were told Russian fables but even with Sanya's translation we had very little chance of understanding them. By about 8 p.m. we had killed a couple of bottles of vodka and everyone was pretty drunk. Sanya's friends had arrived, too, and we were all enjoying the process of watering the vodka down with beer. Then Sanya said, "Okay, time for real Russian experience, the banya!"

We had an idea we might be getting a banya and we were up for it. "Banya" is essentially the Russian word for sauna and they're not all that different. The only major variation from the warm room at your local leisure centre is that this one has a 74-year-old, fully nude man called Sergi in it armed with some leaves, ready to whip you as hard as he can. It was a bizarre experience. There we were all completely tanked up on vodka, fully naked with five or six Russian guys in an exceptionally hot, small steam room. We sat for a while and all was calm until Sergi got out the leaves. Sanya said that Reece and I should get the proper experience one at a time, so we took it in turns to get the full service. Reece and I had actually opted to keep our boxer shorts on but Sergi, who was leading the service, saw them as getting in the way.

I entered the banya and found that Sergi had turned it up to maximum temperature. Just being in there made me lightheaded and gave me pins and needles all over. As I entered, I was instructed to lie flat on my front on the bench. Then Sergi proceeded to hit me repeatedly with the leaves. Every part of my body was covered, and he hit as hard as he could but I didn't really feel any pain, I was in some kind of daze. My boxers were soon pulled down and Sergi proceeded to hit me with the leaves. The next thing I knew, I was flipped over and this time receiving the full treatment on the front, again my boxer shorts didn't stand in Sergi's way. After a few minutes, the whirlwind came to an end. I thought it was over and I was ushered out of the door, only to find the fellas waiting to chuck snow over me and rub the ice into my body. Then I was shoved back into the sauna where Sergi chucked a hot bucket of water over me and, with a few final whips, the ordeal was over. It was seriously intense; I had honestly never experienced anything like it in my entire life.

We spent the rest of the night chatting with the guys and drinking more beers. A couple of them could speak a bit of English and we were able to chat about all kinds of stuff, but mainly we talked about how cool it was that we could come and hang out in their country and learn about their culture. I was keen to talk about some of the key things Russia ends up in the news for, but as soon as I mentioned Putin, Sergi told me I should never talk about politics as all politicians are crooks and the conversation ended there.

Sanya whipped up some eggs for us in the morning, which made a start at getting rid of our hangovers. Then we filled our flask with some extremely strong coffee and hit the road. It hadn't warmed up and we were still in the low minus-thirties. The roads were relatively clear, as it was too cold to snow, so despite having to get inside at any opportunity, we were making okay progress.

We made it about 200 km that day to a small trucker stop where we managed to get the bike indoors. Temperatures dropped even further, to below −40°C at night, and a friend of ours, Tim Sykes, sent us a weather map which showed that, outside of the Poles, we were in the coldest place on the planet. It felt it too. When you walk outside at −40°C your nostril hairs instantly freeze up and it hurts just to breathe. It doesn't take long before you start to get a headache, and if you get on the bike the wind generated cuts right through you.

With the roads still exceptionally icy, we were spending our days feeling freezing cold, scared for our lives and genuinely annoyed with ourselves for continuing. The Russian people were doing their very best to keep our spirits up, though, and they started turning up with gifts. One morning we had a man knock on our door and offer us a Russian flag pin badge and another day we were riding along when we were flagged down by a passing motorist. We thought there must be a problem but, nope, it turned out he was a Siberian mixed martial arts champion who wanted to give us some honey because it keeps you strong. We were also regularly pulled over for selfies while driving along and it was tough to leave a restaurant without pictures being taken or moonshine vodka being offered. It was fun but it was intense. We were like mini celebrities and could barely get a second to catch our breath and count our toes.

The following day we rode into the town of Kemerovo. As we did, we spotted a Ural sidecar outfit parked by the roadside. Alongside it were a load of guys waving frantically at us to pull in. It turned out it was the Kemerovo biker club and they had been waiting by the roadside in −30°C to see if there was any way they could help us. We pulled in and told them we were all good, but we could grab some lunch if they were up for it, when one of them pointed out that we were leaking coolant. A pipe had become dislodged and pressed against a hot part of the engine, which had melted a hole. Fortunately for us, the fellas were chuffed to bits with the task ahead.

We followed the Ural guy down to a garage, where one of their friends set about fixing the pipe. Meanwhile, we were told it was lunch time. We were bundled in a car and taken down to a local kebab shop where we were treated to the most gorgeous wrap. We returned to find the bike was fixed but while we were there the lads suggested a full service. They checked the oil, tightened some bolts, etc., and also fitted a riding mitt. Using some insulation left over from our curtains they created a mitt to put our hands in so we wouldn't catch any wind. We hadn't bothered with this before, as we actually had some really good snowmobile gloves that did the job but to be fair it was a nice addition.

By the time we were done with the servicing, there was no chance we were getting any further down the road and one of the lads, Max, said we could crash at his gaff. He had seen our Facebook post after Sanya's house and said, "Don't worry there will be no vodka!" When we arrived to his house, he opened the door and said, "Whiskey!!" with a big smile. It was a similar experience to Sanya's house, lots of shots, lots of toasting, and lots of fun, no banyas this time though. Alex, one of the other guys, had brought a crapload of food and drinks in. There was loads of beer, some incredible chorizo, this fantastic stringy, salty cheese, and more salted fish. Max had also prepared a homemade borscht, which was out-of-this-world good, so much better than the roadside stuff. We had a great night chatting away and, bizarrely, halfway through the night we had to go downstairs to find a guy who had ridden his motorbike across town to get our autograph. He was on a solo and in nothing more than a pair of jeans and a normal jacket. It was −20°C and the roads were exceptionally icy. He came upstairs, I signed his jacket with a "Best wishes, Matt Bishop," he had a couple of whiskeys, and then he went back from whence he came.

We broke down the following morning. This time, though, it wasn't Kuishi. We were in Max's car on the way back to our rig, and it took a while for his car to get fixed. In the end, we got towed to the garage. We set off and racked up 100 km in one sitting, something we hadn't done since the first day out of Vladivostok. The secret to our success was new boots. The Kemerovo lads couldn't believe what we had been riding in and took us down to a fishing store where we picked up some arctic, good-to-minus-50°C boots. They were sensational. We pulled into a coffee shop after 100 km and could still feel our toes. It was a game changer. With the weather warming up a bit, too, we were suddenly making brilliant progress. We had a 360-km day followed by a 380-km day, stopping only to eat lunch and get our heads down for the night in roadside motels.

We pulled into the town of Omsk, where we grabbed some lunch and one of the guys was particularly pleased to see us. We had a little chat, but the language barrier was a bit of a problem and we couldn't get to the bottom of what he was saying. He eventually gave up trying to tell us something and we made it about another 50 km through the city and into a roadside motel for the night. When we got there, we were sent a message from a guy called Sergiusz in Moscow who had been sharing our posts to a Russian version of Facebook. It was a picture of a huge sign saying "Matt and Reece" which we hadn't seen and it turned out the guy we had bumped into was called Vyachislav and he was the president of the local scooter club. He had arranged for us to crash at his place and have another real Russian experience. We felt terrible to have driven past but genuinely didn't see the sign and couldn't work out what he was saying. We will never know what kind of experience Vyachislav had in mind!

As we pressed on the following day, we were presented with a new weather problem: thick, freezing fog. It was awesome in that it covered absolutely everything with miniature, sparkling white crystals, but it was awful in that it meant you couldn't see more than five metres in front of you and you couldn't avoid getting soaking wet and freezing cold. We pressed on anyway, and about 20 km outside of the town of Kurgan we were flagged down by a motorist. His name was Vladimir and he spoke no English but had written in Google Translate that he was a biker and we should stay at his house. As we pulled in, we noticed the front sidecar joint was broken again and needed welding up. No problem for Vladimir, who took us straight to his friend's garage for some repairs.

We were driven to a huge barn where we had some coffee and a big group of lads started poking around at our rig. We managed to have a chat through broken English and charades, in which we determined that the front weld was a big problem because it will always keep breaking. "You're telling us, mate," I thought to myself. Vladimir said they would fix it properly, but it would take some time. We had five or six guys working on fixing up the rig for six hours. They fitted a new, super-strong, adjustable joint on the front of the sidecar, repaired our sidecar wheel, which was also broken, and even found the time to fit our wing mirror to the roof so we could see behind us for the first time on the trip. One of the guys had come straight from his office job and did most of the welding in his pants so he didn't damage his trousers. It was a ridiculous sight.

We asked how much money they wanted for all of their help, and the fellas were almost offended. "We just want to help you with your journey," was the response and lots of "Welcome to Russia!" We crashed at Vladimir's place that night and he fed us a massive bowl of dumplings. We'd had them a couple of times already, but these were particularly great; they're like little dim sum dumplings, but they don't taste like Asian food. They're just meaty and you cover them in a kind of creamy, yoghurt sauce coupled with really hot chili sauce, if you can handle it.

The following night we were picked up once again but this time by the Chelyabinsk biker club. With nothing wrong with the bike we were free to enjoy the evening and our host for the night, Ivan, had linked us up with the local bike post, owned by a guy called Vladimir. This bike post was incredible, it had been turned into a fully functioning restaurant and had motorcycle paraphernalia all over the walls. We were brought through to the back room where we were given beers, an amazing bowl of dumplings, incredible salted fish and cheese, and, of course, loads of vodka. The drinks were flowing and Ivan said to us, "We think you are finally starting to realise; it is not Russian weather that is your biggest danger, but Russian hospitality!" I think he was right.

It turned out this place was the full experience, too, because Vladimir, the owner of the bike post, had converted an old truck out back into a banya. After dinner, we were ushered in for a good warm-up. It was just the three of us this time and more chilled out than the Sergi experience. This one was just three blokes sat naked in a really warm, old army truck.

Vladimir couldn't speak any English so we had a very limited conversation. He said "girls" after a while and then pointed at Reece and me.

"Yes, yes, we've got girlfriends, both of us."

"Okay! One, two, three?" he questioned.

He could see we were visibly puzzled. "Girls, here, yes, one, two, three?" he said.

"Oh, Jesus, no mate, no, no, no, no. We're okay, thanks," we replied.

"It's okay—very little money!" he replied.

"Christ, mate, no don't say that, no we're okay, thanks!"

He had clearly been suggesting that he get a few prostitutes in for the evening. Reece and I drew the line at experiencing that part of the culture and said no. It was no problem, though. Vladimir just went a bit quiet and then we all returned to the back room for some more beers and some chess. I was actually playing a game of chess with a local police officer when Vladimir asked if he could speak to Reece outside. Reece followed him out there, where Vladimir started to get a bit panicky.

"I'm sorry, I'm sorry, I'm sorry, I'm sorry, I'm sorry, I'm sorry, I'm sorry. Gay?" he said as he pointed at Reece.

"Blimey mate, no, I just don't sleep with prostitutes," replied a concerned Reece, who thought he could be in for a pasting. After all, it is publicised far and wide in the UK that Russian people aren't too accepting of people who are gay. "Look, I've got a girlfriend!" said Reece as he showed him some pictures of him with Hannah. Vladimir was very relieved. Reece actually says that he doesn't think Vladimir was worried about the fact we might be gay but instead was worried about the fact he might have offended us by offering us the chance to sleep with a woman.

I tried to have this discussion with a few people in Russia and struggled. Partly because of the language barrier but mainly because people didn't want to talk about it. I wanted to find out what was behind the media wall. Is Russia really the exceptionally homophobic, racist place the BBC documentaries would suggest, or are we just getting sold a story about them, like they are about us? I found it very hard to believe that the wonderfully kind, generous people I met would be anything but kind and generous towards anyone of a different race or sexuality, but every now and again there was the odd comment or phrase that just made you think that they've got a little way to go yet. Still, we gave Vladimir the benefit of the doubt and chose not to try and get through to him why he shouldn't be sleeping with prostitutes at all.

We stayed at Ivan's family home that night and were given a calendar of him and his friends. It turned out he was part of a biker club of priests. They were priests on motorbikes, and you could have a different one on your wall for every month of the year. When we left Chelyabinsk the following morning, we were only 1,600 km away from Moscow, where we would stay with Sergiusz, who is part of the motorcycling priest movement and had been putting us in touch with people throughout our journey in Russia. Sixteen hundred kilometres or a thousand miles isn't far to go, and it would mark the symbolic end of our journey across Russia. We were in touching distance, but we had one major challenge left: the Ural Mountains.

The Urals are absolutely gorgeous, although the bit we crossed was less the Ural Mountains and more the Ural Rolling Hills. That was fine, because we didn't need any steep climbs or any serious elevation. Fortunately, the roads were quite clear, so we were able to climb up and drive down, rather than push up and slide down, the hills. We made it 200 km on the first day to a roadside guesthouse and enjoyed a night off the vodka. The following morning, we awoke to another beautiful day in the Urals. At a lovely −16°C and with clear roads we were looking good. The frozen woodlands and snowy hills made for an awesome ride and everything was going fine until I lost all power when accelerating out of the bottom of a steep hill.

Suddenly, we were stranded on the side of the road and caged in by a roadside barrier so there was nowhere to safely investigate the issue. The only place was a lay-by about half a kilometre back up the hill. We had no choice and unstrapped all the bags before pushing the rig uphill to the lay-by and then returning for all of the bags. With trucks barreling past us at 60 mph and with only just enough room for us to squeeze up a hard shoulder, it was a nervy moment. We got to work and decided it must have been the transmission. Sure enough, we cracked it open and found that the driven face had fallen off. The cold must have shrunk the bolt and shook it loose. After an hour or so we had it back together and tightened it up ready to crack on. It was incredible, we had broken down on the side of the road and fixed it all on our own, with no help from a stranger. We realised how much simpler but less fun the trip would have been had we been mechanics.

A few hours later, just as the sunset was disappearing, we realised we weren't mechanics: it happened again. Fortunately, this time it happened as we were passing a lay-by, so we rolled straight in and got to work. An hour later and we fixed it up again but this time we put a load of Loctite in with the bolt. It held, and we made it through another 20 km in the dark to a local roadside trucker stop. It was the 22nd December and the café at the stop was hosting a work Christmas party. It wasn't long until we were booked in for the entertainment for the event. Our fee for the evening, which we tried to turn down, was well over a bottle of vodka and some salted fish. We woke up the following morning with a hangover that suggested the night before had been fun.

We were planning to get on the road bright and early, as we were hoping to make it all the way through to the suburbs of Moscow. We were packed and ready to go by 7 a.m. and were just waiting for first light with some breakfast when a guy walked in and came to sit next to us. He handed us a massive jar of pickles that his mother had made for us and explained that he had driven 100 km that morning to deliver them. He sat and had a chat for about five minutes before getting up and leaving. He didn't even see the scooter. It was truly bizarre but very generous. We tucked into a couple of pickles with breakfast and they were lovely.

The morning's ride started out okay but as the day went on, snow started falling and it got heavier and heavier. With us being so close to Moscow there were trucks every few seconds and they were so close to us. The snow was a few inches thick across the road and we were slipping around everywhere. We decided that we had come too far to die now and checked into the next hotel at around 2 p.m.

It had stopped snowing overnight and the roads had been cleared, too, which left us a free run at getting to Moscow and at about midday we pulled into the Russian capital. It had taken six weeks, but after 9,200 km, we had made it from Vladivostok to Moscow. There wasn't a single day on the drive from Vladivostok to Moscow when I actually thought we'd make it. I was sure we'd end up waiting it out for parts, throwing in the towel, or under a lorry, but here we were. It was without a doubt the hardest thing I had ever done in my life and I hope to never bite off a challenge that big again. Thank heavens we were right about the everyday people of the world and found the kindness we knew was out there. We didn't know it would come quite like it did in Russia, though, and it's safe to say the only reason we made it was because of the exceptionally warm, banya-level, red-hot welcome we received.

It was a warm welcome in Moscow, too, from Sergiusz who had been sharing our posts on the Russian version of Facebook and had been responsible for much of the help we received. It turned out that there had been around 15,000 people following on Russian Facebook, which explained the endless selfies and gifts. Sergiusz had been approached by a local tour guide called Vladimir, who wanted to show us around, so the four of us went out exploring. I can honestly say it was one of the most incredible cities of the entire trip. The architecture is unbelievable and the Christmas lights glittering throughout the snowy city were just mesmerising. We had an absolutely brilliant time exploring the place. They both spoke brilliant English and we were able to finally get some answers. Turns out nobody's racist and everyone's cool with it if you're gay so that was those questions put to bed. Also, they like Putin and it's not a problem he's been in power for so long. "Russians enjoy having long serving leaders, they're used to tsars. And, while we're talking politics, why are the UK being so damn aggressive over this Ukraine thing? We really don't want any wars!"

It was bizarre. At first, I thought Vladimir was a government-trained tourist guide, equipped with the right answers, but then I realised that he really thought these things and was just on the other side of this massive media wall. It was a really interesting night and we had an absolute banging steak on Sergiusz, too.

Then, on Christmas Eve, we set off again. The forecast was good, and we weren't going to hang around and wait for another cold snap. We met Vladimir for a quick coffee before we left, as he wanted to give us some gifts. He sent us on our way with a metal mug each that had the Russian flag on it, two pots of caviar for our parents to try, and two packs of biscuits to give to our girlfriends when we met them in Estonia. We had managed to convince Chels and Hannah to meet us in Tallinn for New Year's Eve, so we were planning to just drive as much as possible every day to ensure we got there. It was very nice of Vladimir, as it sorted out the problem of us getting the girls a Christmas present, too.

After an hour or so riding we had made it out of Moscow and we were on the home straight towards St. Petersburg. However, it had started to snow again, and we were essentially in a white-out. It felt exceptionally dangerous. I was at the handlebars and I decided to call it off. I was two or three days from escaping Russia and seeing Chelsea again. At this point, I had absolutely zero interest in going under a lorry, so I pulled into a Burger King. I said to Reece that I was sitting in the Burger King until it had stopped snowing and the road was clear, and if that meant a week then so be it! I'd had enough. I was just absolutely petrified of meeting my icy doom so close to the end.

Reece was a bit taken aback by my exceptionally strong stance, but agreed we should pull in for a Whopper. Around three hours later it cleared it up and we pressed on once again to a roadside motel. We had a nice meal that night and a couple games of chess. It was still pretty tense, as after fifteen months we were still neck and neck, which either shows we're incredibly well matched or, more likely, neither of us can play and we were just testing the law of averages.

We had a lovely Christmas Day drive through to St. Petersburg where we did actually pick up some presents for the girls. I got Chels a pâté taster set (which I later regretted when I realised it had bear pâté in it) and Reece got Hannah some pickled mushrooms. All terrible presents, which was far riskier for Reece than it was for me. I'd spent four years building up low expectations; his garbage gift was coming right out of the blue.

Boxing Day was our final day's ride in Russia. We just about made it over the border to Estonia, but only just. Our sidecar wheel bearing broke as it had done in the Sahara way back when. Incredibly, it happened outside of a garage and we were able to fix it up within a couple of hours. The following day we pressed on south through the snow to the city of Tallinn, where we met Chels and Hannah. We did gifts straight away. The pâté went down great. The pickled mushrooms, for Reece, not so much. Reece and Hannah actually went their separate ways a few months after the trip and I'm convinced the mushrooms were the start of the end.

We had a fantastic few days relaxing and celebrating in Tallinn. It was awesome to be with Chels for New Year's Eve and we watched the fireworks as the snow fell on us in the city's main square. The year 2019 had arrived and it would have to be an absolute belter to beat 2018. After a few days exploring and generally enjoying a break, we waved Chels and Hannah goodbye and told them we would see them at Ace Café in little under three weeks. It was only 5,000 km to home and we were pretty much done. With proper, cleared roads the whole way back, it would be a doddle and we would make it easily, or so you would think. The scooter had other ideas.

– 23 –

"THE RACE TO ACE"

"Christ, mate, this is like Siberia again!" I shouted to Reece through the sidecar curtain. It was our first day's ride in 2019 and we were heading south towards Latvia. There was seriously heavy snowfall and it was the stuff that settles. I found myself at the helm, slipping and sliding my way through a white-out. I reminded myself that most people who die on a mountain do so on the way back down. We had got to Moscow and summited our Everest, now it was time to take it easy and be even more cautious than ever. We pulled in after about 130 km at the coastal town of Parnu. It was a ghost town but there was a biker bar and it was playing the Manchester United match, so I was very happy with what it had to offer.

The weather cleared up a touch the following day and we could at least see where we were going. We decided to try and make it through to Riga where we would take a day off, do some admin, and give the bike a good clean-up. Unfortunately, our scheduled maintenance was scheduled in too late and as we crossed the border from Estonia into Latvia, the sidecar bearing blew up on us again. There's no border control between the two countries anymore but the old checkpoint buildings are now used to serve you coffee. A much better use of space, if you ask me. We popped our heads in and were told that the nearest garage was a kilometre down the road. The bearing was already mangled so we just made it worse and drove down there. It was a tiny village and there was nobody around but eventually we found a workshop and got it sorted. We had no idea what was causing the bearing to keep failing, but we were so close to home now that we decided to just keep on trucking.

We spent a couple of nights in Riga before riding a whopping 49 km to the town of Jelgava. A guy called Marcis had contacted us online and asked if we wanted to stay at his house and use his workshop to try and solve our bearing problem. We of course took him up on the offer and were very pleased we did. He was the president of the local bike club and had a full-on clubhouse in his back yard. It was equipped with a huge workshop, games room, and, you guessed it, a sauna.

We spent the day fixing up the bike. Marcis put a new set of bearings in for us and told us they would hold until we got back to the UK. We had an interesting chat about life under Soviet rule and how tough times had been for him and his family when he was growing up. He said it made him a hard worker and that's why he was doing so well for himself today. He was doing well, too; he had a lovely house and a garage full of motorbikes and sidecars, that's pretty much the end goal for anyone, isn't it?

We explored the town of Jelgava and went for dinner with Marcis' friends before returning to the clubhouse for a night of drinking and warming up. We had a Siberia-style evening with plenty of booze and plenty of nudity. The sauna was a little tamer than Sanya's banya, but it was still fairly intense. We spent most of the night playing a Latvian pub game called Novuss. It's a lot like pool but instead of balls you have disks. It's a lot of fun.

We woke up with horrendous hangovers the following morning and Marcis persuaded us to stay and hang out rather than taking on the bad weather. We ended up going go-karting on ice, which was a lot of fun, too. The following day we pressed on south and made it into Lithuania where we stayed the night in a roadside motel near the town of Marijampole.

Next, we cracked on into Poland. Another day, another country. The weather was terrible for most of the morning and we were getting battered by snow hitting us sideways from some seriously strong winds. By mid-morning it died down a bit, but the countryside was covered in a thick blanket of snow. We thought it would look awesome from above so we threw the drone up to capture us driving through. Unfortunately, something went horribly wrong and the drone started driving itself. I pressed emergency land, as it was right above our heads, and it decided that it needed to climb to a safe distance first. The next thing I knew it had shot off into the clouds above and was gone forevermore. We couldn't believe it. The thing had literally just flown off on its own. The remote was telling us it had landed safely no more than 500 metres away, but 500 metres in any one direction is a huge area to search. There was no chance we would find it. We admitted defeat and went to a trucker stop about 5 km down the road for a warm-up. I started sifting through the app for the drone on my phone and incredibly it gave me exact flight data, including the coordinates of the last landing. We plugged them into Gary and drove back 5 km to find the drone about 500 metres away from where we were stood, safely resting in the middle of a snowy field.

We stopped that night in the town of Grajewo before pressing on the following morning to the country's capital city, Warsaw. Marcis had arranged for us to stay with a biker friend of his in the city. This was a real rarity, because Marcis' friend was a lady called Marina. We had stayed at a lot of family homes and guesthouses run by women, but Marina was the first female biker who put us up for the night, which made a nice change. There was no macho vodka-drinking or sauna-sitting, it was just a drop of red wine, a lovely meal, and a chat about the world. Marina had some really out-there views on the world, the strongest of which was that smoking isn't at all related to cancer or any kind of illness. I heard her out but left unconvinced.

We left Warsaw the following morning, heading for Poznan, the next big city on route. We joined the A2, the Autobahn, and chalked off an easy 95 km to our lunch stop. We had got away late so hadn't got far. It wasn't a problem though, as we had made it to within a thousand miles of the Ace Café. For the first time we could count our remaining miles using three digits and we would be home in no time. Plus, we were on the Autobahn, the final thousand would probably be the quickest thousand.

After lunch, we pressed on with no problems for a couple of hours when, out of nowhere, there was an almighty crunching sound. Luckily, it happened right next to a lay-by so Reece rolled us into it.

"What the hell was that, mate?" I said to Reece, as I took off my helmet.

"I've got no idea, but I've got no power and it sounded really nasty," he replied.

We figured it must have been the transmission again. We got straight to work, took off the crankcase, and, to our horror, we found that everything was in perfect condition.

"Oh my word, mate, this could be game-over," Reece said as we stared at the pristine drive belt. We knew that there was no way we had it in our locker to fix anything now, so we started working out how to get the rig to a garage. We were still 120 km away from Poznan, where we would be staying with the Poznan sidecar club. Yes, incredibly that's a thing and Bartosz, one of their members, had messaged us and asked if we would like to stay with him while we were in town. Unfortunately, our arrival fell on a day when Bartosz was having a big celebration with lots of family over, so there was no space to stay but he insisted that he would book us into an Airbnb around the corner so we could still hang out. So, we had a place to stay, a helpful local person, and a big city, potentially with spare parts just 120 km away. We just had to get there.

There was a roadside SOS phone in the lay-by, so I gave that a go. Incredibly, the person on the other end spoke perfect English and said she would send a recovery truck right away. Problem solved. The recovery truck arrived an hour later and the guy driving it told us that he could take us to Poznan for a fee of EUR350. We politely told him that we were more likely to carry it to Poznan than pay that much and he should crack on with the rest of his day. We were stumped. Our phones didn't have the right SIM for the area, so we asked the recovery guy if we could use his phone to ring our friends. He said yes and I managed to get through to Bartosz and explain the situation. I asked him if he knew any local recovery trucks that might be able to get us for a more decent rate. He asked to be put on to the recovery truck driver and then said to me, "Stay where you are, we are coming to get you."

Two hours of sat in the snowy lay-by passed and the sun disappeared over the horizon as we waited. Then, out of the dark came a small car towing a small trailer, which screeched to a halt right in front of us by the curbside. Out stepped an extremely enthusiastic guy who looked like a combination of Charley Boorman and the bloke from Back to the Future, and a calmer but equally friendly person whom I recognised as Bartosz. We were introduced and it turned out the other guy's name was Gerard. He was also part of the sidecar club and this was his trailer that he used specifically for sidecar outfits.

Sure enough, we got it straight on the trailer and it was the perfect fit. We piled all the kit in the car and Reece and I squeezed in the back, with Gerard and Bartosz up front. Bartosz handed us a Screwdriver each. No, not the tool, the cocktail. Vodka and orange juice. He said everything was now under control and they had managed to get a local scooter shop to open up for us that night to take a look at the problem. An hour and a bit later, we arrived at the scooter shop and instantly started stripping the bike down. It was 8 p.m. and the shop had closed hours earlier. No problem for these guys, though, and it wasn't long until we found the issue: a completely mangled final drive cog. In fact, the entire final drive was ruined. It was completely mashed up. It turned out a bearing had gone and it had been running metal on metal for miles, perhaps even thousands of miles, and it had finally given way.

Gerard and Bartosz looked worried. "It's bad guys, very bad!" The scooter shop owner said it couldn't be repaired and we'd need a brand new part but even then, it would be a huge job to get it repaired and sealed properly. He said that there was a strong chance that even with the new part he would be unable to seal off the unit properly and it would just break again.

"What, so we need a whole new engine?" Reece asked.

"Yes, could be," replied Bartosz.

We couldn't believe it. We had ridden Kuishi 33,000 miles around the world and now 950 km from the finish line, it had finally given up. We were so close to home that we had arranged a small ride into the Ace Café and coined it the "Race to Ace." Well, it now looked like we would certainly lose the race. People had already made plans to see us come in and many had said they would ride in with us from the Channel tunnel. That was all firmly off the cards, we were no longer sure if we would make it at all.

We admitted defeat for the night and said to the guys we would work it out in the morning. We spent all day Thursday searching for parts on the internet with limited success. The best chance we had was to buy them from Honda France for EUR700 and hope that the scooter guys could get the job done. It would be a week for them to arrive and we would miss the ride in, but we might just make it in general. We didn't order them straight away though, as we had some friends and family scouring part shops in the UK. Hopefully they could get them cheaper and have them with us quicker. No luck though, and we went to bed Thursday night expecting to order the parts in on Friday morning. Then at 9 a.m. Bartosz burst through the door.

"Guys, I have found it!" he exclaimed.

"It" was a scrapped Honda SH300i engine that had been restored and was available to buy on a Polish version of Gumtree just 100 km down the road. It was remarkable. They don't even have Honda SH300is in Poland, it was most likely one that had been in an accident in the UK and shipped over here to be "recycled." Well this one really was going to be recycled. It was in perfect condition and according to MotoBob, its current owner, it had only done a few thousand miles. It was up for sale for a cool EUR400, 300 cheaper than the part alone and we were getting a whole new engine!

So again, that night we found ourselves in the back of Gerard's car racing around the countryside, scared for our lives, sipping on Screwdrivers. The engine looked good so we took it back to the guys at the scooter shop and they said they would fit it on Monday morning as they had to go away that weekend. That was no problem for us because if it got fixed on Monday we still had a chance to make it to Ace Café the following Saturday for our ride in. Plus, it just so happened we were in town on the weekend that the Poznan sidecar club were going out to the countryside to do some trail riding on their rigs. They asked if we'd like to join them and we of course jumped at the chance. It was a bit of a busman's holiday, as on the Saturday morning we found ourselves sat in a sidecar, cheesing it down the highway in horrible conditions. It was a lot more fun, though, and at times far too exhilarating. I was riding in Gerard's rig and it was deadly, we were whipping in and out of the traffic and going far too fast for my liking.

We eventually made it to the farm we would be staying at for the weekend and we convened with about six or seven other guys, all riding sidecars, most of them old Russian Ural outfits. We had some coffee and something to eat before getting back in the rigs and hanging on for a day on the trails. It was proper white-knuckle riding and there was a strong chance we would come off. Gerard didn't speak much English but he managed to tell me that he doesn't tip the sidecar every time. Which meant to me that he does a lot of the time. I was ready to bail. I told him he was crazy and he said, "No, I'm not crazy, I'm an athlete. Push limit!" Well, he was certainly pushing the limits. I looked back in envy at Reece, who was getting a comfortable ride in Bartosz's seat.

We spent an hour racing up the trails and Gerard only tipped it once. Fortunately, I wasn't in it and nobody got hurt. We returned that night to the farmhouse where our host for the weekend poured out the vodka and cooked pork chops on top of his log burner. It was a great setting. I asked Gerard what it was all in aid of and he looked at me funny as if to say, you don't know, and said, "Bartosz birthday!" I was shocked but it made sense. It turned out that Bartosz hadn't just left a family visit to pick us up on the side of the road, he had left his own bloody birthday party! What a guy.

We had more than enough shots of vodka celebrating Bartosz's birthday and then returned to Poznan that night to stay with Bartosz. He had room for us at his house now and we met his lovely wife and two-year-old son. His son was exceptionally cute and sadly he had Down's Syndrome. Bartosz told us that was part of the reason he'd got so into sidecars, because he wanted his son to be able to ride a motorbike with him one day. They were a really cool family.

We got to work with Bartosz and the scooter guys the following day and expected to set about rebuilding our engine. I thought we would take the part out and put it in ours but no, the plan was to swap out the entire engine and put the new one in. We were a bit unsure about that. It took the idea of Kuishi being "Trigger's Broom" to a whole new level but the lads said we had little choice. There was a chance we'd mess up the change and render both engines useless, but this was the only way. We got to work swapping it out, well, Reece and I mainly stood and watched as the fellas actually knew what they were doing. It took all day, but we finally managed to get the engine going and in position. We turned the dial to start it up and there was a small struggle before the bike died. We tinkered with it again but had no luck. The scooter guys had no idea what to do, Bartosz wasn't sure either and we were as clueless as ever. We agreed to leave it with them while we got some dinner and had a think.

When we returned a couple of hours later, Gerard was under the rig and he was setting fire to the ignition. That's what it looked like to me; I don't really know what he was doing, but it looked like some kind of mad, exceptionally dangerous experiment. He eventually determined it was broken and he swapped our ignition in off the old engine. We turned the dial and Kuishi roared back to life. The transplant had worked, and we had a rideable bike!

We had a final night hanging out with Gerard and Bartosz where we celebrated fixing the bike and then, the next morning, we rode east, back to where we broke down. Race to the Ace or no Race to the Ace, we were doing every inch of this trip by scooter and sidecar. The new engine was purring nicely, and it even felt a bit meatier than our previous one. Which was impressive because we were carrying the weight of two engines, literally. We strapped the old one to the back of the sidecar, there was no way we could leave it behind now. Just as we were about to make it to the point at which we broke down, we, again, broke down. This time it was the bearing problem but this time there was no lay-by. We pulled off to the side of the road down a small grassy bank and started trying to fix it. With no phone and no

SOS option either, we would have to sort it ourselves. We soon got the wheel off but getting the bearing out was another matter altogether. It had got mangled up and had fused to the inside of the wheel. We needed a workshop to get it out but that wasn't an option, so we got our screwdriver and our hammer and just starting bashing the thing up. With heavy snow falling down on us we were getting battered by the elements as we tried to batter this thing out of shape. It was no use. After around thirty minutes we had only succeeded in shortening our best screwdriver.

A car driver saw we were in trouble and pulled in to help out. It was a man on his own and he got out of the car and started telling us off. He was saying that we shouldn't drive that type of vehicle on the highway. We shot him down right away and said, "Listen, mate, we've driven this thing on a fair few highways, we know what we're allowed to do!" Which, incredibly, he accepted and proceeded to completely change his tack before offering to get us a recovery truck. It turned out his name was Piotr and he ran that particular stretch of the Autobahn. He asked us to put the wheel back on and then sit in his car to keep warm. Twenty minutes later a recovery truck turned up and took us to the local highway maintenance centre. We were given a cup of coffee and the bike was handed over to the resident mechanic. It was all fixed within an hour. We asked how much money we owed, expecting it to be a ludicrously expensive EUR350, and he said they were just happy to help and sent us on our way.

With all the faff, we only made it back to Poznan, where we just got our heads down in a guesthouse before cracking on again the following morning. We were now just days away from making it back to the UK. Next we had a trouble-free ride into Germany where we stopped in a motel before pressing on again for our penultimate night's stay of the whole trip and a visit to the last stranger we would meet on our adventure. Although this guy wasn't really a stranger because he had found us online before our departure and had followed every step of the way. His name was Manfred Jung and I think he had lived and breathed every bit of the ride with us. We pulled into his house and were treated like old friends. He introduced us to his lovely family, and his wife Andrea had cooked up a corker of a meal ahead of our arrival. It was

Thursday night and all we had left to do was wake up in the morning, ride to Calais, crash for the night and then ride to Ace. We decided we weren't risking any more breakdowns and we preemptively changed the bearings in the sidecar wheel before getting settled in for the night.

We had a great evening that night, chatting about travel and enjoying the great food and beer. One particular topic caught my attention and that was the pig farm down the road. Manfred told us that it had grown somewhat in recent years and it now slaughtered 30,000 pigs a day. Imagine that, 30,000 a day. How on earth do you even kill that many pigs in a day? There are tens of thousands of pigs there at any one time, all locked in tightly together. Apparently, there is so much pig poo that it has actually poisoned the local water supply and the town is now reliant on water being tanked in from other parts of Germany. How bad is that? Worse still, Manfred is convinced it's fueled by modern slavery. I can't confirm anything through any of my research, so I don't claim it is at all, but Manfred says he's spotted the signs: poor working conditions, lots of people who can't speak German or English, they very rarely leave the compound, and when they do, they look like they're in really bad condition. Crazy stuff.

We left Manfred's the following morning and rode 515 km all the way to Calais, with no trouble whatsoever. We passed through the Netherlands, only stopping for fuel; we were on a mission to get home! We found ourselves a cheap motel right by the Channel Tunnel and then went for a pizza to celebrate. We had a final two games of chess and Reece won them both, which meant we tied the entire trip. Then we went off to bed ready for the last ride of the trip.

I remember lying in bed and feeling so excited to get back. It had been the experience of a lifetime but there's nothing like driving home via a Siberian winter to make you not miss the road. We were both completely ready to hang up our helmets and were looking forward to the final ride. We boarded the Channel Tunnel as planned in the morning and on the other side we met a small group of supporters. There was John, our trainer from Metropolis; Gemma, the lady who had led us out; and a group of other supporters and followers who picked us up online.

We rode off north to Brands Hatch in convoy, just how we liked it. We led this time, but Gemma jumped in front with the steward lights any time we needed to make a turn. At Brands Hatch, we met a few other supporters including the one and only Gerry, whom we had last seen "heading north with the bear" back in Paris. We picked up a few more followers too, and had a convoy of at least twenty or thirty strong. We took the scenic route through London and Reece had to keep jumping off the bike to film us riding past landmarks. Eventually, we made it to the Mall and once we had driven up it and past Buckingham Palace, we were in spitting distance of the North Circular that would take us all the way to the famous Ace Café. I was driving as we got onto the North Circular and I remember feeling actually sick with nerves. I feel sick just writing and thinking about it. I was nervous because Reece and I had essentially organised our wedding, everyone we knew in the world was going to be there, but more so because this was it. The end of the road. The end of the adventure that I dedicated the last three or four years to. We really had done it.

We pulled off the slip road and got stuck at the lights just a hundred metres or so from the Ace. We were just out of sight, but as the lights turned green the whole convoy started honking their horns in celebration.

We had arrived.

We pulled into the car park to an overwhelming scene of friends and family awaiting our arrival. I pulled in and said, "Hi guys, we made it." I wish I had thought of something better. Fortunately, my victory speech was bolstered by Reece falling over as he tumbled out of the sidecar and then we stood there for a split second before Paddy Tyson of Overland magazine came over, shook my hand, and said, "Welcome home!" I was so grateful for Paddy for doing that because I was so awkward and had no idea who to greet first. Next on the list, and rightly so, was of course Chels! I wish I had picked her up and swung her around like something out of the movies, but it was just a quick hug and a kiss before I was dragged away to somebody else. I gave my mum a hug as she was crying with joy to have us back, and then I shook Richard, Charlie, and Mal's hands and thanked them for everything. I then made my way around the whole crowd, only stopping to do an interview and eat a sausage and mash. I think I was hugging and saying, "Thanks for coming!" to people until around midnight.

We went off to bed in the same Travelodge we had stayed in before we left and I felt a huge sense of relief rush over me. I had made it home and I hadn't died. It sounds melodramatic, but for a long time on that last leg I genuinely didn't think we would make it back, and then after we had got through the bit where I thought it was likely we would die, I thought we would most likely die just for the sake of irony. It had become a genuine fear. I think it was the only time in my life I've been genuinely scared. Scared beyond hysteria, just an accepting, deep-set fear that I might not see the end of the day. I felt like that more or less every day for six weeks across Russia, and I look back now and think, "Why on earth didn't I just throw the towel in?" Honestly, I think the answer to that is the Russian people. If I had sat every night just thinking of the morning, I would have eventually had a breakdown, but their generosity and hilarious company kept morale so high in the evenings that it counteracted the extreme lows I felt in the day. We got super lucky to have not had a serious accident and we were so fortunate to meet all of the incredible people who carried us along the way.

I woke up the following morning next to Chels and it felt nice to not have to think about the fact that she would be gone in a few days. Then we went for breakfast at Ace and met a group of bikers who had come from Banbury to ride us in. Charlie and Gareth Nicholls had arranged for us to receive a mayoral reception on our arrival and we rode into yet another welcoming party. The Banbury town mayor welcomed us into the town hall on our arrival and awarded us with a bottle of champagne for our achievement. We took it outside and of course sprayed it over ourselves and the bike before sharing it around. Everyone eventually dispersed and appropriately Reece, Charlie, and I were the last to leave. Reece then dropped me back at my house in Sibford before cracking on to ride home himself. Getting dropped off was bizarre, because that really was it. I was home and ready for a Sunday night in front of the telly.

And there it was. We had circumnavigated the globe on a scooter and sidecar. We racked up 34,000 miles through thirty-five countries across five continents and became the first people to ever get around the planet on that very specific, very niche kind of vehicle. We had broken the Guinness World Record for the longest journey by scooter and sidecar seven times over and, honestly, it was the privilege of a lifetime. I very much doubt I will ever be lucky enough to do such a thing like it again (nor would I want to). On the trip, I learnt a huge amount about so many things. I learnt so much about the world in general, so much about myself, and far too much about Reece. He had been a great person to travel with, but no two people should ever spend that much time with each other. I can assure you that he is a truly grotesque bloke, I'm sure he'd tell you the same about me.

I had seen so much incredible scenery, visited so many beautiful places, and hung out with some of the world's most brilliant people. I'd also learnt so much about the bad things that happen in our world; I had seen struggle, witnessed desperation, and heard first-hand of the terrible human rights abuses that I knew still existed, including slavery. But overwhelmingly and without doubt the biggest thing I had learnt was that Reece and I had been completely right. That's not something you often say about us two. In preparing for this trip we had been called naïve and stupid so many times. People said it could never be done, and especially not by us. They would have been right had it not been for the one sentiment that we believed so strongly in from day one: the world is a good place, full of great people.

All of the naysayers had been entirely correct; we were two completely naïve, stupid guys, who didn't stand a chance, and couldn't do anything. Fortunately for us, we didn't have to. From the stranger down the road who built us a rig, to the udder-eating host in Egypt who got us through customs, to the Bolivian grandma who took us in and out of the mountains, to the Bigfoot-believer who welded us up, to the vodka swiggers who lifted our spirits, and to the birthday boy who missed his party, the kindness of everyday people was the unrelenting super-power that gifted us success and made us achieve the unthinkable. Thank you to all of you.

So, there you have it, the proof you needed. The world is a good place full of great people. Don't believe me? Slap on a smile, walk out your door, and find out for yourself! You can even borrow the sidecar if you like.

ACKNOWLEDGMENTS

This book in itself reads almost as a constant flow of acknowledgements for the people who made the trip happen as well as for those we met who helped us continue on our trip. The kindness of complete strangers is what powered the journey and as you read in this book there are far too many of those to list them all here. I will pick out a few people who deserve an extra mention, though.

I will first thank Reece. His willingness to blindly do something so ridiculous was instrumental in getting us around the world. If you're planning your own circumnavigation of the globe on a scooter and a sidecar, considering taking him along, he's a good egg—thanks, mate.

Second, I would like to thank my parents who always support me, however ridiculous my ideas may seem. Reece says, "Ditto." To Reece's four-person parenting team, I would also like to extend my thanks for your support, and in Debbie's case, haircuts. Thanks also for the help we received from other family members, including brothers, sisters, cousins, aunts, uncles, and others.

Third, I would like to thank Charlie and Richard Prescott, along with their team of mates, including Malcolm Kew, who together built the only sidecar to ever circumnavigate the globe while attached to a scooter. Without the Prescotts, this trip would still only be a ridiculous idea, not a reality.

Equally, thanks to all of our supporters and followers. Your encouragement and belief kept us going. Thanks to those of you who became our patrons, too—you'll never know how much those cold weather boots helped! Thanks also for those who didn't believe we could do it—your comments were the ultimate inspiration.

Thanks to all of our friends who put up with the constant bombardment of fundraisers and requests for help. A special thanks to Todd Specht for joining the team and volunteering so much time to help build our website.

Next, I would like to thank the motorcycle and overlanding communities of the world. This gets talked about in the book a lot, but it's truly wonderful to have experienced the full force of the multi-cultural, global community of overlanders who helped us en route. Thanks to Paddy Tyson and Saul Jeavons of the Overland Event and *Overland Magazine* for introducing us to the community.

Similarly, thanks to Sam Manicom, Steph Jeavons, Austin Vince, Ted Simon, and many, many others within the UK overlanding community for the advice and inspiration.

On that note, thanks to Roseann and Jonathan Hanson who, along with everyone associated with the Change Your World Fund, are the reason you are holding this book. Their advice and expertise was invaluable in producing this book.

Also, in the production of this book, I would like to thank Susan Dragoo for her extraordinary patience and attention to detail in the copy editing. If you think I say 'it was incredible' a lot now you should have seen the first edit. A massive thanks as well to Oliver Bennet of More Visual who did the brilliant artwork for the cover of this book.

Thanks, too, to our incredible sponsors whose belief in us was misplaced—we were destined to fail and without you, we certainly would have. That includes: David, Liz, and the team at Flight Centre UK; Tom and the team at Devitt Insurance; Vasillis, Mark, and everyone at Ace Café; Luigi and Jan at Gazeboshop; Munya and everyone at Kuishi na Kuishi; Stewart and the gang at SnugPak; Iain at Honda UK; Colin at Alpkit; Richard and the team at Survival Wisdom; Simon at Oxford Products; Chris and John formerly of Metropolis Motorcycles; Mark and the guys at Greenwoods; everyone at Hagon Shocks; and those at Michelin Tyres, too. Thanks!

Last and certainly not least, I would like to thank Chelsea, my partner in crime. Your support and advice keeps me on the straight and narrow and your hilarious mind keeps our lives full of laughter.

Cheers all!

The Change Your World Fund

This book was produced with the assistance of the Change Your World Fund, a project of ConserVentures Charitable Organization. The Change Your World Fund was established in memory of Australian motorcyclist Alistair Farland, who tragically died in an accident while on his first overland adventure, riding from Alaska to Ushuaia. Alistair was born in 1990 so he was roughly our age. He was a firm believer that exploration has the power to change things, and we agree.

Exploration challenges stereotypes. It means you come face to face with people from different backgrounds and it provides more opportunities for learning about others and yourself than it is given credit for. We, too, believe that more people our age need to get involved with exploration and adventure, which hold the key to combatting many of the issues we face as a global society.

We were awarded the Change Your World Fund grant to complete this book in 2019 by Roseann and Jonathan Hanson, co-founders of ConserVentures and Overland Expo. The intention of this book is to inspire you to go out and explore the world with the same level of enthusiasm and curiosity as Alistair had. We hope it has.

Without the help of Roseann and Jonathan Hanson and the Change Your World Fund, this book would still just be an idea. Their help and advice in the editing and production of this book has been invaluable. Thank you both!

The support of the Change Your World Fund has enabled us to donate £1 from every sale of the paperback of this book to Unseen UK. We hope that this donation is able to help Unseen change the world for survivors of modern slavery and enable them to live happy, free lives.

Modern Slavery Around the World

On our journey we visited a range of different organisations that are fighting the issues of modern slavery and human trafficking in their country and beyond. As part of this, we were able to raise £7,215 for the charities. This £7,215 was raised via our website and at fundraising events. It is the total of all money donated by the general public, and because we received funding from corporations to pay for the costs of the journey, 100% of donations from the general public went toward the fundraising total. The money was distributed to the following organisations:

Unseen UK, who we met in the UK – Unseen run the UK's Modern Slavery Helpline (08000 121 700) and safe houses for victims in the South West of the UK. They're working to free the thousands of people living in slavery in the UK.

We donated £1,500 to Unseen UK's emergency appeal to keep the UK Modern Slavery Helpline open. The £1,500 paid for the helpline for a full day. In 2019, the helpline identified 1,812 cases of modern slavery in the UK. Taking an average that equates to five cases a day. That's five people who were identified and able to receive help as a result of donations from supporters of the trip.

Utopia 56, who we met in France – Utopia 56 aren't directly a modern slavery charity, but they prevent it by supporting people caught in the migrant crisis in Europe. Refugees are exceptionally vulnerable to being trafficked into modern slavery.

We donated £635 to Utopia 56, which used the funds to provide shelter to refugees on the streets of Paris.

The Smile of the Child, who we met in Greece – Smile of the Child are a children's charity in Greece who work to support child victims of human trafficking in Greece. They also work to try and stop children getting trafficked out of the many migrant and refugee camps in Greece.

We donated £635 to The Smile of the Child and they used the money to support unaccompanied minors in refugee camps in Greece.

Melissa Network, who we met in Greece – Melissa is an organisation supporting female refugee and migrant workers in Athens. Founded by a group of inspiring women including Click Ngwere, who escaped from slavery in Greece, the Melissa Network does fantastic work in providing vulnerable women with the tools they need to support themselves and their families.

We donated £635 to Melissa, which used it for education programmes for female refugees in Greece.

People's Legal Aid Centre Sudan (PLACE), who we met in Sudan – PLACE work to prevent human trafficking within Sudan and provide legal aid in the fight for justice for survivors.

We donated £635 to PLACE, which used the funds to provide legal aid for survivors of human trafficking.

HAART Kenya, who we met in Kenya – HAART Kenya work to prevent slavery in Kenya and help Kenyan nationals enslaved around the world. Unfortunately, the safe house they had just opened as we drove past in 2018 has just had to close its doors through lack of funding. HAART hope to re-open the shelter when more funding becomes available.

We donated £635 to HAART Kenya, which will use the contribution to support survivors of modern slavery in Nairobi. This can include medical costs and providing food and shelter.

A21 South Africa, who we met in South Africa – A21 are forming teams of abolitionists to warn South Africans, as well as people around the world, about the risks of human trafficking. At the same time, they run the South Africa Modern Slavery Helpline, which has led to 62 rescues to date.

We donated £635 to A21 South Africa, which used the funds to support awareness-raising programmes in South Africa.

ENCA, who we met in the UK – The Environmental Network of Central America helped us with advice to get this project on the road since we started planning. They fight for social and environmental justice in Central America by supporting grassroot organisations throughout the region. We were unable to visit any organisations associated with ENCA in the end because of logistical problems we faced in Central America. However, the organisation still supports many initiatives that limit modern slavery and human trafficking in the region.

We donated £635 to ENCA, which put the funds towards an education programme ran by CENDAH in the Guna Yala. CENDAH work to empower the Guna people to live in their traditional way rather than risk travelling to the mainland in search of work and being at risk of human trafficking.

El Pozo de Vida, who we met in Mexico – El Pozo de Vida fight to eradicate human trafficking through working with the children, families, and communities who are most vulnerable to being trafficked so that they can experience freedom and restoration to rebuild their lives.

We donated £635 to El Pozo de Vida, who used the funds to support their safehouse for underage victims of trafficking. The house is now full, including some women with young children. The funds were specifically used to cover medical costs and doctor visits.

New Friends, New Life, who we met in the USA – Through providing access to education, job training, interim financial assistance, mental health, and spiritual support, New Friends New Life helps victims of slavery restore their lives.

We donated £635 to New Friends, New Life who used the donation to provide food, toiletries, and cleaning products to survivors of trafficking they support in Dallas.

The donations made by supporters of this project enabled us to make a small but nonetheless genuine contribution to the fight against modern slavery.

In buying this book you have also donated £1 to Unseen UK who we continue to support. If you would like to support all of the organisations listed here you can still donate on our website AsSeenFromTheSidecar.org/donate.

Aside from the financial contribution, this project made a commitment to raising awareness of the issue of modern slavery around the world. Every single anti-slavery organisation we met en route told us that raising awareness of the issue is as important as raising money. Few people know about the true extent of the issue and many still don't recognise its existence or understand its prevalence.

Modern slavery is in every country on earth. You and I are both complicit in it through the activities we do, things we buy, and services we use. Aside from donating financially to organisations fighting the cause, you can help end modern slavery in a number of different ways. Firstly, learn about how you can limit how many people you enslave by visiting SlaveryFootprint.org. Use the information you get from the site to make active life choices that limit the amount of people you enslave. Further to that, you can take action to pick suppliers who actively engage in the fight against modern slavery like Tony's Chocolonely for your chocolate or Manumit Coffee for your coffee. It's so engrained in society that we can't always escape products that involve modern slavery, but making conscious choices when there is an alternative makes a real difference.

The other major thing you can do to fight modern slavery is keep an eye out for it in your community. Spot the signs and report any concerns to the appropriate authorities where you are. Here in the UK you can call the Modern Slavery Helpline on 08000 121 700.

MODERN SLAVERY: SPOT THE SIGNS

Here are some tips on how to spot the signs in your local community.

Physical Appearance

Shows signs of physical or psychological abuse, look malnourished or unkempt, anxious/ agitated or appear withdrawn and neglected. They may have untreated injuries.

Isolation

Rarely be allowed to travel on their own, seem under the control, influence of others, rarely interact or appear unfamiliar with their neighbourhood or where they work.

Relationships which don't seem right – for example a young teenager appearing to be the boyfriend/ girlfriend of a much older adult.

Poor Living Conditions

Be living in dirty, cramped or overcrowded accommodation, and / or living and working at the same address.

Restricted Freedom of Movement

Have no identification documents, have few personal possessions and always wear the same clothes day in day out. What clothes they do wear may not be suitable for their work

Have little opportunity to move freely and may have had their travel documents retained e.g. passports.

Unusual Travel Times

Be dropped off / collected for work on a regular basis either very early or late at night

Unusual travel arrangements - children being dropped off/ picked up in private cars/ taxis at unusual times and in places where it isn't clear why they'd be there.

Reluctant to Seek Help

They avoid eye contact, appear frightened or hesitant to talk to strangers and fear law enforcers for many reasons, such as not knowing who to trust or where to get help, fear of deportation, fear of violence to them or their family.

If you spot these signs in the UK then call the Modern Slavery Helpline on 08000 121 700.

If you spot these signs in the USA then call the National Human Trafficking Hotline on 1 888 373 7888

If you are outside of the UK and the USA and you spot the signs, then report it to the local authorities or your national anti-slavery helpline number if there is one. If you don't feel you can find help and can't find a local organisation then call the UK Modern Slavery Helpline who may be able to help or direct you to another local organisation to you.

Organisations we supported financially:

Unseen, UK| https://www.unseenuk.org | +44 303 040 2888

Utopia 56, France http://www.utopia56.com/en | +33 640 9916 45

The Smile of The Child, Greece | https://www.hamogelo.gr | +30 210-3306140

The Melissa Network | https://melissanetwork.org | +30 210 821 8486

PLACE, Sudan | rmakkawi@yahoo.co.uk

HAART Kenya | https://haartkenya.org | +254 738 506 264

A21 South Africa | https://www.a21.org | +27 21 551 0971

CENDAH (via ENCA) | https://enca.org.uk

El Pozo de Vida | https://www.elpozodevida.org.mx | info@elpozodevida.org.mx

New Friends, New Life | https://www.newfriendsnewlife.org | +01 (214) 965-0935

Other places to learn about modern slavery:

Freedom United - https://www.freedomunited.org

Made in a Free World - https://madeinafreeworld.org

Slavery Footprint - https://slaveryfootprint.org

End Slavery Now - https://www.endslaverynow.org

The Global Slavery Index - https://www.globalslaveryindex.org

ABOUT THE SIDECAR GUYS

As Seen From The Sidecar

You can visit www.AsSeenFromTheSidecar.com to see weekly videos and blogs from our trip around the world by scooter and sidecar. You can also read more about the organisations we met as well as donate to the organisations we support.

The Sidecar Guys

Visit www.TheSidecarGuys.com to see what's new with us. We're always up to adventurous stuff and The Sidecar Guys website is where you can read all about everything we do.

The Armchair Adventure Festival

Since returning home, we've been talking about our adventures to groups of all sizes all around the UK. We love telling stories from the road and we love hearing from other adventurers, too. That's why, during the lockdown for the COVID-19 pandemic, we set up The Armchair Adventure Festival—the world's first virtual adventure festival.

The Armchair Adventure Festival features top adventurers like Charley Boorman, Ted Simon, Steph Jeavons, Claudio von Planta, Tiffany Coates, Natalia Cohen, and many, many others. With live Q&As, presentations, adventure films, and panel discussions, there is all kinds of adventurous content to enjoy. The first festival raised £8,170 for the NHS Charities Together Fund for the fight against COVID-19.

Tune in to our next festival for some top quality armchair adventure entertainment at www.ArmchairAdventureFestival.com.